OXFORD HISTORICAL MONOGRAPHS

Saving and Spending

*The Working-class Economy
in Britain 1870–1939*

PAUL JOHNSON

CLARENDON PRESS · OXFORD

1985

Oxford University Press, Walton Street, Oxford OX2 6DP
Oxford New York Toronto
Delhi Bombay Calcutta Madras Karachi
Kuala Lumpur Singapore Hong Kong Tokyo
Nairobi Dar es Salaam Cape Town
Melbourne Auckland
and associated companies in
Beirut Berlin Ibadan Nicosia

Oxford is a trade mark of Oxford University Press

Published in the United States
by Oxford University Press, New York

© Paul Johnson 1985

British Library Cataloguing in Publication Data

Johnson, Paul
Saving and spending: the working-class economy
in Britain 1870–1939.—(Oxford historical monographs)
1. Labor and laboring classes—Great Britain—History
2. Social problems—Economic aspects—Great Britain—History
3. Great Britain—Social conditions—19th century
4. Great Britain—Social conditions—20th century
I. Title
305.5'62   HD8390
ISBN 0–19–822933–X

Library of Congress Cataloging in Publication Data

Johnson, Paul.
Saving and spending.
(Oxford historical monographs)
Bibliography: p.
Includes index.
1. Great Britain—Economic conditions—19th century.
2. Great Britain—Economic conditions—1918–1945.
3. Labor and laboring classes—Great Britain—History.
4. Saving and thrift—Great Britain—History.
5. Consumer credit—Great Britain—History.
I. Title. II. Series.
HC255.J62 1985 305.5'69'0941 85–11406
ISBN 0–19–822933–X

Set by Eta Services
Printed in Great Britain
at the University Press, Oxford
by David Stanford
Printer to the University

TO MY PARENTS

Acknowledgements

MY primary debt is to Ross McKibbin and Nick Crafts who supervised the thesis on which this book is based, and who have provided constant guidance, encouragement, and judicious criticism over the last six years. Brian Harrison and Barry Supple examined the thesis and made many valuable suggestions as to how to make the text less indigestible. Lewis Johnman checked the notes and references; Leslie Hannah, Michael Hart, and Mary MacKinnon have read and commented on some or all of the chapters. Kenneth Hudson generously made available the material he had collected for his own history of pawnbroking, the Family Welfare Association gave me access to Charity Organisation Society case papers, and I received much hospitality from the staffs of the Foresters and Oddfellows friendly societies, and from the Britannic, Pearl, and Prudential assurance companies, for which I am most grateful. Finally, I would like to thank the Warden and Fellows of Nuffield College, Oxford, for electing me to a research fellowship which allowed me both to complete this book and to avoid the moral hazards of indebtedness.

London School of Economics and Political Science   PAUL JOHNSON

Contents

List of Tables

Abbreviations

AFS	Affiliated Friendly Societies
ASE	Amalgamated Society of Engineers
AOF	Ancient Order of Foresters Friendly Society
COS	Charity Organisation Society
CWS	Co-operative Wholesale Society
FCS	Friendly Collecting Society
HMSO	His Majesty's Stationery Office
IA	Industrial Assurance
IOOFMU	Independent Order of Oddfellows, Manchester Unity Friendly Society
M-O	Mass-Observation Archive, Sussex University
NHI	National Health Insurance
NIESR	National Institute of Economic and Social Research
NSC	National Savings Certificates
OFS	Ordinary Friendly Societies
POSB	Post Office Savings Bank
PP	British Parliamentary Papers
PRO	Public Records Office
SC	Select Committee
SID	Special Investment Department of the Trustee Savings Bank
SSRC	Social Science Research Council
TSB	Trustee Savings Bank
UAB	Unemployment Assistance Board

1

Introduction

Annual income twenty pounds, annual expenditure nineteen
nineteen six, result happiness. Annual income twenty pounds,
annual expenditure twenty pounds ought and six, result misery.

(Mr Micawber in *David Copperfield*, 1850)

For many low income households, the borderline between success and disaster in planning expenditure is extremely narrow
and to be as little as ten shillings on the wrong side may have
serious consequences.

(Crowther Committee on Consumer Credit, 1971)

THE problem of balancing income with expenditure, of making
ends meet, is common to all societies and all classes. Resources
and needs fluctuate between seasons, and from good years to
bad. Individuals have to prepare for periods of ill health and
declining physical powers in old age; families bear a heavy
economic burden when supporting dependent children. The
balance is easier to maintain for some people than others: a
large income and a high level of savings can provide a cushion
against sudden shortfalls; substantial inherited wealth does the
same. A regular and constant income, even if small, facilitates
budgeting by preventing fluctuations on one side of the scales,
and allowing long-term planning for fluctuations on the other.
When income is erratic and irregular as well as small, the difficulties of balancing it with fairly stable subsistence demands are
acute, the area of manœuvre is limited, and the costs of failure
are great.

Misery was Mr Micawber's term for the cost of failure, the
misery of debt, deprivation, and, in Victorian Britain, ultimate
resort to a semi-punitive Poor Law. The financial scales of
low-income households were finely balanced on a knife edge of
sufficiency, always threatening to plummet into the arms of the
relieving officer or rise towards some brief moment of frippery.

Few manual workers in Victorian and Edwardian Britain
could be confident that their financial reserves were sufficient
to withstand the costs of sickness or unemployment, and if both
coincided then the most prudent, thrifty, and abstinent could
quickly find themselves destitute, dependent upon charity or
state welfare.

Take, for instance, the case of John M, a twenty-seven-year-
old bricklayer from Fulham who made an application for
charitable assistance in February 1895 when he was recovering
from an illness.[1] Although John was a member of the Bricklayers' Society and receiving sick pay of 14s. 5d. a week, the
charity caseworker reported that 'he needs more nourishment
now than the Club pay allows. Fire has to be kept night and
day burning 2½ cwt. a week and he has 8d. to 10d. a day in milk
and two new laid eggs.' Part of John and Mary M's financial
troubles sprang from the fact that 'when they married they had
to get part of their furniture on hire and these payments have
thrown them back, they have paid off £3 and have 25s. to pay
at 2s. or 3s. a week'. By April, John was recovering slowly,
although after thirteen weeks his sick pay was reduced to 8s. 5d.
In January 1897 he was again asking for relief during sickness.
He was suffering from congestion of the lungs but 'is not at
present attended by club doctor because he is in arrears. This
is owing to the strike in the summer when he was not able to
pay the levies.' The case papers have attached the following
note:

The foreman of the Bricklayers employed at the Vere Hotel says
applicant has been known to him a considerable time: has worked for
them since the job started. Will be employed again as soon as he is
able, as he is a very decent steady man: has run out of the Bricklayers'
Society through previous illness, his wife also has been ill. A collection
would have been made for him among the men, but over 40 hands
were discharged yesterday.

In April 1900 he was again ill with rheumatic fever. Although
he was back in the Bricklayers' Society and receiving 14s. 5d. a

---

[1] Charity Organisation Society (COS) Case Paper, area 1, box 1, case 10409. These
case papers are lodged with the Greater London Council Record Office.

week sick pay, the rent was four weeks in arrears, £1 worth of other debts were outstanding, and £5 worth of goods were in pawn. The 19*s*. that had been painfully accumulated in a savings bank had been drawn on since September and the account was now empty. A new application in 1908 reported neither club membership nor savings; another in 1910 stated: 'Was in Bricklayers' Union—got behind hand and could not rejoin because of health'.

John M's troubles stemmed from his own poor health which undermined and eventually precluded attempts to obtain adequate insurance cover during sickness, but his case shows well the way a number of separate financial difficulties could combine to overwhelm a family. Rent arrears, hire-purchase debts, pledges to be redeemed, the loss of income during a strike, the exhaustion of savings bank funds, the extra costs associated with illness, the laying-off of workmates who normally would help one of their colleagues in distress—when all of these coincided with much reduced income during a period of sickness, it was inevitable that hardship would result.

The case of John M is not typical—most workers did not suffer from chronic illness in this way—but the phenomenon of recurring periods of want was undoubtedly widespread. The number of paupers in Britain before 1914 is just one indicator of how many people failed to balance their income with their expenditure, and there are other measures, such as the number of county court plaints for recovery of small debts, which tell the same story—that many, perhaps most, manual workers could expect at some time in their lives to face acute financial crisis. This experience was not pleasant, and the physical want that went hand in hand with this poverty (poverty which Charles Booth found to be the lot of one-third of the population of London at the turn of the century) was even less agreeable. Not surprisingly, most families took some precautions against lapsing into this state of dependency.

These precautions, the way in which families saved in good times and borrowed in bad, form the subject of this study. They are of interest in their own right, since around them evolved a set of saving and lending institutions which impinged upon the lives of most people yet which have been largely neglected by social and economic historians.[2] The weekly call of the industrial insurance agent to almost every worker's home, the small-scale but none the less important attempts to save in local clubs and societies, the common resort to shop credit and the pawnbroker—this was a vital part of working-class experience. It was vital because it provided the wherewithal to live an independent life, and the study of this behaviour can provide much information and some understanding of an unexceptional (and therefore important) side of working-class existence. The problem of paying rent or the doctor's bill may appear to be less interesting than the great historical moments of wars, elections, and strikes, but for most people these conflicts were passing distractions from the real business of life, of earning enough to pay the bills and having a little bit extra left over. One need only turn the pages of *The Ragged Trousered Philanthropists* to see just how much the problem of making ends meet absorbed the thoughts of working men and women.[3]

Owen the housepainter never had a convincing response to the taunt that socialism would not pay next week's rent. In Mugsborough, as in other towns, the exigencies of balancing income and expenditure dulled minds to any sense of an alternative way of organizing life. A study of the material conditions of life may itself appear to be dull and humdrum, but it is crucial to an understanding of why people thought and behaved as they did. The common middle-class complaint that the poor were feckless and never looked more than a few days ahead,

[2] There is no study of friendly societies beyond the mid-Victorian period, save for a discussion of their response to the introduction of pensions and national insurance. See P. H. J. H. Gosden, *The Friendly Societies in England 1815–1875* (Manchester, 1961), and Bentley B. Gilbert, *The Evolution of National Insurance in Great Britain* (London, 1966). The only post-war work on industrial assurance is the apologia by Dermot Morrah, *A History of Industrial Life Assurance* (London, 1955); the history of savings banks has not been updated for almost forty years since H. Oliver Horne, *A History of Savings Banks* (OUP, London, 1947). The co-operative and trade union movements have been better served with institutional histories, though it has been more often the political than the economic face that has been studied. There is no work on retail finance—the development of hire-purchase and other forms of credit—and no study of moneylending. The outline history of pawnbroking has been recently if briefly told by Kenneth Hudson, *Pawnbroking, An Aspect of British Social History* (London, 1982), and has received more imaginative treatment from Melanie Tebbutt, *Making Ends Meet* (Leicester, 1983).

[3] Robert Tressell, *The Ragged Trousered Philanthropists* (St Albans, 1965). See in particular chapter 3, 'The Financiers'.

and the socialist lament that workers so seldom co-operated in
a constructive way, both owe something to the fact that today's
debts weigh more heavily on the mind than tomorrow's pros-
pects. A knowledge of individual responses to material or financial problems can inform a discussion of topics that are social
and collective, and a constant theme in the chapters that follow
is that behaviour which is apparently determined by selfish
economic motives can significantly affect and be affected by
social and non-economic forces. The aim of most households
was not just to balance income and expenditure to make ends
meet, but to do so in a way that brought various social benefits
in an intensely competitive world in which position or status
had constantly to be reasserted.

In the main, these intentions and desires went unvoiced. The
population dealt with in the following pages, the great grey
shapeless mass of the manual work-force, was inarticulate, and
left few extensive sets of records beyond census returns and
gravestones, so a good deal of what will be said here about
intentions is inferred from actions. This is a path fraught with
dangers for the unwary traveller, and it is worth stating at the
outset what precautions have been taken against wrong turn-
ings. The aim has been to build up an image of working-class
saving and borrowing from a number of different perspectives,
and to see whether a consistent picture emerges. Institutional
records give details of the numerical and financial strength of
particular saving methods, and of their overall costs and benefits. Social surveys tell of the hierarchical structure of credit and
thrift agencies in a particular community, and how they were
used by different groups. Autobiographies and interviews
reveal the way in which different types of saving and borrowing
were carried on by individuals simultaneously to meet different
problems.

Where a consistent pattern of behaviour can be identified
from the range of available sources, it needs to be explained.
Two broad but interrelated explanations are offered here. The
first is individualistic and economistic, and rests on the principle that poor families with many unfulfilled wants will not
waste money on some type of saving or borrowing repeated
week by week if they derive little or no advantage from it. To
dismiss such consistent behaviour as feckless, an indication of

stupidity or moral degeneracy, can only lead to a repetition of the censorious views of many contemporary middle-class observers. But to confine any explanation to a rigid economic framework of absolute rationality and an unvarying goal of utility-maximization seems to be historically inappropriate. It is inappropriate because it ignores or diminishes the social determinants and results of saving and spending decisions. Individuals or families did not take these decisions in isolation, but as part of a larger community or work group with its own customs, conventions, and codes of conduct, and an important aspect of many financial decisions was the potential social integration or alienation that might result. Because financial security was difficult for most working-class households to achieve before the First World War, individual attempts to promote such security by some form of accumulation acquired a social symbolism often out of all proportion to their true economic worth—saving designed to permit the ritualistic wearing of a Sunday suit or the ostentation of a 'decent' burial are two examples that will be discussed in some detail below. Conversely, the economic dependence represented by the use of the pawnbroker or resort to the Poor Law carried a degree of social stigma often far more oppressive than the financial want involved. A view of economic decision-making must, therefore, be tempered by an understanding of the social symbolism of many expenditure decisions.[4] The worker should be seen not as an ultra-rational (and therefore very simple) individual, but, as Katona suggests:

a human being, influenced by his past experiences. His socio-cultural norms, attitudes, habits, as well as his belonging to groups, all influence his decisions. He is apt to prefer short cuts, follow rules of thumb, and behave in a routine manner. But he is also capable of acting intelligently. When he feels that it really matters, he will deliberate and choose to the best of his ability.[5]

By looking at the workers' choices, this study attempts to establish what really mattered to them, and why.

Before examining the choice between alternative ways of

---

[4] For a stimulating discussion of this idea, see Mary Douglas and Baron Isherwood, *The World of Goods* (London, 1979).

[5] George Katona, *Psychological Economics* (New York, 1975), p. 218.

saving and borrowing, it is necessary both to describe the population being considered and to explain the time period chosen. Since some sort of financial balancing is common to all social groups at all times, the adoption of any particular definition inevitably involves an element of the arbitrary. The starting date of 1870 was determined by the availability of sources. Government inquiries in the early 1870s into pawnbroking and friendly and building societies contain a wealth of information previously unavailable, and the reorganization of the Registry of Friendly Societies in the mid-1870s established a reasonably competent statistical department. The Post Office Savings Bank opened for business in 1861 to provide a safe repository for working-class savings, and it was in the same decade that industrial insurance companies began a phase of rapid expansion. The absence of institutional information about the small savings of workers before the mid-Victorian period cannot be taken to imply that this sort of savings behaviour was a new phenomenon, though it may be true that the extension during the nineteenth century of industrial wage labour forced the pace of development of financial institutions for the low-paid. But, as will be explained in chapters 2 and 3, there were a large number of informal and unregulated (and therefore unrecorded) clubs that catered for the saving and insurance wishes of the work-force, and it seems more than likely that some of the growth of the large-scale thrift institutions was at the expense of the small fry. The work continues up to the 1930s because the inter-war years offer some interesting contrasts with late-nineteenth century experience. Pawnbrokers and friendly societies were on the decline after the First World War, life insurance companies were offering different services, the national savings and building society movements were expanding, hire-purchase was becoming the dominant mode of purchasing consumer durables. Part of this was due to a general increase in prosperity, but part was due also to the introduction from 1908 of state welfare facilities which guaranteed a respectable freedom from want for large sections of the population. This impact of the state on the saving and borrowing habits of working-class people is the major theme of chapter 7.

The determination of a time period for this work was straightforward, the delimitation of a working-class group much less so. Although all groups in society use some means to balance their budgets, there are good grounds for believing that these means will vary greatly between people of different economic standing. Wealth is one factor of obvious importance. A large stock of assets that can be drawn on in times when expenditure is greater than income allows any such fluctuations to be ignored in the short run, and provides a financial cushion that permits a gradual readjustment to any fundamental change in economic circumstances. Substantial wealth also provides the opportunity to hold a diversified portfolio of investments, and therefore gives the expectation of a secure and stable investment income. But the bulk of the population (something over three-quarters if the figures given in chapter 4 are correct) did not possess substantial wealth, and did not derive a stable and secure income from non-human capital. They relied for income upon the sale of labour power week by week or day by day. This income was inevitably precarious—it depended upon the state of trade, the sentiment of the employer, the productivity and health of the worker. The assets held by this group amounted to little more than household goods and insurance policies, neither large enough nor flexible enough to support a family through a long period of deficient income. With a precarious income and few assets to provide a financial safety net, achieving some sort of financial balance was at once a more complex, a more difficult, and a more pressing problem than for the well-off. Instead of investing surplus income left at the end of the month—a typical response of the well-paid and wealthy—wage-labourers, and in particular their wives, had to make decisions daily about how much to spend, how much to put by for the weekend, for a holiday, for the children's clothes, for insurance money. The financial constraints of families with low incomes and few assets made success in balancing the household budget crucial when the opportunity for striking such a balance was least.

It seems sensible, therefore, to make some distinction on economic grounds between a middle-class group with high incomes and accumulated wealth, and a working-class group with few assets and an income very often little above a subsistence level. But economic differences do not explain all variations in saving and borrowing behaviour. Clerks might have an income no higher than skilled manual workers, but their social and economic life-style tended to be very different. There was an economic reason for this, because the greater certainty and regularity of a monthly salary allowed a different sort of financial planning, and made less necessary the provision for those periods of unemployment or sickness when no wage was coming in. But there was a social explanation too, as lower middle-class people typically eschewed the mutual thrift organizations of manual workers—co-ops, friendly societies, and saving clubs—and instead took to heart the Smilesian doctrine of independent self-help. In the chapters that follow some attempt has been made to investigate the occupation of members and clients of different credit and thrift institutions to test the belief that manual workers adopted a more communal approach to budget management. It will be argued that this communality did not imply a strong consciousness of class position. Mutual organizations were adopted because risk-sharing offered economic advantages, but the goal of each participant was intensely personal, the achievement of financial security and the establishment of personal position and status—concepts intimately linked in an impoverished working-class milieu to material wealth.

The idea of an internal tension in working-class life which is implicit in this description derives in part from the focus of this study on the domestic environment rather than on work, the workplace, and workplace organization. Although there were undoubtedly strong collective forms which emerged from factory life, and which did affect the world beyond the workplace, they did not necessarily dominate that world. The concentration of much labour and social history on unions, workers, and work makes little allowance for the influence of social life in the home and community on working-class sentiments and actions; this book goes some way towards reinstating the 'social' in working-class social history.

The working class to be studied is, therefore, delimited both by economic factors (wealth and size and stability of income), and also in part by social behaviour, by the extent to which use was made of mutual institutions for credit and thrift. Although mutuality was often conditioned by economic necessity, it was also part of the inherited cultural equipment of working-class people. It came to play an important part in working-class community life, and has often been seen by historians as exemplifying a national working-class solidarity. This interpretation will be challenged here; in the late nineteenth and early twentieth centuries it will be shown that mutuality tended as much to strengthen the particularism of local communities as to mould a national working-class consciousness.

2

Life Insurance, Death Insurance

THE most popular form of working-class saving was some form of contingency insurance. In 1859, Samuel Smiles had concluded that the 'three chief temporal contingencies' for which a man should provide were 'want of employment, sickness and death',[1] and by 1911 at least, according to Lloyd George, the working classes were fully alive to the need for making some such provision. But the high level of pauperism, and the obvious economic distress of the ill and unemployed, were clear enough signs that 'very few can afford to pay the premiums, and pay them continuously, which enable a man to provide against those three contingencies'.[2] On these grounds, Lloyd George proposed a limited compulsory national health and unemployment insurance scheme; burial insurance, being already 'very thoroughly covered', he left well alone, despite a strong plea from the Liberal back benches for it to be brought within the compass of the state scheme.[3]

The aim in this chapter is to trace the development of burial insurance to see how thorough the coverage was by 1911, and to discover why it was such a popular form of saving. The Victorian celebration of death was a widespread phenomenon, as popular in the slums of the East End as in the royal household. Public display of grief and mourning was almost a social duty, though one no longer recognized in Britain today.[4] Before the First World War, according to one East Ender:

[1] Samuel Smiles, *Self-Help* (London, revised edn. 1878), p. 294.

[2] Hansard, 5th ser., vol. xxv, col. 611 (4 May 1911).

[3] The plea was made by Leo Chiozza Money on the grounds of beneficent economy. If house-to-house collection could be superseded, he thought 'the gain to the community at large would be simply enormous, because 6d., and in some cases I believe more than 6d., in every 1s. would be saved out of their contributions for that particular benefit'. Hansard, 5th ser., vol. xxvi, col. 792 (29 May 1911).

[4] As pointed out in Geoffrey Gorer, *Death, Grief and Mourning* (London, 1965), chs. 3 and 4. For a provocative interpretation of changes in attitudes to death and grief over the last century see David Cannadine, 'War and Death, Grief and Mourning in Modern Britain' in Joachim Whaley (ed.), *Mirrors of Mortality* (London, 1981), pp. 187–242.

Funerals were a common sight in Wapping. They were always very grand affairs, for no matter how poor a family might be it always gave its members a good funeral. The body was kept at home for a week after the death and put on show for people to see. It had to be displayed for a full week in case people thought you were hurrying the body away. Funerals were horse drawn. The animals would be glossy and black with long black plumes on their heads and velvet palls hanging on either side of them. The top of the hearse was completely covered with plumes and was attended by bearers in long black coats and tall crepe-covered hats. People from throughout the district would gather outside the house of the dead man and line upon either side of the pavement to give him a good send-off.[5]

The social significance of burial customs will be returned to at the end of this chapter in order to put into context the expense and ostentation of working-class funerals; first must come an examination of the cost and structure of the burial insurance system.

Dying is and was an expensive affair. In London, the average cost of burying a working-class adult in 1870 was £5.9s., and a child could be buried for £2.2s.[6] By 1937 this had risen to an average of £22 for an adult in London, although provincial town charges were about 15 per cent lower, and in country parishes where parish churchyards could be used for interment, the cost was sometimes below £10.[7] As a proportion of income, the cost of an adult's funeral in London rose over this period, from about seven to about nine times the weekly earnings of an unskilled male worker.[8] But this was not the total cost of a burial. Wreaths and flowers, headstones and memorials, mourning dress and refreshments all added to the expense. Whether or not claims about working-class extravagance are accepted, the bald statistics of the average expenditure make it clear that burial could not be paid for in a lump sum from a few

---

[5] Grace Foakes, *Between High Walls* (London, 1972), p. 71.

[6] J. M. Goldstrom, 'The cost of disposal of the dead in Metropolitan London, 1830–1870', p. 25. Appendix to unpublished SSRC Final Report HR 2662, 1977.

[7] Sir Arnold Wilson and H. J. Levy, *Industrial Assurance: An Historical and Critical Study* (Oxford, 1937), p. 135.

[8] Taking these earnings at £43 p.a. in 1870 and £129 p.a. in 1935. See Guy Routh, *Occupation and Pay in Great Britain, 1906–79* (London, 1980), p. 120, and E. H. Phelps Brown, *A Century of Pay* (London, 1968), appendix 3.

weeks' saving. Nor could there be any substantial drawing upon capital, since personal holdings of wealth were so small. Nine-tenths of all Britons who died between 1899 and 1904 left so little property that no affidavit was sworn; a contemporary estimate put the average value of these estates at less than £16.[9] The most common way to cope with the inevitable financial burden of death was to take out some form of life assurance.

This security could be purchased in conjunction with sickness or unemployment benefit through ordinary and affiliated friendly societies and trade unions, but the widest coverage was that provided by Industrial Assurance Companies and Friendly Collecting Societies. They operated a system which came to be known officially as industrial life assurance, unofficially as death or burial insurance.[10] Its distinguishing feature was that premium payments were collected from the home at intervals of less than two months (usually weekly) by itinerant collectors or agents. The sums were low, and in certain cases limited by statute, the costs of collection and management were high, and the return on investment was poor. So poor, in fact, that even in 1944, after great advances had been made in reducing the costs of administration, it could still be said that

---

[9] L. G. Chiozza Money, *Riches and Poverty* (London, 3rd edn. 1906), p. 51.

[10] These were in law quite separate institutions, although they carried out exactly the same sort of work. The Industrial Assurance Companies were joint-stock profit-making companies controlled by shareholders; policyholders had no right to intervene in the operation of the company. Friendly Collecting Societies were in theory controlled by the policy-holding members. In fact, though, the control of the Societies was entirely in the hands of managerial staff and agents who could pack general meetings and fix votes at will (see, for example, the Report of the Chief Registrar of Friendly Societies on the Royal Liver Friendly Society, PP 1886 lxi (C. 4706)). Despite criticisms of high dividends paid by the proprietary Companies, they tended to offer a better return to policyholders than the supposedly democratic Societies. The Companies, led by the Prudential in 1907, admitted policyholders to a share in the profits to which they had no legal right, and by 1939 most of the Companies had reduced their expenses ratios to levels significantly below those of the Societies. The Companies had to submit annual returns to the Board of Trade, the Societies to the Registry of Friendly Societies. Since aggregate statistics were collected separately by these different government departments, they are presented separately in Table 2.1.

A note on terminology. To avoid needless repetition, the terms 'industrial assurance companies' and 'industrial life offices' will be used to refer to all institutions selling industrial insurance, whatever their legal status, whilst the terms 'Industrial Assurance Companies' and 'Friendly Collecting Societies' refer to those specific legally-constituted bodies. Also, since there seems to be no agreement in the literature, the terms 'assurance' and 'insurance' will be used interchangeably.

'half the pitiful sums [the poor] pay goes in expenses and lapsed policies. Not six pennyworth of value do they get for any shilling so hardly spared.'[11]

The pennies and shillings that were spared each year amounted to a very large sum. The Cohen Committee on Industrial Assurance pointed out that the monies collected in 1930 exceeded the annual cost of the navy, or, to make a more apposite comparison, exceeded the total of workers' and employers' contributions to the National Health Insurance and State Pension schemes.[12] The annual premium income rose from about £2m. in 1880 to almost £19m. in 1910 and over £66m. in 1936. The aggregate figures for membership, income, and capital are presented in Table 2.1.

The rate of growth of this sort of insurance is almost certainly overstated by the data in this table, since these refer only to the officially registered or incorporated Industrial Assurance Companies and Friendly Collecting Societies, and it is clear that similar insurance facilities were provided by small, unofficial burial or slate clubs which sometimes provided sickness benefit as well as burial money. In 1872 the secretary to the Provident Association of Warehousemen, Travellers and Clerks estimated that there were 'no less than 900 provident and benevolent associations in London alone, of which neither the government nor anyone has any knowledge whatever, except what is gathered casually at their annual meetings'.[13] Fifteen years later a witness before another official inquiry claimed that navvies and casual labourers seldom joined friendly societies proper; instead 'they largely belong to their own little fund; they give a little to some ganger in whom they have confidence, and he receives sixpence a week from them'.[14] John Benson's work on English coal-miners has shown that 'nearly every worker seems to have been a member of at least one local unregistered friendly society' around 1870, but that by the end of the nineteenth cen-

[11] John Hilton, *Rich Man, Poor Man* (London, 1944), p. 106.
[12] Committee on Industrial Assurance and Assurance on the lives of children under ten years of age [Cohen Cttee.], PP 1932–3 xiii (Cmd. 4376), Report, pp. 4–5.
[13] Royal Commission on Friendly and Benefit Building Societies [Northcote Cmmn.], Third Report, PP 1873 xxii (C. 842), Evidence, q. 26991.
[14] Select Committee on National Provident Insurance [Maxwell Cttee.], PP 1887 xi (257), Evidence, q. 373.

tury, more and more miners were insuring with trade unions, permanent relief funds, and industrial insurance companies, especially the Prudential.[15] This supports the view that part of the apparent growth of industrial assurance was due to the success of the aggressive canvassing of the societies and companies in attracting members away from local unregistered burial societies. There is, after all, no increase in mortality rates, no evidence of substantial increase in the cost of burial, and no widespread and fundamental change in personal economic circumstances that might otherwise explain this new departure. There was, however, a long history of local friendly societies and clubs failing (more through actuarial incompetence than fraud)—in 1874 a government investigator claimed that 'The Burial Club which survives a generation is an exception'[16]—and the size and apparent financial strength of the large institutions, coupled with widespread advertising, were effective in attracting custom.

Nevertheless, it is clear that the unregistered societies were of importance well into the twentieth century. In 1906, Sir Edward Brabrook, the former Chief Registrar of Friendly Societies, told the Poor Law Commissioners that at the end of 1904 ordinary and affiliated friendly societies had 5.7m. members, Friendly Collecting Societies had 7.5m. members, and, deducting generous amounts for overlapping, unregistered societies might represent another 6m. people.[17] And Seebohm Rowntree, in his second survey of York, found the membership of registered friendly societies in the city at the end of 1938 to stand at 17,305, whilst a careful inquiry into non-registered clubs showed a membership of about 14,000.[18] These estimates suggest that the official statistics in Table 2.1 overstate the rate of growth of the number of burial insurance

---

[15] John Benson, 'The Thrift of English Coalminers, 1860–1895', *Economic History Review*, 2nd ser., xxxi (1978), pp. 416–17. See also his *British Coalminers in the Nineteenth Century* (Dublin, 1980), chap. 7, and G. J. Barnsby, *Social Conditions in the Black Country 1800–1900* (Wolverhampton, 1980), p. 48.

[16] Northcote Cmmn., Reports of the Assistant Commissioners: Southern and Eastern Counties, PP 1874 xxiii pt. ii (C. 997), p. 27.

[17] Royal Commission on the Poor Law [Hamilton Cmmn.], appendix, vol. iii, PP 1909 xl (Cd. 4755), qq. 35174–81. This 6m. would include people insured for sickness as well as death benefit.

[18] B. Seebohm Rowntree, *Poverty and Progress* (London, 1941), pp. 208–10.

Table 2.1. Membership, income, and funds of Industrial Assurance Companies and Friendly Collecting Societies

	(1) IA paid-up policies (m.)	(2) IA free policies (m.)	(3) IA new policies (m.)	(4) IA premium income (£m.)	(5) IA funds (£m.)	(6) FCS paid-up policies (m.)	(7) FCS free policies (m.)	(8) FCS new policies (m.)	(9) FCS premium income (£m.)	(10) FCS funds (£m.)
1870	0.673[a]									
1871	0.812[a]									
1872										
1873										
1874										
1875										
1876	2.64[a]									
1877										
1878	3.66[a]									
1879						2.96				1.56
1880				1.94	1.48					
1881	4.82[a]			2.25	1.91					
1882				2.60	2.17					
1883				3.05	2.83					
1884	6.30[a]			3.28	3.58					
1885	6.67[a]			3.55	4.39	3.63				2.06
1886	9.14	0.058[a]		3.74	5.36					
1887	9.20	0.089[a]		4.00	5.91					
1888	9.41	0.128[a]		4.36	6.87					
1889	9.43	0.171[a]		4.85	8.02					
1890	9.87	0.208[a]		5.03	8.87					
1891	12.83	0.246[a]		5.46	9.59	4.08				2.95
1892	13.21	0.288[a]		5.70	10.20					
1893	13.32	0.338[a]		5.92	11.16					

Year										
1894	14.99	0.398[a]	6.38		12.47					
1895	15.30	0.448[a]	6.61		13.55					
1896	15.86	0.499[a]	7.15		14.40					
1897	17.23	0.549[a]	7.57		15.84					
1898	17.85	0.604[a]	8.07		17.22	5.56				4.83
1899	18.65	0.663[a]	8.42		18.77	5.92				5.21
1900	20.00	0.713[a]	9.29		20.47	6.30[c]				5.59[c]
1901	21.21	0.771[a]	9.61		22.1	6.68				5.97
1902	22.51	0.836[b]	10.26		24.1	7.01				6.55
1903	23.81	0.912[a]	10.60		26.3	6.97				7.22
1904	24.66	1.00[a]	11.09		28.5	7.45				7.86
1905	25.54	1.10[a]	11.61		30.9	7.88				8.46
1906	26.85	1.19[a]	12.44		34.4	8.45[c]				9.20[c]
1907	27.81	1.29[a]	13.09		37.2	9.01				9.94
1908	28.54	1.40[a]	13.33		39.6	6.73[d]				8.47
1909	29.14	1.50[a]	14.12		43.6	6.83		1.88		9.11
1910	31.17	1.82	15.70		46.2	7.16			2.92	9.7
1911	35.47	1.95	16.27		49.3	7.49			3.09	10.2
1912	36.16	2.09	16.69		53.0	7.74			3.18	11.0
1913	37.55	2.20	17.29		55.8	7.48[e]			3.19	11.3
1914	36.37[b]	2.29[b]	17.98		58.7	7.61			3.29	12.1
1915	38.30[b]	2.36[b]	18.56		61.4	8.27			3.59	12.5
1916	39.68[b]	2.41[b]	19.57		65.0	8.80			3.84	13.1
1917	41.06[b]	2.45[b]	20.96		69.4	9.22			4.22	14.0
1918	42.68[b]	2.49[b]	22.34		74.0	9.69			4.63	14.8
1919	44.95[b]	2.54[b]	25.35		80.5	10.85			5.44	16.2
1920	47.26[b]	2.62	29.27	6.08	89.7	13.21[f]			6.53	17.9
1921	47.76[b]	2.62[b]	31.09	5.69	100.3	13.51			6.71	20.1
1922	48.75	2.62	31.58	6.63	111.5	13.67		1.74	7.09	22.5
1923	48.76	2.74	33.21	6.84	123.2	13.71		1.96	7.59	25.4
1924	49.29	2.85	34.13	6.30	136.4	14.92		2.07	8.36	30.9
1925	52.32	2.97	36.61	6.69	151.8	15.50	0.01	2.20	8.82	33.7

Table 2.1 (continued)

	(1) IA paid-up policies (m.)	(2) IA free policies (m.)	(3) IA new policies (m.)	(4) IA premium income (£m.)	(5) IA funds (£m.)	(6) FCS paid-up policies (m.)	(7) FCS free policies (m.)	(8) FCS new policies (m.)	(9) FCS premium income (£m.)	(10) FCS funds (£m.)
1926	52·97	3·13	6·03	36.80	165.8	15·93		2·06	8·92	36.8
1927	53·46	3·41	7·47	38.80	179.1	16·37		2·45	9·56	40.0
1928	54·00	3·65	7·35	40.88	192.0	16·86		2·45	9·98	43.6
1929	54·83	3·89	7·72	42.00	203.1	17·50		2·58	10.41	46.7
1930	56·74	5·23	8·00	43.81	217.3	17·79	0.35	2·64	10.86	50.2
1931	57·53	6·42	8·25	45.41	226.3	18·89	0.84	2·55	11.30	53.9
1932	57·72	7·41	8·38	46.35	243.0	19·61	1.32	2·68	11.70	57.3
1933	58·63	7·97	8·47	47.66	259.2	20·58	1.78	2·73	12.12	61.5
1934	59·86	8·47	8·53	50.07	277.5	21·75	2.30	2·78	12.84	65.7
1935	61·64	9·34	8·18	51.50	296.7	22·80	2.80	2·73	13.40	69.6
1936	62·87	9·78	8·25	53.63	317.1	23·78c	3.14	2·70	14.09	74.5
1937				55.79		24·75			14.97	79.9
1938				58.00					15.49	

Notes

a These figures relate only to the Prudential Assurance Company. In 1886 the Prudential had 7.11m. policies outstanding, 78 per cent of the total.

b These figures for all Industrial Assurance Companies have been estimated from the Prudential figures. Between 1913 and 1922 the Prudential share of paid-up policies fell from 56 per cent to 49 per cent of the total; its share of free policies fell from 86 per cent to 79 per cent.

c Gaps in the series have been estimated from the two adjacent observations.

d This fall was caused by the conversion of the Royal London Friendly Society into a mutual company.

e This fall was caused by the conversion of the Blackburn Philanthropic Friendly Collecting Society into a company.

f This increase was mainly due to the change in enumeration from members to policies (see p. 21).

Sources

Col. 1 (1870–8₅) and Col. 2 (1886–1909): Annual Reports of the Prudential Assurance Company.

Cols. 1–5 (to 1914): Statement of Accounts of Life Insurance and Annuity Business, PP 1882 lxv (187), and then annually.
(1914–26): Reports of the Industrial Assurance Commissioner for 1927, PP 1928 x (18), pp. 152–7.
(1927–36): Ibid. for 1937, PP 1937–8 xii (163), pp. 46–51.
(1936–8): Eighty-third Statistical Abstract, PP 1939–40 x (Cmd. 6232), pp. 274–5.

Cols. 6 and 10 (1879): Report of the Registrar of Friendly Societies for 1880, part ii(B), PP 1883 lxviii (212–I), pp. 118–19, 152.
(1885): Ibid. for 1886, part ii(F), PP 1887 lxxvii (103–V), pp. 38–9.
(1891): Ibid. for 1892, part D(2). PP 1893–4 lxxxiv (513–I), p. 186.

Cols. 6, 9, and 10 (1898–1909): Fifteenth Abstract of Labour Statistics, PP 1912–13 cvii (Cd. 6228), pp. 254–5.
(1910–21): Eighteenth Abstract of Labour Statistics, PP 1926 xxix (Cmd. 2740), pp. 200–1.
(1922–35): Twenty-second Abstract of Labour Statistics, PP 1936–7 xxvi (Cmd. 5556), pp. 160–1.

Cols. 6 and 10 (1937): Report of the Chief Registrar of Friendly Societies for 1938, PP 1939–40 iv (12), section 3.

Cols. 7 and 8: Report of the Industrial Assurance Commissioner, PP 1933–4 xiii (116), pp. 84–5; ibid. for 1937, pp. 46–7.

Col. 9 (1936–8): Eighty-third Statistical Abstract, pp. 274–5.

Col. 10 (1936): Report of the Chief Registrar of Friendly Societies for 1937, part 2, (HMSO, 1939), p. 27.

policies in existence but understate the total number of such policies, particularly in the nineteenth century.

It is quite clear that the number of policies in force is not the same as the number of people insured, since from around 1914 there were more policies in force than there were resident Britons. This was not a new phenomenon; in the early 1870s, Preston supported nine local burial societies with 92,269 members, a number of agencies of the Royal Liver and Liverpool Victoria Collecting Societies, and 9,679 policies in force with the Prudential. Since the population of the town was little more than 86,000 there was 'clearly a great deal of re-insurance going on'.[19] How general this behaviour was it is impossible to say; Brabrook thought not more than one per cent of members belonged to more than one society,[20] but even if this is correct, it gives no idea of how much multiple insurance took place within each Society or Company. Such multiple insurance was common since the way to increase the sum assured for an industrial policy holder was not to rewrite the original policy, but to take out another one. This is how the president of the National Federation of Insurance Workers described the procedure to the Parmoor Committee on Industrial Assurance in 1920:

perhaps a policy is issued to an assured for quite a nominal figure to start with, and with as low a denominator as 1*d*. or 2*d*. Then in process of time responsibilities increase and the assured feel they want more assurances, and the first policy is augmented by a second, third or fourth policy, until they feel they have enough insurance to cover what they require.[21]

So particularly in periods of rising real income or price inflation, an increase in the number of policies does not necessarily imply an extension of business to the previously uninsured.

There was a further reason for multiple insurance: the existence of life-of-another policies, these being policies other than ones taken out by individuals on themselves or their spouses.

---

[19] Northcote Cmmn., Asst, Cmmrs.; Cheshire, Derbyshire, etc., PP 1874 xxiii pt. ii (C. 996), p. 106.

[20] Hamilton Cmmn., app., vol. iii. q. 35157.

[21] Departmental Committee on the Business of Industrial Assurance Companies and Collecting Societies [Parmoor Cttee.], PP 1920 xviii (Cmd. 614), q. 318.

The legal controversies surrounding this insurance have a long and complex history, and need not be pursued here,[22] but the effect of allowing anyone to insure their child, parent, grandparent, grandchild, brother, or sister was to enable several people to take out life assurance policies on one particular person. Any claim paid on this life-of-another insurance was supposed to be confined to covering the cost of 'funeral expenses', but the companies made no effort to establish whether the insurer had any liability for the funeral expenses for which he or she was nominally insuring. So it was possible for, say, an aged parent to be insured by perhaps a dozen children and grandchildren, for most of whom the policies would be viewed as a financial gamble rather than as a way of securing a private burial.

The extent of multiple insurance cannot be stated with any certainty as there is so little reliable information about it. In 1920 the annual returns of Friendly Collecting Societies required by the Registry of Friendly Societies called for an enumeration of the number of policies issued, rather than the number of members as hitherto required. Not all the returns were accurate; those of the Liverpool Victoria appear to be, and they show that on 31 December 1919 the society's 4,537,326 members were paying for 6,117,013 policies; in other words, it had just over four policies for every three members. Evidence for the years 1923 to 1940 comes from the Royal Liver Friendly Society, which listed both the annual number of death claims it received, and the number of policies claimed on. Nearly all children under 10 were covered by just one policy; for other members the average rose from $1\frac{3}{4}$ policies per death in 1923 to two in 1940.[23] Whether the level of overlapping

---

[22] By the Assurance Companies Act of 1909, about 10m. illegal life-of-another assurances were retrospectively validated, according to an estimate by the then President of the Board of Trade, Winston Churchill. That this did not stop illegal insurances from being issued is clear from the mass of evidence collected by the Parmoor and Cohen Committees. For a brief review of this question, see Social Insurance and Allied Services [Beveridge Report], PP 1942–3 vi (Cmd. 6404), appendix D, pp. 266–71.

[23] It seems from the returns that many Friendly Collecting Societies had never bothered to give exact statements of their membership. This was certainly the case with the Royal Liver; its official returns only enumerated policies. See the Annual Returns of the Royal Liver and Liverpool Victoria Collecting Friendly Societies. PRO FS 16/38 and FS 16/57 and 58.

insurance was the same in other Societies or Companies there is
no way of knowing. A glimpse of the extent of multiple insurance between companies comes from a saving survey of Slough
conducted in 1940, which found that 30 per cent of families
which bought insurance paid into more than one company, 7
per cent paying into three companies.[24]

This all makes any estimate of the number of individuals
covered by industrial assurance policies a very tentative
matter. Impressionistic evidence suggests that coverage was
wide. Clara Grant observed that 'the Poor Law Guardians
grant burial where really necessary, but insurance is practically
and rightly universal', and this in an area of Poplar coloured
black (lowest class) and blue (very poor) by Booth.[25] In 1914
Mrs Bosanquet thought burial insurance was 'a misdirection of
expenditure so general that it seems hopeless to try to remedy
it'.[26] Sidney Dark's investigation into London thrift at the turn
of the century convinced him that 'the burial club is a far more
popular institution than the organization which provides funds
to tide its members over bad times'.[27] And this was not confined to London. A number of witnesses before official inquiries
claimed that industrial assurance was extensive in the agricultural parts of the country of which they had knowledge.[28] The
large Companies and Societies boasted of their nationwide
business; in 1911, the Britannic, the fifth largest of the Companies, was conducting operations in 282 different towns in
England and Wales, from Dover to Llandudno, from Penzance
to Carlisle.[29] Several of the social surveys carried out in the
1930s give further evidence of widespread industrial assurance.
In York in 1936 life assurance premiums were 'paid weekly by

[24] Charles Madge, *War-time pattern of saving and spending* (NIESR Occasional Paper
iv, Cambridge, 1943), p. 45.
[25] Clara Grant, *Farthing Bundles* (London, c.1931), p. 105.
[26] Review by Helen Bosanquet of Mrs Pember Reeves, 'Round About a Pound a
Week', *Economic Journal* xxiv (Mar. 1914), p. 110.
[27] Sidney Dark, 'London Thrift', in G. R. Sims (ed.), *Living London* (London, 1902),
ii. 257.
[28] For instance, Royal Commission on the Aged Poor [Aberdare Cmmn.], PP 1895
xiv (C. 7684–I), qq. 7089–91; Hamilton Cmmn., app., vol. i, PP 1909 xxxix (Cd.
4625), q. 4375; ibid., app., vol. vii, PP 1910 xlvii (Cd. 5035), q. 69047.
[29] Details drawn from the policy registers for 1911 of the Britannic Assurance Co.,
held at the Birmingham headquarters of the company.

practically every family, even the very poorest'.[30] The Bristol
survey of 1937 found that 79.8 per cent of all working-class
families in the sample had industrial life policies, a figure confirmed by an NIESR survey which revealed the following percentages of working-class families making weekly life assurance
payments in the years 1940 to 1943:[31]

Islington	80	Bradford	75
Coventry	85	York	88
Blackburn	82	Slough	85
Bristol	75	Glasgow	95

Aggregate figures point to the same scale. The Parmoor
Committee estimated in 1920 that, taking account of some
double or multiple insurance, the 51m. policies then in force
represented a clientele of about 35m., or about 75 per cent of
the UK population.[32] Linking the Committee's statement that
the business 'appeals chiefly to the working classes' with Guy
Routh's estimate that in 1921, 77 per cent of the British work-
force was employed in some form of manual labour, it appears
that industrial assurance was indeed 'practically universal'
among the working class.[33] By the end of the Second World
War, the Industrial Life Offices could confidently announce
that industrial life policies of one sort or another were held in
nine out of ten working-class homes.[34] It is not possible to
make any such estimate for the nineteenth century; how many
people joined *ad hoc* clubs organized at the workplace or public
house will never be known.

Of course, to say that most working-class people were, from
the 1890s at least, purchasers of industrial life assurance, does
not necessarily mean that they were the only purchasers,
although on a priori grounds it seems likely that higher income
groups would pay the quarterly or annual premiums required
by ordinary life assurance companies if they desired this form of

[30] Rowntree, *Poverty and Progress*, p. 200.

[31] Herbert Tout, 'A Statistical Note on Family Allowances', *Economic Journal* 1
(Mar. 1940), p. 58; Madge, *War-time pattern of saving*, p. 45.

[32] Parmoor Cttee., p. 2.

[33] Routh, *Occupation and Pay*, p. 7.

[34] Industrial Life Offices, *Twenty Questions about Industrial Life Assurance* (London,
1949), p. 3. See also Philip Snowden's introduction to J. G. Sinclair, *Evils of Industrial
Assurance* (London, 1932), p. viii.

contingency saving. This feeling is confirmed by the membership records of the Blackburn Philanthropic Friendly Collecting Society. The conversion of this society into a joint-stock
company in December 1913 necessitated the compilation of a
list of members' names and addresses, and for about 60 per cent
of members an occupation is also stated. Table 2.2 presents an

*Table 2.2. Occupations of members of the Blackburn Philanthropic Friendly Collecting
Society living in Bolton and Preston in September 1913 (5 per cent sample)*[a]

Housewife	107	Agent	4
Millhand	65	Carpenter/Joiner	4
Child	52	Servant	4
Weaver	47	Mechanic	4
Labourer	47	Machinist	3
Engineer/Fitter	20	Foreman	3
Spinner	16	Barman	3
Housekeeper	13	Gardener	3
Bricklayer/Plasterer	10	Tailor/Hatter	3
Clerk	10	Shopman	2
Miner	9	Draper	2
No occupation	7	Other	80
Cabman	6	Not given	375[b]
Grocer	6	TOTAL	905

Notes

[a] The work of the society was confined almost solely to Lancashire.

[b] No occupation was listed for just over 40 per cent of people included on the list of
membership. It seems likely that many of these were children, as most burial clubs had
a membership distribution that reflected the age structure of the population. In 1911,
the under-16s made up about one-third of the British population.

Source

Records of Names and Addresses of persons who were members of the Blackburn
Philanthropic Friendly Collecting Society at the Date of the Certificate of Incorpora-
tion of the said Society as a Joint-Stock Company, namely on the 2nd day of
September, 1913. Vols. for Bolton and Preston. Liverpool Municipal Library,
uncatalogued.

occupational analysis of a 5 per cent sample of the 18,000 or so
members living in Preston and Bolton. Little had changed, it
seems, since 1871, when a representative of the society told the
Friendly Society Commissioners that his members were 'factory
workers, nearly all of them'—very few belonged to the higher
class of artisan.[35] The small size of subscriptions—the average

[35] Northcote Cmmn., Second Report, pt. 2, PP 1872 xxvi (C. 514–I), qq. 2506–7.

per member in 1913 was less than 2*d.* per week—does nothing to detract from this view.

Given the need to make some provision to cover expenses of burial, the extent of industrial life assurance is, perhaps, not surprising. What is surprising is that so many social observers could so whole-heartedly condemn the working classes for their improvidence and fecklessness. Even Charles Booth held the view that 'Provident thrift, which lays by for tomorrow, is not a very hardy plant in England', although in the same paragraph he writes: 'I understand that death clubs with a weekly sub-scription of ½*d. to* 2*d.* per head are very commonly subscribed to.'[36] Part of the condemnation occurred because the commen-tators did not comprehend the true extent of thrift, especially thrift through insurance, part because they objected to the extravagant way the insurance benefits were spent. Even in 1937 it could still be said that 'the governing classes in this country are for the most part unaware of the nature and scope of industrial assurance'.[37]

Of prime importance was the ethic of self-help that was the point of reference for most middle-class Victorian social investi-gators. They saw a mass of poor people continually struggling to get out or to stay out of debt, seldom able to save a large enough sum to safeguard their future in times of sickness or unemployment. These were the people Samuel Smiles had branded 'thriftless persons ... They waste their money as they do their time; draw bills upon the future; anticipate their earn-ings; and are thus under the necessity of dragging after them a load of debts and obligations which seriously affect their actions as free and independent men.' It was their own moral failings that led to their position in society, since 'any class of men that lives from hand to mouth will ever be an inferior class'.[38] Almost fifty years after Smiles wrote these words, Margaret Loane, a district nurse who presented an otherwise sympathetic series of pictures of working-class domestic life, could continue the moral tale with as much force as ever:

Broadly speaking, the people who become and remain rich are those who accept all the responsibilities that life brings them, and even seek

[36] Charles Booth, *Life and Labour of the People in London* (London, 1892), 1st ser., i. 46.
[37] Wilson and Levy, *Industrial Assurance*, p. 118.
[38] Smiles, *Self-Help*, pp. 297, 293.

for more; those who continue or who become poor, are those who shirk these responsibilities, those who, almost unknown to themselves, are seeking to shake off some burden which it is for the 'safety, honour and welfare' of their manhood that they should bear.[39]

The poverty of the poor was itself proof enough that they were improvident; hence the standard Charity Organisation Society view that 'the level of the lower *couches sociales* cannot rise until foresight has displaced the hand-to-mouth habit of mind which takes no account of the future'.[40]

If burial insurance was considered at all, it was to condemn it for its inefficiency and expense rather than to praise it for its contribution to thrift. There seemed to be ample reason for this condemnation. Both the cost of management and the rate of lapsing of industrial assurance policies were very high compared with alternative saving methods. In fact, it was largely in an attempt to counter these twin evils that Gladstone introduced the Government Annuities Act in 1864, whereby individuals could purchase life assurance through the Post Office on conditions more advantageous than those offered privately. The industrial insurance companies originally offered no surrender value on policies terminated before maturity, and in this respect the terms of contract were more severe than those offered on ordinary life assurance policies. As Gladstone explained to the Commons:

among the higher classes, a holder of a policy who is unable to continue his payments has a certain proportion, generally about one third of his premiums, repaid to him; but no such right is conceded in the case of the industrial classes. Now, is the lapsing of policies a token of improvidence on the part of the labourer? How can any labouring man answer for payments throughout every week or every quarter of his life. He has no guarantee against want of employment, sickness, the duty of providing for an aged and decrepid parent, or extending generous aid to a friend, or any of the ten thousand calamities to which they are subject. If the poor man fails in any such case—not to speak of improvidences and kindred errors—to pay one premium, the policy drops, and he loses everything he has paid.[41]

[39] Margaret Loane, *From their point of view* (London, 1908), p. 62.
[40] C. H. d'E. Leppington, 'The Charity Organisation System Today', *Economic Review* viii (Jan. 1897), p. 35.
[41] Hansard, 3rd ser., vol. clxxiii, p. 1575 (7 Mar. 1864).

The numbers losing everything they had paid seem to have been very large. In the early 1870s for instance, the Royal Liver was losing 13 per cent of its members each year, and in the period 1877 to 1888 its lapsing rate averaged 11.3 per cent p.a., with the highest rates coinciding with peaks in the numbers of unemployed.[42] The cumulative effect of this high annual lapse rate was that something between 65 per cent and 90 per cent of all industrial assurance policies lapsed before maturity.[43]

The figures need to be looked at carefully. The immediate and obvious implication is that the number of policies in force at any one time represents only a fraction of policies issued, and that the number of people who at some time have purchased industrial assurance will certainly exceed the number insured at any moment. To give an example, between 1916 and 1926 the Companies and Societies together issued 87.7m. new policies, whilst the number of policies in force rose by about 20m.[44] Making due allowance for those policies terminated by death or other means, it is clear that well over half of all policies ending during these eleven years did so through lapse. The figure for Collecting Societies alone for the three years 1924–6 show that 78.7 per cent of terminations were due to lapsing, as against 16.3 per cent that terminated upon the death of the insured.[45] These millions of lapsed policies suggest that some large number of people must have repeatedly taken up a policy and then let it lapse. This was certainly Sidney Webb's view in 1915 when he wrote:

lapsing occurs again and again to the same person or family. Policies are taken out and allowed to lapse; again taken out, and again allowed to lapse; sometimes in the same or other office, even a dozen times within as many years. There is almost a habit of lapsing. It seems from the statistics, and from the testimony of those in touch

[42] Northcote Cmmn., Second Report, q. 1437; Select Committee on the Friendly Societies Act, 1875, PP 1889 x (304), appendix 5, p. 308. The peaks in the lapse rate—14.6 per cent in 1880 and 18.1 per cent in 1887—lag by one year the unemployment peaks of 10.7 per cent and 10.2 per cent. This is no doubt in part due to the period of grace—often up to thirteen weeks—between the commencement of arrears and the lapsing of a policy.

[43] See, for instance, Northcote Cmmn., Third Report, qq. 24987, 25320, 25874–6, 25894–5.

[44] Report of the Industrial Assurance Commissioner for 1927, PP 1928 x, p. 156.

[45] Ibid., p. 154.

with the business, that a large proportion of the wage-earning population all over the kingdom—a proportion comprising literally millions of persons—are incessantly 'in and out' of insurance.[46]

It was just this sort of behaviour which seemed to confirm observers' views of the lack of foresight of many working-class households. They could not look far enough ahead either to safeguard their weekly policy payments by building up a store of savings, or to realize that long-run payment of premiums would be impossible. And their inability to learn this fact from repeated lapsing was yet more proof of financial naïvety or stupidity.

Whether these dismissive views were justified is discussed below, but it was certainly not the case that most lapses involved the policyholder in a large financial loss or the company in a large financial gain. As Table 2.3 shows, the majority of lapses occurred within two years of issue, before any large number of premiums had been paid, although as Wilson and Levy pointed out, 'the aggregate loss to the payers of premiums must nevertheless be considerable'.[47] There were, however, cases of people falling out of benefit after years of payment. To alleviate this problem, the Prudential pioneered in 1878 a system of granting a 'free policy'—that is, a fully paid-up policy for a reduced sum at maturity—to any person who lapsed after five years' payment.[48] By 1886 the Prudential had granted 58,099 free policies; by 1923, when free policies after five years of premium payments for lives over 15 years of age were made compulsory by the Industrial Assurance Act, the Prudential already had granted 2.2m. of them.[49] By the mid-1930s the competition between industrial assurance companies had led to most of them granting free policies upon any lapsed policies

[46] *New Statesman* iv, no. 101 (13 Mar. 1915). 'Special supplement on Industrial Insurance by the Fabian Research Department', edited by Mr S. Webb, p. 10.

[47] Wilson and Levy, *Industrial Assurance*, p. 191.

[48] Free policies were granted after ten years' payment on lives that had attained the age of 21 from 1878, and this was reduced to five years in 1882. Prudential, *A Century of Service* (London, 1948), p. 133.

[49] Annual Reports of the Prudential Assurance Co. The Royal Liver started granting free policies on lapse in 1903. See *A Brief Survey of the History, Objectives and Achievements of the Royal Liver Friendly Society* (Liverpool, 1950), p. 7.

Table 2.3. Examples of industrial assurance policies lapsed in 1913 and 1923, showing the years in which such policies were issued

Lapsed in 1913 Issued in:	1913	1912	1911	1910	1909	1908 and before	TOTAL
Liverpool Victoria	286,169	205,181	41,375	25,700	16,600	58,663	633,688
Pearl	485,492	380,180	66,091	27,667	13,445	27,576	1,000,391
Prudential	373,231	370,411	58,185	26,170	14,239	67,194	909,430

Lapsed in 1923 Issued in:	1923	1922	1921	1920	1919	1918	1917 and before	TOTAL
Liverpool Victoria	161,219	231,503	102,780	78,136	52,199	37,445	97,957	761,239

Sources

For 1913: Parmoor Committee, appendix A, table IV.
For 1923: Returns of the Liverpool Victoria Friendly Society, PRO FS16/57.

more than two years old, though often these would be for trifling sums of just a few shillings at death.[50]

Despite the appearance of being money for nothing, most lapsed policies did not bring large windfall profits to the companies, since the heavy initial cost of agents' commission and clerical work at head office more than outweighed the first few months' premium payments. In 1889 the actuary to the Registry of Friendly Societies could safely assert that 'for some years after policies are taken out ... the societies and companies lose by secession',[51] and an estimate made in 1912 by a trade guide was that expenses in the first year of a policy took 120 per cent of the first years' premiums.[52] Companies often went to great lengths to prevent policies lapsing; for instance, during the Lancashire cotton famine of 1862–4, the Royal Liver extended its period of expulsion,[53] and most companies seem to have given special consideration to policyholders affected by the coal strikes of 1921 and 1926—apparently, some 5 per cent of the Prudential's industrial assurance policyholders took advantage of these special facilities in 1926.[54] The Prudential also initiated in 1870 a scheme whereby agents received commission only on net increase in business, rather than on each new policy issued, as hitherto. This immediately reduced the lapsing rate by one-third by removing the incentive for agents to poach on each other's policyholders, and it was thereafter adopted by most other companies.[55]

Since the companies lost as much from lapsed policies as the

---

[50] Wilson and Levy, *Industrial Assurance*, p. 191.

[51] SC Friendly Societies Act, appendix 4, p. 303. See also the evidence of the General Manager of the Prudential, ibid., q. 4436.

[52] *Insurance Guide and Handbook* (London, 5th edn. 1912), i. 119.

[53] Northcote Cmmn., Second Report, q. 1415.

[54] *Insurance Mail Yearbook for 1928* (London, 1928), p. 15. The Royal London extended its expulsion time by up to eighteen months. Parmoor Cttee., q. 6329. Britannic policyholders who could not pay arrears had the sum assured reduced to compensate for the lost premium payments. The alterations can be seen in the surviving policy registers, with the words 'Industrial Distress 1921' or 'Industrial Distress 1926' written in the margin in red ink.

[55] Northcote Cmmn., Third Report, qq. 25878–9, 25894–5. For a description of poaching, and the harmful effects it had on both policyholders and agents, see Arthur James Berry, 'Notes on the History of the Pearl Assurance Co. Ltd.', an undated typescript held in the history section of the Pearl library at the company's London headquarters.

policyholders themselves, they made strenuous efforts to reduce the rate of lapse. But the same was not always true of management costs—as these went up, the employees and shareholders benefited to the direct cost of the policyholders, and it was on the grounds of high cost that the criticisms of industrial assurance seemed most substantial, and the short-sightedness of the subscribers most acute. Even by 1940, after determined attempts to reduce administrative costs, these took 35 per cent of all industrial assurance premiums, compared with 16 per cent for ordinary life assurance business, where premiums were paid at quarterly intervals or longer.[56] In the nineteenth century, costs of collection and management had been much higher. In 1887, for instance, the expenses of the Prudential were 41.5 per cent of premium income, those of the Royal Liver were 40 per cent, and the small Yorkshire Provident Industrial Assurance Co. was using an amazing 90 per cent of premium income to pay commission and expenses.[57] The general reduction in expenses from over 40 per cent to around 35 per cent that occurred between 1918 and 1940 was due primarily to the efforts of the Prudential in substituting salaried collectors for free-ranging agents paid by commission. This allowed the Pru. to continue to expand its business while reducing the number of agents from 17,524 in 1913 to 12,725 in 1918 and 10,455 in 1932.[58] By dividing towns into separate blocks, each to be served by one salaried collector, the company overcame the problem of its own collectors competing with each other in very large, overlapping areas. It was claimed in 1920 by a former insurance agent that one long street in Hull, housing some 3,500 people, was served by about one hundred insurance agents, of whom twenty or more were employed by the same company.[59]

This step towards greater efficiency could not obscure the fact that weekly door-to-door collection of premiums was a

[56] Beveridge Report, appendix E, p. 279.

[57] SC Friendly Societies Act, appendix 1, p. 295; appendix 5, 308. The affairs of the Yorkshire Provident were investigated by a Select Committee in 1889, and criminal proceedings were taken against the management. Select Committee on Yorkshire Provident Insurance Company, PP 1889 xvi (262).

[58] Parmoor Cttee., qq. 3254–6; Cohen Cttee., appendix B, p. 110.

[59] Parmoor Cttee., q. 1815.

much more expensive way to buy insurance than was the payment of quarterly or annual instalments, an expense which
millions of families appeared to be willing to bear. The rates of
commission paid to agents varied from company to company,
with higher rates on new business compensating for lower rates
on weekly collections, but the average was something over 25
per cent of all premium payments.[60] This sytem of door-to-
door collection and canvassing was seen by many critics as the
curse of industrial assurance, a means whereby 'speculators and
sharpers' could deprive 'the thrifty and respectable working
classes of a considerable portion of their savings'.[61] For people
involved in the business, weekly collection was seen as the *modus
vivendi*. Joseph Degge, one of the founders of the Royal London
Friendly Society, told the Friendly Societies Commissioners
that 'discontinuance of collectors by societies who now employ
them would be tantamount to lapsing the whole of their business in a few years to come'; burial insurance depended upon
'agents, and agents alone'.[62] Industrial assurance catered for
people with small incomes paid at short intervals, therefore premiums were collected in small amounts each week, so as to
coincide with the weekly pay packet. Friday was good only for
canvassing new business, not for taking in money. A manual of
life assurance pointed out that the agent 'gets paid best by those
policyholders upon whom he calls earliest after their wages are
received'.[63]

The role of the collector, for good or evil, was hotly debated
by critics and advocates of industrial assurance. For the critics,
the number of lapsed policies was a clear indication that the
collectors, or 'penny-a-week death hunters' as they were pejor-
atively called,[64] were using their powers of persuasion to enrol
many people who did not really want or who could not afford
the life assurance on offer. Both the Parmoor Committee in
1920 and the Cohen Committee twelve years later concluded
that business was being pushed too far, and at the outbreak of

[60] *New Statesman* supplement, p. 4; *Insurance Guide and Handbook*, i. 119.

[61] Anon., *Useless Thrift, or how the poor are robbed* (London, n.d., *c.*1893), p. 56. See also J. Frome Wilkinson, *Mutual Thrift* (London, 1891), p. 268.

[62] Northcote Cmmn., Third Report, qq. 24995, 25099.

[63] J. Redman Ormerod, *The Essentials to Success in Life Assurance* (London, 2nd edn. 1906), p. 88.

[64] Les Moss, *Live and Learn* (Brighton, 1979), p. 5.

the Second World War 'the scale of abortive insurance was as large as ever'.[65] The reason for this over-persuasion was the commission earned by the agents. There had been little change in the seventy-five years since Gladstone described them as 'preachers and denominational missionaries, who, animated by the golden vision of 25 per cent on the premiums paid, find their way into every cottage in the country'.[66] Agents, according to a critical account written in the 1930s, had 'convinced themselves, by long years of self-persuasion, that it is little short of immoral for a man to be underassured', and they tended to view lapses not as a sign of a real inability to pay, but as an indicator of the financial recidivism of the masses.[67]

It was true that incessant seeking after new business was necessary if an agent were to increase his income, and trade journals seldom counselled moderation. Advice to agents would often be of this sort:

Try to Induce every Person to Assure. Take a proposal for the least possible amount where you cannot get a larger sum, and then follow it up as prudently as you can to get it increased to a larger sum. There are few persons who assure as much as they can, or as they ought, and there are fewer still whose first assurance is as large as they may be induced to make it.[68]

For every cautionary tale about the dangers of extending business in a house already in arrears can be found the contrary opinion that the policy should be increased 'so as to make the contract between the Company and the assured of more importance', as then 'it would be looked upon as a valuable undertaking, and worth looking after'.[69] This sort of high-pressure selling must have led to some over-extension of industrial assurance, but not all the business or all the lapses could be dismissed simply as the consequence of the selling methods. As a critical

[65] Beveridge Report, appendix D, p. 266.

[66] Hansard, 3rd ser., vol. clxxiii, p. 1565 (7 Mar. 1864).

[67] Wilson and Levy, *Industrial Assurance*, pp. 206–7.

[68] Advice in a letter sent to all new agents of the Refuge Assurance Society from James Procter, Managing Director 1872–88. Cyril Clegg, *Friend in Deed* (London, 1958), p. 50. The message was quoted approvingly by *The Assurance Herald* I, no. 3 (1 Mar. 1887), p. 17.

[69] Frederick H. Gisborne, *Life Assurance. How to Conduct an Agency* (Windsor, n.d., c.1897), pp. 4–5. This is directly at odds with Ormerod, *Essentials to Success*, p. 108.

Fabian essayist wrote in 1943, 'the flow of new policies has been stimulated by the high-pressure salesmanship methods of the agents, but the procuration of 10 million new policies every year can hardly be ascribed to an artificially induced demand alone. The public want burial insurance'.[70] There is also clear evidence that unemployment caused a fluctuation in family income which was a major factor in the lapse rate. The actuary to the Prudential thought that the small number of lapses that the company experienced between 1916 and 1918 was due to 'the considerable means of the general population; money was so plentiful'.[71] The lapses of the Liverpool Victoria shown in Table 2.3 support this view. The much higher rate of lapse in 1923 than 1913 of policies over five years old—17.8 per cent against 9.3 per cent—points to a higher than usual rate of continuation during the years of wartime prosperity, whilst the depression from the end of 1921 forced many of the long-term policyholders to renege on payments. In 1924 a district manager of the Pearl Assurance Co. asserted that 'there is no doubt that in a general sense, the primary or principal cause of arrears is low paid work or unemployment'.[72] And during the Second World War, the number of lapses fell to one-third of the pre-war level, 'quite definitely due to the greater economic security of the people in wartime'.[73]

The advocates of industrial assurance could counter criticism by showing that without the pressure of the collector calling each week, millions of people would go without any insurance at all. A number of companies allowed policyholders to claim back about 20 per cent of the annual premium if they acted as their own collectors, bringing or posting their subscriptions weekly to the central office, but they all found that 'people who live nearest the office as a rule lapse their policies when they undertake to bring the money themselves'.[74] It was, however,

[70] Louis Ginsberg, 'Industrial Life Assurance', in William A. Robson (ed.), *Social Security* (London, 1943), p. 262.

[71] Parmoor Cttee., q. 3209.

[72] H. Higgins, *The District Manager* (London, 1924), p. 22.

[73] Industrial Life Offices, *Industrial Assurance Explained—A Reply to Criticisms* (London, 1944), p. 12.

[74] Northcote Cmmn., Third Report, q. 24994. See also ibid., Second Report, qq. 2144, 10947, 11354; SC Friendly Societies Act, q. 4436.

the experience of the government life assurance scheme, operated through the Post Office, that showed most clearly the need for collectors.

Post Office life assurance was incorporated in Gladstone's Government Annuities Act of 1864, and came into operation in April 1865.[75] It provided for life insurance on individuals from 16 to 60 years of age for sums between £20 and £100, with premiums paid direct to a post office. Aside from the lack of collection, the scheme was quite inappropriate for the bulk of working-class insurers towards whom it was aimed, as the minimum assurance of £20 was well above the figure that most of them could afford.[76] Even in 1926 the average sum assured for by industrial assurance policies was only £15; in 1913 it had been £11, in 1898 £9.[77] The minimum sum assured in the Post Office scheme was in 1884 reduced to £5, the lower age limit to 8 years, and the scheme was linked to the Post Office Saving Bank, so that deposits of any amount could be made at any time during the year, with the annual premium being deducted from the individual's account. Sums assured for a given premium were little more in the Post Office than in industrial assurance companies, but contributions of Post Office insurers ceased at 60 years of age, instead of at 75 with the Pru., or at death with most other companies. Window bills were put up in all Post Offices to advertise the scheme, but with the number of policies issued annually seldom exceeding 1,000, and often standing below 300, its appeal was clearly always very limited. A committee of investigation recommended in 1908 that advertising should be increased, and that weekly premium payment should be made possible by the sticking of postage stamps in stamp premium books,[78] but the subsequent increase in new business in 1914 proved to be transitory. When the Post Office

[75] For an outline history of the government scheme see Morrah, *Industrial Life Assurance*, pp. 29–35, and Parmoor Cttee., qq. 7068–204.

[76] Gladstone's original aim, according to the deviser of the Post Office scheme, was to allow assurances from £5 to £200, but he was compelled to abandon these limits owing to parliamentary opposition organized by the life assurance companies. See Northcote Cmmn., Third Report, q. 27759.

[77] *Insurance Mail Yearbook* (1928), p. 15; *The Insurance Agent and the Insurance Review*, xxxiii, no. 392 (1 Sept. 1898), p. 136.

[78] Departmental Committee appointed to consider the question of encouraging the Life Assurance system of the Post Office [Farrer Cttee.] PP 1908 xxv (311), Report, pp. v–vii.

scheme closed, on 31 December 1928, it had 9,956 contracts in force, assuring a sum of £494,536. On the same date the number of contracts in force in industrial life offices was 73,107,970, assuring a sum of £1,119,436,376.[79] The Post Office scheme did not even provide insurance for the working class on a small scale—the average sum assured for was between three and four times greater than that in commercial industrial assurance, and those who bought Post Office insurance were 'people of a standing somewhat above the lower class of wage earners'.[80]

The only clear advantage the Post Office scheme offered was cessation of payment at 60, but, as the Parmoor Committee pointed out, 'the proposer for assurance looks to the rate of premium and the sum assured, and the question whether, assuming that he survives, he is to pay for 40 years or for 50 is not in his mind and would receive little weight if it were suggested to him'.[81] Of course, it never was suggested to him, whereas the companies were very generous with the doorstep praise they gave their own schemes. The agent was more than willing to explain the few questions asked on the proposal form, and even fill it out for the client,[82] whilst the prospective Post Office insurer was faced with a double sheet of foolscap containing sixteen 'inquisitorial' questions.[83] Furthermore, Post Office advertising literature, according to the chairman of the Brixworth Board of Guardians, was just 'not in the tongue "understanded of the people"'.[84] But the civil servants who ran the state scheme had no doubts—its ultimate failure was due not to poor advertising or complex proposal forms, but the lack of

---

[79] R. B. Walker and D. R. Woodgate, *Principles and Practice of Industrial Assurance* (London, 2nd edn. 1943), p. 4.

[80] Parmoor Cttee., q. 7176.

[81] Ibid., Report, para. 31.

[82] The practice of filling out the form on the client's behalf was sometimes actually advocated, with an ulterior motive in view: 'In filling up the proposal, write replies to *every* question distinctly. Insert the full Christian name of the person whose life is to be assured, with address and occupation. Leave the *amount* blank till he has signed, then in most cases suggest a *larger* sum than that spoken of.' *Memoranda for Life Assurance Agents* (London, 8th edn. *c.*1892), p. 9.

[83] Farrer Cttee., qq. 5–20.

[84] Aberdare Cmmn., qq. 4565–6.

agents: 'we have never done a large business, for the reason that we have never employed canvassers or collectors'.[85] Sir Edward Brabrook agreed. For the Post Office to compete with the companies, it would have to take its insurance to the masses by means of a 'special collecting postman'; in other words, it would have to adopt the very same system that it was established to counter.[86]

Despite all the attention devoted to collectors and the cost of collection, little effort was made to understand why so many million people were prepared to pay upward of a third of their life assurance premiums for the privilege of having the monies collected from their home each week. Did this just represent the cost of the time that would otherwise be spent taking premiums to an insurer or post office, were there other benefits to be gained from collection, or were the critics right to dismiss most of the working population as naïve and profligate in their attempts at domestic money management?

Certainly collection of premiums was a service that many hard-worked housewives might have been prepared to pay for. Industrial assurance was a system built almost entirely on the payments made by women—'they pay these pence, and it is through their instrumentality to a very great extent that burial societies flourish', according to a representative of a Liverpool burial club.[87] As an agents' guide put it, 'The wife is the Chancellor of the Exchequer and not only provides supplies but also saves for each member of the household, including her husband.'[88] To be successful, a collector 'must be a ladies' man, or he'll never do any good'.[89] In defending the collection system before the Friendly Societies Commissioners, the solicitor to the Royal Liver Friendly Society explained that:

the 1*d.* a week to the burial society is generally paid, not by the man himself, who comes home late at night, but by the wife; she keeps the

[85] Parmoor Cttee., q. 7098.

[86] E. W. Brabrook, *Provident Societies and Industrial Welfare* (London, 1898), pp. 78–9.

[87] Northcote Cmmn., Second Report, q. 2405. Also, ibid., Third Report, q. 25944; Hamilton Cmmn., app., vol. iii, q. 35164; *New Statesman* supplement, p. 24.

[88] 'A. Fieldman', *The Industrial Agents' Companion* (London, c.1935), p. 2.

[89] Northcote Cmmn., Asst. Cmmrs. Ireland and Wales, PP 1874 xxiii pt. ii (C. 995), appendix I, p. 27.

money handy somewhere, and she expects the collector to call for it, nor would her domestic duties allow her to leave the distant part of Liverpool to go to Prescott St. to pay over the counter to the Royal Liver. The time it would take her to go that distance would be worth more to her than the farthing she pays for somebody to come to her.[90]

There must be some truth in this view, though it neatly overlooks the fact that most households had children who were frequently called on to run errands, and for large families running an errand with the insurance money could have saved several valuable pence each week.[91]

There was another, and much more pressing, though seldom stated, reason why premiums had to be collected, a reason directly linked to the exigency of balancing the family budget. Income tended to fluctuate considerably from week to week, so that a few days of relative plenty might be succeeded by days of relative want. In order to protect any savings from raids during the periods of hardship they were frequently and quite deliberately made inaccessible by putting the money into some contingency fund—'You want to have it where you can't get hold of it', explained a building labourer's wife in Lancashire just before the outbreak of the Second World War.[92] Attempts to save at home were normally doomed to failure, because, as one advocate of mutual thrift explained,

The everyday demands upon the average workman's wife to spend the weekly earnings are too strong to resist; the nest-egg of a few weeks, collected by great sacrifice and often after bitter reflections as to the wisdom of undergoing present suffering on the chance of reaping future comfort she sees again and again dissipated by some unlooked-for calamity, until the efforts to provide for the future—heroic efforts in many instances—become fewer and less sustained, and the hand-to-mouth existence becomes established.[93]

The importance of the agent was in putting external pressure on the housewife in those weeks of hardship to induce her to

[90] Northcote Cmmn., Second Report, q. 23387.

[91] On these unofficial labours of childhood, see Robert Roberts, *A Ragged Schooling* (London, 1978), *passim*.

[92] Mass-Observation Archive, Sussex University (hereafter M-O), box 17, file A. Responses to the South Lancashire Saving Survey.

[93] I. H. Mitchell, 'Trade Unions', in *Thrift Manual* (London, 1906), p. 66. See also *Insurance Mail Yearbook* for 1908, p. 26.

save even when there was scarcely enough money to feed the family. It was his role to remind the policyholder of long-run goals when immediate financial pressures seemed overwhelming—he imposed the sort of discipline for saving that many people could not exercise on their own, and without this discipline lapsing rates would certainly have been higher.

The agents also had a social function. Each week they visited millions of separate homes—more frequently, as Sidney Webb pointed out, than clergymen, doctors, or any official of the state—and they inevitably came to be a potent force in British working-class life.[94] Within his local collecting area, the industrial assurance agent was a man of standing, and he had an unrivalled opportunity to observe the economic well-being of each family, and to pass this information on to his other subscribers. According to Lloyd George, there was 'nobody more acceptable in the houses of the working people than these agents'.[95] The insurance man was one of the first to know if a family was insolvent, and his entrée into a house each week allowed him to see whether there were any additions or losses to the stock of possessions—changes often jealously guarded from neighbours' eyes. He was the controller of a grapevine of information about personal economic conditions, and he had the ability to elevate or slur the family's character. 'The fact is', said one friendly society secretary, talking about collectors, 'that these men go round and gossip, and the thing is talked about in the district, and everybody is proud of paying to the man.'[96]

The overriding reason for insurance was, however, financial—people wanted enough money for a decent burial. Table 2.4 gives a few examples of the sums that were paid on death. It is immediately clear from this that seldom were any two policies issued by different companies identical in all respects, and the fine actuarial calculations needed to establish which policy offered the best return on investment were too difficult for the layman to attempt. The choice between companies therefore

[94] *New Statesman* supplement, p. 4.
[95] Hansard, 5th ser., vol. clxxiv, col. 115 (18 May 1925). I would like to thank Brian Harrison for drawing my attention to this reference.
[96] Northcote Cmmn., Third Report, q. 24625.

Table 2.4. Terms of insurance offered by different companies in 1928

Child Whole-Life Assurance
Age next birthday 1 year; weekly premium 1*d.*

If death after:	0–13 weeks	14–26 weeks	27 + weeks	10 years
Blackburn Philanthropic	£1.10s.	£3	£6	£12.10s.
Britannic	£1.10s.	£3	£6	£15
Co-operative	£1.10s.	£3	£6	£16. 3s.
Liverpool Victoria	none	none	£6	£15
Pearl	£1.10s.	£3	£6	£13
Prudential	£1.10s.	£3	£6	£15
Royal Liver	£1.10s.	£3	£6	£15
Royal London	£1.10s.	£4.10s.	£6	£15

Adult Whole-Life Assurance
Age next birthday 21 years; weekly premium 1*d.*

If death after (weeks):	0–13	14–26	27 +	With profits	Free policy after:	Payments continue until:
Blackburn Philanthropic	¼	½	full = £ 9. 4s.	X	5 years	death
Britannic	¼	½	full = £ 8.18s.	X	5 years	death
Co-operative	full	full	full = £10.16s.	√	5 years	75 years
Liverpool Victoria	¼	½	full = £ 9.17s.	√	5 years	death
Pearl	¼	½	full = £10. 9s.	X	5 years	death
Prudential	¼	½	full = £10.11s.	√	3 years	75 years
Refuge	¼	½	full = £10.16s.	X	5 years	death
Royal Liver	¼	½	full = £10. 4s.	√	5 years	70 years
Royal London	½	½	full = £ 9.14s.	√	5 years	death

Adult Endowment Assurance
Age next birthday 21 years; weekly premium 6*d.*, twenty-year endowment assurance

If death after (weeks)	0–13	14–26	27 weeks to 20 years, or at maturity
Blackburn Philanthropic	¼	½	full = £20.19s.6d.
Britannic	¼	½	full = £22. 3s.
Co-operative	full	full	full = £21. 3s.
Liverpool Victoria	¼	½	full = £23. 2s.
Prudential	¼	½	full = £21. 6s.
Royal Liver	¼	½	full = £20. 2s.

Conditions of bonus, etc., as for adult whole-life policies

Source: Stone and Cox Industrial and Monthly Tables (London, 1928), *passim.*

rested very much on advertising, word-of-mouth recommenda-
tion, and the personal charm of the agent. This perhaps
accounts for the apparent paradox pointed out by Beveridge,
that despite having the lowest expenses ratio of any industrial
assurance office, the Prudential grew more slowly between the
wars than any other large Companies and Societies.[97]

One other point needs to be made briefly about this financial
aspect of industrial assurance. There was a marked change in
the type of industrial assurance being purchased after 1918—in
fact this was the only major change in the demand for this sort
of assurance in the seventy years covered by this survey, aside
from continual growth. Originally the companies sold only
whole-life assurances—that is, policies maturing on the death
of the insured—but in the 1880s they began to offer endowments (maturing after a given number of years) and endowment assurances (maturing after a given number of years, or at
death if sooner). In 1895 there were under 100,000 such assurances in force, but this figure rose sharply from 1897 to reach
3.5m. by 1912. Thereafter the growth was very rapid—to 7.2m.
in 1922, and 13m. in 1931. Between 1920 and 1930, total industrial assurance premium income rose by about 66 per cent,
endowment and endowment assurance income rose by 350 per
cent, from one-ninth of the total to one-quarter.[98]

Two reasons may be adduced to explain this marked change
in insurance habits. First, the fall in mortality rates (especially
infant mortality) in the twenty years either side of 1900, and
the concomitant increase in longevity, made death insurance
less financially worthwhile, whilst an endowment for old age
became increasingly attractive, particularly after the introduction of state old-age pensions if the arguments made about
savings thresholds are to be believed.[99] The abrupt fall in infant
mortality rates may be especially significant here, as child
insurance was a large and important part of industrial assurance business—important because the offer to insure a new-

[97] Beveridge Report, appendix D, pp. 257–8.
[98] Figures from: Statement of Accounts of Life Insurance and Annuity Business, PP
1897 lxxxi, 1899 xc, 1926 xii; Statistical Abstract, PP 1914–16 lxxvi; Cohen Cttee.,
Report, p. 5.
[99] See below, pp. 201–2.

born baby was one of the best ways for the agent to get a foot across the doorstep,[100] and large because the proportion of children in the population was very high. Companies were always anxious to take on child insurance because it was highly profitable. The maximum sum assured on child lives was limited by the Life Assurance Companies Act of 1870 to £6 for children under 5 and £10 for those between 5 and 10 (increased by the 1923 Act to £6 under 3, £10 under 6, and £15 under 10).[101] However, the actuarial worth of a 1*d.* a week insurance on a child rose much more rapidly than this: according to the English Life Table No. 6 (Male) the sum assured for one penny a week rose from £1.5*s.*3*d.* in the first year, when infant mortality was high, to £10.10*s.*4*d.* for a two-year-old, and to over £77 for a nine-year-old.[102] The companies were in the peculiar position of being forced by law to restrict competition and take handsome profits on all child insurance for two-year-olds and above. It is not true to say, however, as some critics did, that industrial assurance was principally infant or child insurance; as Sidney Webb remarked, 'both the aggregate of policies in force and the new business in any one year of any of the colossal offices do not greatly differ in age distribution from the census population'.[103]

Second, the increase in endowments and endowment assurances may reflect a general increase in prosperity. An analysis of a Prudential agent's collecting book carried out for the Cohen Committee showed that the average weekly premium on whole-life policies was 2¼*d.*, on endowments it was 6½*d.*[104] The ability to pay these higher premiums could come not only from increased real family income, but also from the decreasing number of children per family.[105] Whatever the reason for it, the growth of endowment assurance in the twentieth century may be seen as an indicator of greater long-term financial planning, particularly planning for greater sufficiency in old age.

To say that the prime motive for the purchase of industrial

---

[100] Northcote Cmmn., Second Report, q. 22560.
[101] Morrah, *Industrial Life Assurance*, pp. 50, 96.
[102] *Insurance Guide and Handbook*, i. 121.
[103] *New Statesman* supplement, p. 27.
[104] Cohen Cttee., Report, pp. 5, 7.
[105] R. M. Titmus, 'The Position of Women', in *Essays on 'The Welfare State'* (London, 1958), p. 89.

assurance was financial does not explain why this particular method of accumulation was, despite its inefficiencies, so overwhelmingly popular. To comprehend this, we have to look beyond economic factors, or else we come up against the same barriers of incomprehension as those contemporary commentators who could decry the profligacy of burial insurance but not explain its entrenched position in working-class life. We need look no further than the pauper funeral. In a detailed study of burial practices, published in 1938, Wilson and Levy wrote:

> though a pauper funeral may be 'decent', it is still felt to be a slur on the dead and on their relatives ... The feelings of shame aroused by the common grave are enhanced by the idea that such interment represents the loneliness of the corpse for whom nobody cares except the Poor Law Authorities, who are simply fulfilling a statutory or sanitary obligation. These feelings are, to our knowledge, as strong as ever today. The poorer the individual, the lower in the social scale, the deeper his sense of guilt and shame if he cannot promise a decent burial for his relatives.[106]

The same was true in the 1870s, when Samuel Smiles remarked that 'the desire to secure respectable interment for departed relatives, is a strong and widely-diffused feeling among the labouring population', though he censoriously added, 'Such an expense, at such a time, is ruinous, and altogether unjustifiable. Does putting on garments of a certain colour constitute true mourning? Is it not the heart and the affections that mourn, rather than the outside raiment?'[107]

To which the obvious answer was 'no', because funerals were not just affairs for private mourning, they were the 'greatest festivals of all' in working-class life.[108] The Mass-Observation study of Bolton (alias 'Worktown') in the 1930s led Tom Harrison to conclude that 'Death was the biggest Peace-time drama in Worktown. Many poor people saved all their lives to have impressive funerals and tombstones ... The fascination of dying, sickness, and above all, funerals and cemeteries commands an extraordinary interest. Watching other people going

---

[106] Sir Arnold Wilson and H. J. Levy, *Burial Reform* (Oxford, 1938), pp. 63–4.
[107] Samuel Smiles, *Thrift* (London, 1875), pp. 256–7.
[108] Helen Bosanquet, *Rich and Poor* (London, 2nd edn. 1898), p. 124.

to their graves was as good as a film and cheaper.'[109] There was an intensely competitive edge to the ceremony of death which seemed wildly extravagant to the outside observer, but which was customary to most local communities. When death occurs,

according to the fierce code of honour prevailing in the district, this is a time for display ... and who knows better than the widow that a score of eyes are watching events through broken Venetian blinds and dirty Nottingham lace curtains, which screen something yet more sordid, in order to see how the Joneses or the Williamses come through the ordeal.[110]

The fear of a pauper funeral was something that clearly drew on the widespread Victorian dislike of pauperism and the Poor Law, but it came to signify much more than this, so that whilst the sense of shame at receiving grants from the Public Assistance Committee in the 1930s was much less than that experienced by mid-Victorian paupers, Rowntree could still claim in his second survey of York that 'the dread of a parish funeral is as great as ever it was'.[111] What people wanted was a 'respectable' funeral, and in general greater expense was held to confer increased respectability. A respectable funeral had to have all close relations dressed in black, horse-drawn (later motorized) carriages and hearse, and afterwards, 'a social gathering and more or less eating and drinking for which it affords occasion'. And quite clearly, the more the better; it was on this that the majority of industrial life assurance money was spent.[112] Sometimes the debts incurred on one showy funeral were so great that they prevented the payment of further insurance premiums on surviving members of the family.[113] How far this idea of a respectable funeral was of ancient inheritance it is difficult to say. It is true that the undertaking trade had little prominence until the 1860s except in large towns, and Wilson

---

[109] *Britain in the 1930s—Worktown by Camera*. Photographs by Humphrey Spender, commentary by Tom Harrison (Royal College of Art, 1975, limited edition). The quotation comes from a commentary on a photograph of a funeral cortège lined up in a Bolton street.

[110] Bertram S. Puckle, *Funeral Customs: their origin and development* (London, 1926), p. 96.

[111] Rowntree, *Poverty and Progress*, p. 212.

[112] *New Statesman* supplement, p. 7.

[113] D. N. Paton, J. C. Dunlop, and E. M. Inglis, *A Study of the Diet of the Labouring Classes in Edinburgh* (Edinburgh, 1901), p. 20.

and Levy have inferred from this that there was little demand for expensive funeral display until grasping undertakers foisted this on an unsuspecting public.[114] But one can look with equal or greater reason to the supersession of the local walking funeral by the horse-drawn hearse when distant municipal cemeteries had to be used instead of the overcrowded parish burial grounds, and also to the evolution of the role of the funeral in urban working-class culture—a development still awaiting historical study.[115]

The desire for respectability, for flamboyant display that would impress friends and neighbours, provided the positive incentive to save in any way that would make this possible—and, of course, the most accessible way was through some sort of burial insurance. To this desire for display was linked the negative impulse of avoiding a pauper funeral—the worst sort of pauperdom, a stigma not only on the dead, but on those living who could not pay for a more becoming interment. Families would break up their home and sell off their furniture if struck by the calamity of the death of an uninsured child.[116] They would even go short of food and hasten their deaths in order to afford the insurance premiums. Of a sample of 267 York families living below the poverty line in 1936, Rowntree found 99 paying up to 5 per cent of their income on life insurance, 93 paid between 5 and 10 per cent, and 30 paid between 10 and 20.9 per cent of income.[117]

The revulsion against being buried 'on the parish' came not only from a hatred of the stigma of pauperism in general,[118] but from the specific conditions of pauper burial. This is how they were described by the Secretary of the British Undertakers Association in 1932:

A common interment is a grave dug ten, fifteen or twenty feet deep

---

[114] Wilson and Levy, *Burial Reform*, p. 89.
[115] Although this is touched on in a stimulating article by Gareth Stedman Jones, 'Working-Class Culture and Working-Class Politics in London, 1870–1900; Notes on the Re-making of the Working Class', *Journal of Social History* vii (1974), esp. pp. 473–4.
[116] Liverpool Joint Research Committee, *How the Casual Labourer Lives* (Liverpool, 1909), p. 5; COS Case Papers, area 1, box 2, case 15194.
[117] Rowntree, *Poverty and Progress*, p. 213.
[118] Edwin Cannan, 'The Stigma of Pauperism', *Economic Review* v (July 1895), pp. 380–91.

and the bodies are put in one after another. There will be about eight adult persons in that grave, and they will finish off the top with a layer of four children so there may be twelve to sixteen people in one grave ... People talk about pit burials, that is what are called common interments.[119]

Little wonder, then, that even workhouse inmates would strive to secure a private burial by getting their relatives to pay insurance money for them. This relieved the Guardians of a financial burden they were pleased to be rid of, so they made no objection. If the experience of the Swansea and Yeovil Unions is at all representative, then around half of all workhouse inmates who died in the first decade of this century were buried privately on the proceeds of insurance policies.[120] This, of course, was decried by middle-class advocates of working-class thrift. If there was enough money to pay for the old folks' burial, there should be enough to keep them out of the workhouse.[121] But it was sensible behaviour for the families involved—if the shame of pauperism was to fall on a family, then at least it could be minimized at reasonable cost by ensuring that the final send-off was glorious.

The enormous edifice of industrial life assurance, with its millions of policies and members, its vast annual income and capital, rested on a desire for the social display involved in the working-class idea of a respectable funeral. In time, some sort of social distinction, albeit minimal, came to be vested in the act of paying the insurance money—people were 'proud' of doing so. The social distinction arose because friends and neighbours could watch the payment—or rather, the call of the insurance man. If he stopped calling, it was a clear sign of economic distress in a particular family. Consequently, the insurance policy itself acquired a social importance; many families would hang the insurance book up where it could be seen and so talked about by visitors.[122] The importance of the policy was

[119] In evidence to the Cohen Committee. Quoted in Wilson and Levy, *Burial Reform*, p. 28.

[120] Hamilton Cmmn., app., vol. v, PP 1909 xli (Cd. 4888), q. 50438(4); ibid., app., vol. vii, qq. 69643–7. The same was true of outdoor paupers; see R. G. Garnett, *A Century of Co-operative Insurance* (London, 1968), p. 97.

[121] Wilkinson, *Mutual Thrift*, pp. 276–7.

[122] *Insurance Mail*, no. 578 (29 May 1915), p. 341.

enhanced by its technical language. Policyholders may not have understood any of the fine points of the contract,[123] but 'they appreciate the high-sounding words used on the present-day policies. They would not consider themselves properly insured unless their policy was full of words such as "Whereas", "Aforesaid", "Hereinafter", "Notwithstanding", etc.'[124]

'It will be very difficult', wrote Samuel Smiles in 1875, 'to alter the mourning customs of our time . . . Still, common sense, repeatedly expressed, will have its influence; and, in course of time, it cannot fail to modify the fashions of society.'[125] Seventy years was not enough time; but his sort of thrifty 'common sense' was never applicable to the economic life of mean streets.

[123] *New Statesman* supplement, p. 24.

[124] *Insurance Mail*, no. 597 (9 Oct. 1915), p. 665. From a paper read to the Manchester Insurance Institute by a Prudential Co. actuary.

[125] Smiles, *Thrift*, p. 257.

3

Sickness, Unemployment, Old Age

SICKNESS was often a double blow to the economic well-being of a working-class family. Medical assistance was costly; the question of 'whether one should call in the doctor, at considerable expense ... was often an agonizing decision in a family already stricken with poverty'.[1] If professional advice could not be afforded, the experience of local amateurs could be hired or patent medicines purchased, but even this was an expensive business.[2] If it was the main wage-earner who was stricken, diminished income made it yet more difficult to meet medical fees, and so savings had to be drawn upon or debts incurred. Even the healthiest of families had to face the costs of confinement and the perennial infantile diseases like measles and whooping cough.

Cash saved under the mattress, on the mantelpiece, or in the bank could provide a reserve to pay these necessary fees, but the haphazard incidence of injury or sickness made the pooling of risks and resources through an insurance fund sensible. The primitive nature of actuarial calculation before the middle of the nineteenth century had not prevented the development of mutual societies for insurance against loss of earnings due to sickness. Eden found friendly societies in every corner of England in 1795, and J. M. Ludlow believed they had their roots in the medieval guilds.[3] Many societies revelled in tracing a dubious lineage back to Roman times; one claimed to predate the Flood.[4] The first relevant piece of legislation, 'An Act

---

[1] Roberts, *Ragged Schooling*, p. 20. See also Lady Bell, *At the Works* (London, 1907), p. 80.

[2] On the use made of patent medicines and the cost of doctors, see F. B. Smith, *The People's Health 1830-1910* (London, 1979), pp. 345, 369-78.

[3] Gosden, *Friendly Societies*, pp. 2, 4. This is the standard institutional history, and is based largely on evidence presented to the Northcote Commission.

[4] Or so its name suggests—The Royal Antediluvian Order of Buffaloes. For the myths surrounding the beginnings of the Oddfellows, see R. W. Moffrey, *A Century of Oddfellowship* (Manchester, 1910), pp. 11–13. See also Bye-Laws of the Caution Lodge of the Ancient Noble Order of United Odd-Fellows, Neptune Inn, Hebden Bridge (Todmorden, 1868), p. 2. Calderdale District Record Office, TU 9/8.

for the Encouragement and Relief of Friendly Societies', was passed in 1793, and major consolidation and extension of the law took place in 1875 and 1896, very much as a response to autonomous developments within the societies themselves.[5] Governments assisted working-class mutual insurance by granting tax exemptions and legal protection of funds, but the nineteenth-century *laissez-faire* tradition precluded any more direct official support for these attempts at self-help. None the less, by the early 1870s, friendly society insurance was common throughout Great Britain, and it was expanding. As the first two columns in Table 3.1 show, friendly society membership more than doubled between the mid-1880s and the Second World War.

These aggregate figures must be viewed with great caution, because the broad term 'friendly society' encompassed a number of functionally distinct institutions, from doctor's clubs to savings banks, which performed very different roles and had quite distinctive standing in the working-class hierarchy of thrift. They were grouped together by the government because they all came within the ambit of friendly society legislation— that is, they were mutual societies designed to give to their members a wide range of non-trade benefits, the most common of which were 'the relief of members in sickness' and 'the payment of a sum of money on death, generally only for funeral expenses'.[6] If the statistics of friendly society membership are subdivided by functional group, the pattern of constant growth up to 1939 becomes much less obvious. The most popular societies were accumulating societies, so called because they accumulated in a reserve fund the annual excess of contributions over benefits in order to provide for increased sickness claims in old age and, in a few cases, an old-age pension. Accumulating societies were themselves divided by legislation into two classes, known as affiliated societies and ordinary societies. Affiliated societies were those organized on a branch

[5] This has been clearly shown by Barry Supple, 'Legislation and Virtue: An Essay on Working Class Self-Help and the State in the Early Nineteenth Century' in Neil McKendrick (ed.), *Historical Perspectives: Studies in English thought and society in honour of J. H. Plumb* (London, 1974), pp. 211–54.

[6] *The Guide Book of the Friendly Societies Registry Office* (HMSO, 1912), sections 41–3.

Table 3.1. Membership and funds of ordinary and affiliated friendly societies; membership and annual lapse rate of the Independent Order of Oddfellows, Manchester Unity, and of the Ancient Order of Foresters

	(1) OFS members (m.)	(2) AFS members (m.)	(3) OFS funds (£m.)	(4) AFS funds (£m.)	(5) IOOFMU members (000)	(6) IOOFMU annual secessions (%)	(7) AOF members (000)	(8) AOF annual secessions (%)
1870					405	3.49	356	
1871					412	3.00	374	
1872					423	3.10	397	
1973					436	2.37	419	
1874					447	2.78	438	
1875					459	3.26	460	
1876					468	3.00	476	
1877					475	2.73	487	
1878					480	3.12	495	5.02
1879					483[a]	3.35[a]	504	4.95
1880					486	3.65	515	4.77
1881					493	3.40	519	4.66
1882					502[a]	3.62[a]	534	4.47
1883					511	3.84	553	4.41
1884					522	3.50	571	4.44
1885	1.96				531	3.67	579	4.38
1886		1.8[b]	8.53	11.6[b]	542	3.60	592	4.45
1887		1.9[b]		12.2[b]	550	3.79	602	4.53
1888		1.9[b]		12.7[b]	558	3.54	612	4.27
1889		2.0[b]		13.4[b]	568	3.62	622	4.11
1890		2.1[b]		13.8[b]	579	3.48	637	3.73
1891	2.02	2.1[b]	9.07	14.2[b]	594	3.22	645	3.96

Year								
1892		2.2ᵇ		14.8ᵇ	612	4.00	652	4.18
1893		2.2ᵇ		15.3ᵇ	627	3.76	655	4.07
1894		2.2ᵇ		16.0ᵇ	637	3.57	658	3.97
1895		2.2ᵇ		16.4ᵇ	653	3.71	655	3.72
1896		2.3ᵇ		17.1ᵇ	665	3.42	658	3.43
1897		2.4ᵇ		17.9ᵇ	682	3.41	660	3.49ᵃ
1898	2.73	2.56	13.17	18.5	698	3.47	661	3.55
1899	2.81	2.41	13.75	19.0	711	3.42	666	3.31
1900	2.87	2.46	14.37	19.7	724	3.23	667	3.02
1901	2.94	2.54	15.0	20.5	736	3.52	675	3.09
1902	2.99	2.61	15.4	21.0	744	3.45	675	3.19
1903	3.06	2.61	15.9	22.5	752	3.62	672	3.25
1904	3.13	2.61	17.0	23.4	755	3.69	664	3.68
1905	3.23	2.67	18.1	23.9	755	3.64	657	3.69
1906	3.23ᵃ	2.69ᵃ	18.7ᵃ	24.7ᵃ	754	3.51	648	3.40
1907	3.42	2.71	19.3	25.6	752	3.29	639	3.32
1908	3.47	2.70	20.0	26.4	753	3.33	629	3.31
1909	3.53	2.70	21.0	27.2	751	3.44	618	3.28
1910	3.52	2.78	21.8	27.9	749	3.16	612	2.95
1911	3.62	2.89ᶜ	22.5	28.6ᶜ	753	3.19	601	3.04
1912	3.83	3.00ᶜ	22.7	28.8ᶜ	752	3.39	688	2.65
1913	3.82	2.98ᶜ	23.0	29.1ᶜ	884	4.73	669	4.21
1914	3.70	2.92ᶜ	23.6	29.7ᶜ	862	4.61	648	3.80
1915	3.65	2.88ᶜ	24.6	30.7ᶜ	832	3.09	632	2.54
1916	3.66	2.88	25.6	31.8	811	2.02	619	2.21
1917	3.68	2.88	27.2	32.5	794	1.45	608	1.26
1918	3.71	2.90	28.6	32.9	781	1.11	599	1.31
1919	3.97	2.98ᵃ	30.2	34.2ᵃ	769	1.59	603	1.57
1920	4.16	3.06	32.0	35.5	777	3.11	600	2.39
1921	4.27	3.09ᵃ	34.6	36.8ᵃ	773	2.86	590	2.74
1922	4.34	3.13ᶜ	37.3	38.2	762	2.97	575	3.17
1923	4.50	3.13ᵃ	40.5	39.4ᵃ	750	2.75	566	2.78

Table 3.1 (continued)

	(1) OFS members (m.)	(2) AFS members (m.)	(3) OFS funds (£m.)	(4) AFS funds (£m.)	(5) IOOFMU members (000)	(6) IOOFMU annual seccessions (%)	(7) AOF members (000)	(8) AOF annual seccessions (%)
1924	3.77[d]	3.12	41.0	40.6	742	2.47	558	2.66
1925	3.95	3.12[a]	45.0	41.8[a]	737	2.39	552	2.58
1926	4.11	3.13	48.2	43.1	734	2.18	545	2.40
1927	4.21	3.08[a]	51.3	44.2[a]	731	2.34	538	2.60
1928	4.30	3.04	54.5	45.4	728	2.12	532	2.21
1929	4.43	3.01[a]	57.7	46.3[a]	726	2.11	527	2.21
1930	4.54	2.98	61.1	47.3	724	2.10	523	2.29
1931	4.63	2.96	64.4	48.3	723	2.15	520	2.21
1932	4.67	2.93	68.7	50.1	720	2.17	513	2.53
1933	4.89	2.91	73.8	51.3	715	2.08	508	2.36
1934	4.98	2.91	78.2	52.0	712	1.92	506	2.29
1935	5.26	2.90	82.8	52.5	712	1.84	502	2.38
1936	5.33	2.89	87.6	53.5	712	1.93	500	2.39
1937	5.46	2.88	92.1	54.0	718	2.03	501	2.27
1938	5.63		97.1		722	1.97	498[a]	2.29[a]
1939					724	1.97	494	2.32

Notes

[a] Gaps in the series have been estimated from the two adjacent observations.

[b] These figures have been estimated from the returns of the following societies:

Independent Order of Oddfellows, Manchester Unity

Ancient Order of Foresters

Independent Order of Rechabites, Salford Unity

Loyal Order of Ancient Shepherds, Ashton Unity
National Independent Order of Oddfellows
National United Order of Free Gardeners
United Ancient Order of Druids
The Order of Druids
Nottingham Order of Oddfellows
British Order of Ancient Free Gardeners
The Sons of Temperance.

In 1898 these eleven societies accounted for 90 per cent of affiliated society funds and 77 per cent of membership.

[c] AFS figures for 1911–15 have been estimated using the actual growth rates of OFS membership and funds.

[d] This decline was the result of the transfer of 866,927 members and £2.4m. to the Collecting Society category on 1 Jan. 1924, under the provisions of the Industrial Assurance Act, 1923.

[e] This increase is due to the inclusion of juvenile members previously omitted from the returns.

Sources

Cols. 1 and 3 (1885): Report of the Registrar of Friendly Societies for 1886, part ii(F), pp. 38–9.
(1891): Ibid. for 1892, part D(2), p. 186.
Cols. 2 and 4 (1886–97); Returns of Fourteen Large Friendly Societies in the Sixth Abstract of Labour Statistics. PP 1900 lxxxiii (Cd. 119), pp. 52–7; ibid. (fifteenth), PP 1912–13, pp. 256–61.
Cols. 1–4 (1898–1909): Fifteenth Abstract of Labour Statistics, pp. 254–5.
(1910–24): Ibid. (eighteenth), PP 1926, pp. 200–1.
(1924–38): Eighty-third Statistical Abstract. PP 1939–40, p. 271.
Except Cols. 2 and 4 (1916): Report of the Registrar of Friendly Societies for 1931, part 2 (HMSO, 1932), p. 31.
(1917 and 1918): Seventy-fifth Statistical Abstract. PP 1931–2 xxiv (Cmd. 3991), p. 223.
Cols. 5 and 6: Independent Order of Oddfellows, Manchester Unity. *Quarterly Reports* (April). Annually.
Cols. 7 and 8: *Directory of the Ancient Order of Foresters*. Annually.

system, with both insurance liability and administrative responsibility divided between individual branches and regional or national groupings; by far the largest affiliated societies were the Independent Order of Oddfellows, Manchester Unity (IOOFMU) and the Ancient Order of Foresters (AOF). Ordinary societies were those that had only one office—most of them were small and localized, but some, like miners' relief funds, would operate throughout a particular coalfield, and others, called centralized societies, had a head office (usually in London) and conducted a nationwide insurance business by post.

Some societies were restricted to members of a particular profession, industry, or trade, and in 1899 these provided for over half a million members, nearly all of whom worked in mining or for railway companies.[7] The Rechabites enrolled only teetotallers, but the affiliated orders and most local societies had a broad membership—as the word oddfellow suggests—excluding only those applicants such as lead-workers, miners, and publicans, who followed particularly hazardous pursuits. Details of membership costs and benefits will be discussed below; here it needs to be stressed that members were predominantly—and in many societies exclusively—male. This was partly because of the different sickness experience of women, partly because they were deemed incompatible with the type of fellowship which was an important element in many nineteenth-century friendly societies, but mainly because they could not afford to join. Contributions were high, and this usually limited membership to the chief wage-earner. This needs to be remembered when looking at membership statistics; it would not be too far from the truth to say that each friendly society member covered by sickness benefit represented a family for whom the worst extremes of income fluctuation were avoided. Inevitably, therefore, total membership was much lower than that of Friendly Collecting Societies and Industrial Assurance Companies, though the fact that most ordinary and affiliated societies included some sort of death benefit in the services offered means that burial insurance was even more extensive than suggested by the figures given in chapter 2.

[7] Report of the Chief Registrar of Friendly Societies for the year ending 31 December 1900, part A, appendix (K), PP 1901 lxxii (35–I), pp. 300–3.

Although the principle of accumulating a reserve fund to pay sickness benefit was common to many societies, and was thoroughly publicized by the two dominant ones, the Oddfellows and the Foresters, it did not guide the actions of all societies. Some ordinary societies were nothing more than burial clubs, but, because they did not do any business more than ten miles from their headquarters, they did not come within the compass of Collecting Society legislation. Some were simply doctors' or hospital clubs which provided medical attendance but no sickness pay. Others were deposit societies, which, as will be explained below, were primarily private savings banks. The fourth exceptional group were the dividing societies or slate clubs. These usually provided some sort of sickness and funeral benefit, but instead of accumulating a reserve fund to meet future insurance liabilities, they divided surplus funds among members at the end of the year. Such societies could not offer the same long-run security as those which had large reserves, and they particularly discriminated against old and infirm subscribers who, after a year of heavy sickness claims, would often be refused renewal of membership in order to maximize the annual distribution of funds for other members. Table 3.2 shows the relative importance of these different sorts of ordinary friendly society from 1899. The number buying sickness insurance from ordinary friendly societies (columns 1 and 2) is more or less constant, with the result that the proportion of the male population over 19 years of age who purchased sickness insurance from either affiliated or ordinary societies was actually declining from the turn of the century, not increasing as the official figures suggest (see Table 3.3). This means that the estimate of Bentley Gilbert that in 1891 'nearly half the adult males in Great Britain were members of societies' is too high, since it includes some people who were paying only for burial insurance or other limited cover; it adds more weight, though, to his view that sickness insurance 'made no appeal whatever to the grey, faceless, lower third of the working class. Friendly society membership was the badge of the skilled worker.'[8]

---

[8] Gilbert, *Evolution of National Insurance*, pp. 166–7.

Table 3.2. Ordinary friendly society membership by type of society

	(000s)						
	(1) Accumu- lating	(2) Dividing	(3) Burial	(4) Deposit	(5) Medical	(6) Hospital	(7) Miscel- laneous
1899[a]	1,672	133	757	c.50	?	?	?
1910	1,289	332	856	381	329	36	403
1911	1,258	370	890	398	332	37	409
1912	1,339	359	921	526	311	35	498
1913	1,313	370	918	549	138	37	538
1914	1,220	385	900	566	144	37	490
1915	1,164	394	857	599	135	37	495
1916	1,135	389	855	625	130	35	510
1917	1,115	380	855	657	130	35	518
1918	1,121	369	863	687	130	35	517
1919	1,135	376	908	747	134		646
1920	1,143	410	938	816	135		692
1921	1,132	429	998	856	135		688
1922	1,125	444	1,021	901	132		689
1923	1,084	426	270[b]	954	135		726
1924	1,088	445	280	1,027	138		741
1925	1,149	461	211	1,102	144	40	780
1926	1,138	478	239	1,175	148	175	702
1927	1,146	487	240	1,257	147	177	696
1928	1,145	506	231	1,377	143	189	640
1929	1,144	512	232	1,471	147	190	668
1930	1,152	499	218	1,574	148	200	686
1931	1,174	500	215	1,644	148	203	668
1932	1,194	405[c]	326[c]	1,730	145	206	638[d]
1933	1,166	404	324	1,820	146	216	580
1934							
1935							
1936							
1937	1,140	425	327	2,172	144	510	
1938							
1939							

Notes

[a] Statistics for this year are suspect. It seems likely that about ½m. members who in later years are listed under dividing or miscellaneous societies are here enumerated under accumulating societies.

[b] This decline was due to the transfer of 866,927 members to the category of Collecting Societies under the terms of the Industrial Assurance Act, 1923.

[c] In 1932 about 95,000 members were transferred from the dividing to the burial society list.

[d] From 1932, annuity, endowment, and accident societies were listed separately from miscellaneous societies in the official returns. In this table, the original system of aggregation is continued.

Sources

For 1899: Report of the Chief Registrar of Friendly Societies for 1900, part A appendix(K), PP 1901 lxxii (35–I) pp. 300–3.
From 1910: annual reports of the Chief Registrar of Friendly Societies, part 1.

Table 3.3. *Apparent and actual extent of friendly society sickness insurance*

	(1) Males in England and Wales 20 years and over (000)	(2) Official number of OFS and AFS members (000)	(3) (2) as % of (1)	(4) Number of OFS and AFS sickness benefit members (000)[a]	(5) (4) as % of (1)
1891	8,517	4,110	48.3		
1901	10,043	5,470	54.5	4,140[b]	41.2
1911	11,562	6,420	55.5	4,430	38.3
1921	12,445	7,350	59.0	4,700	37.7
1931	14,063	8,380[c]	59.5	4,530	32.2

Notes

[a] The sum of AFS members (Table 3.1, col. 2) and OFS accumulating and dividing members (Table 3.2, cols. 1 and 2).

[b] Figures for 1899 have been used. It has been assumed that 200,000 members listed under accumulating societies in Table 3.2 did not receive sickness benefits.

[c] For consistency, the members transferred to the Collecting Society list in 1923 are here counted as OFS members.

Sources

As for Table 3.2.
B. R. Mitchell and Phyllis Deane, *Abstract of British Historical Statistics* (Cambridge, 1962), p. 12.

It is difficult to go beyond this sort of generalization about the social class of members; little work has been done by historians, and there seem to be few sources. Gosden's work is essentially institutional, and the only other studies come from the work of Crossick and Gray on the local 'labour aristocracies' of Kentish London and Edinburgh, which deals mainly with the pre-1870 period.[9] In 1893, a fellow of the Institute of Actuaries reckoned that friendly societies providing sick pay included:

not more than one third or one fourth of the workers; they certainly do not include that large mass of pure labour for whom it is most desirable that these schemes should be propounded; they do not take in the dockers and . . . they take in only a very limited proportion of the agricultural labourer, therefore nothing . . . that the friendly

[9] R. Q. Gray, *The Labour Aristocracy in Victorian Edinburgh* (Oxford, 1976), pp. 122–6; Geoffrey Crossick, *An Artisan Elite in Victorian Society* (London, 1978), pp. 174–98.

societies could do, even if their finances permitted it, would touch the mass of the population of this country.[10]

This is the general impression conveyed by the evidence heard by the Northcote Commission in the early 1870s. Members were 'rather a respectable class—what are called respectable artizans', 'mechanics and tradesmen', 'very largely of the mercantile class, clerks, and warehousemen, and the skilled artizan class', 'of the ordinary artizan class', 'for the most part handicraftsmen'.[11] There was some disagreement about the possibility of unskilled labourers paying the subscriptions required. Officials of the IOOFMU claimed that 'in our strictly rural districts we have at least one-half agricultural labourers' with wages as low as 12s. a week,[12] and a social survey of the agricultural village of Corsley in Wiltshire conducted in 1906 found that 'nearly every working class householder and most of the young men belong to a benefit society, to secure medical attendance and a weekly allowance in case of their own illness, and burial money on the death of themselves or their wives'.[13] On the other hand, Sir George Young, Assistant Commissioner for the South and East, found that 'with very few exceptions the lodges of a society like the Manchester Unity are practically closed against agricultural and other unskilled labourers by the high rate of contribution demanded',[14] and this latter view seemed to prevail. The only detailed information the Friendly Society Commissioners received was an occupational breakdown of IOOFMU membership handed in by Henry Ratcliffe, the Order's Corresponding Secretary, but this was no more than a rewrite of a similar analysis relating to the 1840s and did

---

[10] Aberdare Cmmn., q. 11792. The finances of most friendly societies were decidedly shaky by the end of the nineteenth century, largely because of the increased longevity of the insured population. See Bentley B. Gilbert, 'The Decay of Nineteenth-Century Provident Institutions and the Coming of Old Age Pensions in Great Britain', *Economic History Review*, 2nd ser., xvii (1965), pp. 553–8.

[11] Northcote Cmmn., Second Report, qq. 9659, 9877, 10991, 11428; ibid., Asst. Cmmnr. South and East, p. 2.

[12] Ibid., Second Report, qq. 96–100.

[13] Maud E. Davies, *Life in an English Village* (London, 1909), p. 250. Support for this view comes also from F. G. Heath, *British Rural Life and Labour* (London, 1911), pp. 56–74.

[14] Northcote Cmmn., Asst. Cmmnr. South and East, p. 2.

not reflect the current membership distribution.[15] Twenty years later, the Royal Commission on Labour found a great deal of local variation. In Melton Mowbray, for instance, very few agricultural workers were in clubs of any sort, in Basingstoke the affiliated societies were popular among the young workers, and in Woburn 'most of the young men are in a benefit club of some kind, but many of the old men are not in any, the small local clubs to which they formerly belonged being broken up'.[16] In the seven central and southern English counties investigated for the Commission by Cecil Chapman,

the actual proportion of agricultural labourers who belong to benefit societies cannot be given with accuracy, but striking an average for the seven districts it will be fairly correct to say that rather more than half belong to some club or other. The rest depend upon savings in the Post Office or in a stocking or upon nothing at all.[17]

One great problem with such accounts is that they often make no distinction between different sorts of friendly societies, so it is not clear whether club membership implies full sickness insurance or just burial insurance. One limited piece of evidence comes from the family budget survey of forty-two agricultural labourers conducted by Seebohm Rowntree for a typical week in November/December 1912. All but two families reported some form of club membership, but the average subscription of just over $1\frac{1}{2}d.$ per person per week suggests this was mainly low-cost burial society membership rather than payment to an affiliated friendly society.[18] In towns the pattern of mass burial club membership and more restricted friendly society membership was much the same. Miss Butler's 1912 study of Oxford found a clear hierarchy of thrift among the working population. The commonest form of provision was life insurance, but about one in nine of the inhabitants belonged to the 'great friendly societies, which give liberal sick pay and in most cases medical attendance'. These societies 'include here

---

[15] Gosden, *Friendly Societies*, pp. 229–30.

[16] Royal Commission on Labour, report by William Bear on Bedfordshire, etc., PP 1893–4 xxxv (C. 6894–I), pp. 24, 86, 143.

[17] Ibid., report by Cecil Chapman on Berkshire, etc., PP 1893–4 xxxv (C. 6894–II), p. 39.

[18] B. S. Rowntree, *How the Labourer Lives* (London, 1913), pp. 43–292.

among their members all social classes, from labourers up to shop assistants and clerks in good positions, but their chief strength is among the artisan'.[19] The general impression of some degree of economic and social exclusivity among friendly society members was confirmed by Brabrook, who thought that, although membership might include some unskilled and agricultural labourers, it represented 'very fairly the aristocracy of the wage earning classes'.[20]

One rough and ready way to assess the extent of agricultural membership is to examine the geographical distribution of friendly society members. The imprecision of this approach comes both from the somewhat erratic way in which societies were enumerated, and from the fact that statistics were collected according to the location of the registered office of each society, not according to the actual location of the members.[21] No clear pattern emerges from an analysis of the regional distribution in England in 1871; Lancashire and Derbyshire have few agricultural labourers and high friendly society membership, and Hereford the converse, which would seem to support Young's observations. Wiltshire, on the other hand, is one of several counties with a high proportion of agricultural labourers and a high friendly society membership, suggesting that the pattern found in Corsley by Miss Davies in 1906 was neither abnormal nor of recent origin. In general, though, the figures are too crude to tell us much about industrial/agricultural differences, let alone about the specific class of members.

The membership records of an Edinburgh Oddfellows lodge and a Woolwich Foresters court unearthed by Gray and Crossick, although relating mainly to the years before 1870, provide some of the details of occupation that cannot be gleaned from aggregate statistics, and they tell the same story as the Northcote Commission, of a concentration of membership among the skilled trades.[22] Records of a Halifax friendly society in 1902 show that this pattern had changed little; 57 per

[19] Violet Butler, *Social Conditions in Oxford* (London, 1912), pp. 198–9, 241.

[20] Hamilton Cmmn., app., vol. iii, q. 35162.

[21] Paul Johnson, 'Credit and Thrift: working class household budget management in Britain, 1870–1939' (Oxford University D.Phil. thesis, 1982), pp. 57–65.

[22] Gray, *Labour Aristocracy*, p. 122; Crossick, *Artisan Elite*, p. 183.

cent of members were skilled workers, 17 per cent worked in the retail and service sectors, and 22 per cent were unskilled.[23] The reason for this was primarily financial. To secure the benefits of medical attendance, sick pay of about 14*s.* a week, and enough money to provide a decent funeral, cost between 6*d.* and 1*s.* per week, depending on age of entry into the society. These financial benefits could bring broader returns. As one society member recalled:

The contributions of sixpence per week were paid monthly, and each week's portion of the sum required was thriftily separated from the current expenditure in readiness for necessary payments. The benefits of 'the Club', even though small in amount, gave real consolation, for the services of the doctor with ten shillings per week during sickness, together with the assurance that in the case of death there would be ten pounds available for expenses, gave to the labourer and his wife some touch of that peace which passeth bourgeois understanding.[24]

The number of households which could contemplate this sort of expenditure every week for many years was clearly limited; some societies enforced this selection on financial grounds by imposing a minimum wage clause on prospective members. The Royal Standard Benefit Society would not accept anyone earning less than 24*s.* per week, the Hearts of Oak set its minimum at 22*s.*, though by 1898 it claimed that 'these several restrictions have been abrogated'.[25]

It should be said, however, that both the societies named above as imposing minimum wage restrictions on members were examples of centralized societies, so called because they worked their insurance business not through a network of branches, but instead by post from head office. This absence of local organization and fellowship meant that, as compared with affiliated societies, centralized societies were much more a professionally run business, much less a fraternal club. They were notably successful in avoiding the twentieth-century stagnation and decline of the other sorts of accumulating society.

[23] Membership Declaration book of the Rose of Allangate lodge of the British United Order of Odd-Fellows. Calderdale District Record Office, TU 9/8.
[24] Lord Snell, *Men, Movements and Myself* (London, 1936), p. 18. I would like to thank Michael Hart for drawing my attention to this reference.
[25] Northcote Cmmn., Asst. Cmmnr. Cheshire, p. 132; ibid., Third Report, q. 24390; Crossick, *Artisan Elite*, pp. 186–7.

The largest of the centralized societies, the Hearts of Oak, had 26,510 members in 1871. By 1899 this had risen to 239,000 and continued to increase to 303,000 in 1910 and 428,000 in 1933.[26] J. M. Baernreither, a foreign investigator writing in the 1880s, found that the contributions were higher in centralized than in other friendly societies, and members generally earned higher wages and were primarily well-paid artisans, clerks, domestic servants, and the like. 'In point of character', he wrote, centralized societies 'form already the transition to the numerous insurance companies for the middle class. Their whole business assimilates to that of these companies, which they resemble also in this, that their relations with their members are of a purely business kind, and there is no social bond of union.'[27]

Membership returns for the late 1870s are given in Table 3.4 for one centralized society, the Royal Standard Benefit Society, and they seem to confirm Baernreither's remarks about the higher occupational character of this type of society. The proportion of skilled workers is slightly higher than in the Oddfellows and Foresters branches studied by Gray and Crossick, and markedly higher than in the Blackburn Philanthropic Friendly Collecting Society (Table 2.2). What is particularly striking is the much higher percentage of clerks in the Royal Standard—over 11 per cent compared with under 3 per cent in the Oddfellows and Foresters, and little over 1 per cent in the collecting society. This would seem to support the view that clerks avoided benefit clubs which involved fellowship and mixing with manual workers, a form of behaviour incompatible with their aspiration to the respectability of the middle-class household.[28]

The lack of some element of fellowship in these centralized societies, or even a knowledge of who the other members were, was a great break with friendly society behaviour in the nineteenth century. Crossick is quite right when he says 'friendly societies were generally more than just insurance organizations.

[26] Report of the Registrar of Friendly Societies for 1871, PP 1872 liv (394), p. 80; Report of the Chief Registrar of Friendly Societies for 1900, part A, app. (K), p. 84; ibid. for 1910, part A, app. (N), section iii, PP 1912–13 lxxxi (123–IV), p. 19.

[27] J. M. Baernreither, *English Associations of Working Men* (London, 1899), p. 199.

[28] Gregory Anderson, *Victorian Clerks* (Manchester, 1976), p. 132; Geoffrey Crossick (ed.), *The Lower Middle Class in Britain* (London, 1977), pp. 25–6.

Table 3.4. Occupations of members joining the Royal Standard Benefit Society between March 1876 and February 1880 (25 per cent sample)

Carpenter/joiner	75	Foreman	5
Clerk	62	Merchant	5
Printer/compositor	28	Bookseller	4
Engineer/fitter	23	Plumber	4
Bricklayer/plasterer	22	Butcher	4
Butler/groom/footman	22	Draper	4
Shopman	17	Waiter	4
Grocer	16	Hairdresser	4
Baker	16	Gardener	4
Coachbuilder	15	Hosier	4
Tailor/hatter	14	Farmer	4
Publican/victualler	12	Wood engraver	4
Warehouseman	12	Assurance agent	3
Jeweller/engraver	11	Manager	3
Cabinet-maker	10	Photographer	3
Coachman/cab driver	10	Cheesemonger	3
Porter	8	Bootmaker	3
Upholsterer	8	Piano tuner	2
Traveller	7	Oilman	2
Piano maker	7	Cooper	2
Blacksmith	7	Tin-plate worker	2
Packer	6	Pattern maker	2
Bookmaker	6	Other	59
Schoolmaster	6		
		TOTAL	554

Note

The society's business was confined to London, and was at its maximum extent in 1888, when membership reached 9,472. In return for an entrance fee of 3s. 6d. and a monthly subscription of 2s. 6d., members were entitled to claim 18s. per week sick pay, a £20 death grant, and £2 for a wife's lying-in.

Sources

Membership Registers nos. 1–8 of the Royal Standard Benefit Society. Greater London Council Record Office A/RSB/27–34.
Jas. Cox, *Royal Standard Benefit Society. The History of the Society, 1828–1928, with part 2, 1929–1966 by A. C. W. Mell* (London, 1967), pp. 3, 7, 23.

They were also an important part of the social life of their members.'[29] The life of affiliated order branches and most ordinary societies revolved around the monthly or fortnightly club night. In the nineteenth century, most societies met in a public house—in Oldham in 1871, over 200 of the 230 or so

[29] Crossick, *Artisan Elite*, p. 177.

different societies met on licensed premises.[30] Lady Bell observed the same tendency in Middlesbrough thirty-five years later.[31] Temperance friendly societies, of course, always found more sober premises, and many societies in time introduced rules to prevent the expenditure on drink of society funds. The rule-book of the Bath Friendly Society, for instance, stated that:

no feasts, drinking at public-houses, nor any meetings of the members are allowed, by which any payment or charge can be made out of or upon the Society's funds. The *whole* funds, from whatever source arising, are to be applied solely to the payment of allowances for the relief of the members and the necessary management of the business, and to no other purpose whatsoever. The application of money out of the funds for feasts, and drink etc., has been one cause of the failure of so many Friendly Societies, to say nothing of the bad habits, immorality, disease, and consequent application to the fund by the destruction of health.[32]

The affiliated orders, too, were worried by the diversion of funds to social purposes. The Annual Moveable Conference of the IOOFMU discussed the question of wet rents, 'the pernicious system of supplying beer or other refreshments in exchange for rent paid for use of lodgeroom', several times during the 1890s, and threatened to expel any lodges which refused to abandon the practice.[33] This threat, it seems, was effective—wet rents fade from discussion thereafter, though lodges continued to meet on licensed premises. The Mass-Observation survey of Bolton in the late 1930s found all manner of clubs and societies holding meetings in local pubs. Some were informal funds organized by the landlord or a group of regulars, others were branches of the Oddfellows, Foresters, and Buffaloes.[34] In country districts, village clubs were frequently organized by the local landlord, who would act as treasurer and victualler.[35] Rivalry between beer shops could

[30] Northcote Cmmn., Asst. Cmmnr. Cheshire, p. 92.

[31] Bell, *At the Works*, p. 122.

[32] Bath Friendly Society Rules, 11th edn., 1879, p. 5. PRO FS 15/594.

[33] Moffrey, *Oddfellowship*, pp. 129–30.

[34] Mass-Observation, *The Pub and the People* (London, 1943), pp. 274–82.

[35] Michael Winstanley, 'The Rural Publican and his Business in East Kent before 1914', *Oral History* iv, no. 2 (Autumn 1976), p. 72.

be the reason why some villages had several competing clubs, all of them too small to be actuarially sound.[36]

The social life of the friendly society involved more than just drink. Wilkinson, writing in 1886, put it like this:

From the moment of his entry into a Friendly Society Order to the moment when his body is laid in its last resting-place, a member ceases to be regarded as an isolated unit, but is from first to last placed in relations of brotherhood, not merely as regards the working of a money insurance scheme, but as regards his whole life and conduct.[37]

Brotherhood was especially strong on lodge night, when subscription payments featured less prominently than various forms of lodge ritual and other entertainments. Lodge business was itself considered to be valuable as a training in the conduct of public business,[38] and it was this element of self-government that was seen by many middle-class observers as the most important feature of these societies—it exercised a 'wholesome influence on the character',[39] or, in the more forthright terms of J. M. Ludlow, kept active working-class minds away from politics and 'the social democracy or the anarchic socialism of the Continent'.[40] The affiliated orders were particularly conscious of their claims to political neutrality. Members who used the society name in their political canvassing were reprimanded,[41] and when aid was granted to members who, because of strike activity, were liable to lapse, it was stressed that this did not imply taking sides in the dispute.[42] Reflecting on the industrial turmoil of 1926, the High Chief Ranger of the AOF said, 'I am exceedingly glad that the Friendly Societies keep right away from politics'.[43]

One of the prime purposes of the regalia and ritual of the nineteenth-century friendly society was public display.

---

[36] Northcote Cmmn., Asst. Cmmnr. South and East, p. 16.

[37] J. Frome Wilkinson, *The Friendly Society Movement* (London, 1886), p. 204.

[38] *Oddfellows' Magazine* xxxix, no. 407 (Nov. 1908), p. 548. For the same views thirty-six years earlier, see *The Foresters' Miscellany* viii (1872–3), pp. 35–6.

[39] Miss C. F. Yonge, 'Friendly Societies', *Economic Review* xvi (July 1906), p. 295.

[40] Maxwell Cttee., PP 1884–5 x (270), q. 1458.

[41] *AOF Quarterly Reports of the Executive Council* (Jan. 1900), pp. 10–11.

[42] *Oddfellows' Magazine* xxix, no. 285 (Sept. 1898), p. 293; *AOF Quarterly Report* (Jan. 1894), p. 49; ibid. (Oct. 1898), p. 8.

[43] *AOF Quarterly Report* (Oct. 1927), p. 32.

Friendly society membership was 'the badge of the skilled worker', but the badge had to be properly paraded if the maximum amount of social prestige was to be gained. For this reason, whether the society was a local or national affair, some sort of show was arranged each year. On Whit Monday or Easter Monday, the members of local dividing societies:

> may be seen mustering in front of the inn in their Sunday clothes, with sashes and scarves, behind the band which is to 'play them' to church. The strong box is carried by the treasurer, and two or three wands and baubles, dignified by the outlandish name 'regalia', are distributed into the custody of the stewards, and away they go to church, where the vicar says the prayers, and preaches an appropriate sermon.[44]

The affiliated orders could summon more pomp and circumstance, but they differed little in the type of display. In the second week of August, 1893, the fiftieth High Court of the AOF met at the Colston Hall, Bristol. On the Saturday evening, there was a mayoral reception for about 700 delegates and their wives, at which 'An excellent musical programme was gone through in an artistic manner. Light refreshments were provided. Speeches were delivered by the Mayor, the High Chief Ranger, and Mr. Justice Grantham.' And on the Sunday:

> At 2.30 p.m., a Procession of delegates of the Order, and kindred Societies, headed by the Executive Council, Permanent Secretary, and the Incoming Executive Council, with six bands of music, proceeded from Old Market Street, to Bristol Cathedral, where an eloquent and powerful sermon was preached by Bro. the Rev. A. A. Matthews, Vicar of Holy Trinity, Swansea.[45]

The proceedings, part business, part pleasure, continued until the following Friday. Even humble local burial societies aspired to some sort of show, with velvet sashes for treasurer and secretary and other oddments of decoration and regalia.[46]

---

[44] Revd J. Y. Stratton, 'Farm Labourers, their Friendly Societies, and the Poor Law', *Journal of the Royal Agricultural Society*, 2nd ser., vi (1870), p. 102. See also Mary Chamberlain, *Fenwomen* (London, 1975), p. 31.

[45] *AOF Quarterly Report* (Oct. 1893), p. 27.

[46] See the records and other remains of the Halifax District Juvenile and Adult Burial Society of the Independent Order of the Golden Fleece, Bradford Unity, Friendly Society. Calderdale District Record Office, TU 33.

Many lodge meetings were, in theory at least, shrouded in mystery. Passwords had to be given to secure admission, and doors were closed before discussion began to prevent outsiders from overhearing business.[47] Even as late as 1939, new recruits to the AOF were taken through an elaborate initiation cere- mony at which they were taught the secret word, grip, sign, and password of the order.[48] This was all part of a deliberate design to inflate the members' sense of their own self- importance and exclusiveness, and to attract the attention of curious outsiders. Robert Roberts, reflecting wryly on his father's activities in the 'Buffs', wrote: 'Lodge members met fortnightly in great public secrecy at a local pub.'[49]

The social superiority that the members undoubtedly felt, and which rested ultimately on the financially exclusive nature of friendly society membership, was heightened by the links societies were able to forge with notable local or national worthies. As Crossick has noted, it was not patronage the societies wanted, but that type of social approval which would emphasize the exclusivity and respectability of the members.[50] The AOF would do nothing that interfered with that 'spirit of independence, and ... earnest desire on the part of the indivi- dual to help himself' which lay at the heart of Forestry,[51] but by 1906 over 200 Members of Parliament were honorary Foresters, including Haldane, Balfour, and Campbell- Bannerman.[52] These honorary members had to do little other than lend their names and speak approvingly of independent thrift. It was a painless coincidence of wants—of the respec- table middle class for more working-class thrift, of thrifty work- ing men for the trappings of respectability.

In the inter-war years, not even the long-established affiliated orders could manage to maintain the tradition of mutuality and fellowship. Two independent surveys of friendly

---

[47] *AOF Quarterly Report* (Oct. 1895). The quarterly password and rules are printed on the inside front cover of the 'Court Copy' of the Quarterly Report.

[48] Proceedings and Ritual of the Ancient Order of Foresters Friendly Society, pub- lished by the Executive Council, 1939. Calderdale District Record Office, TU 10/3.

[49] Roberts, *Ragged Schooling*, p. 46.

[50] Crossick, *Artisan Elite*, pp. 196–7.

[51] *AOF Quarterly Report* (Oct. 1889), p. 32.

[52] Yonge, *Economic Review* (1906), p. 295.

societies carried out at the end of the Second World War both highlighted the same trends—of an ageing membership and less participation. The impression of the Mass-Observation surveyors was that 'the membership of Friendly Societies today . . . is very largely a passive one',[53] and this was confirmed by the statistical study conducted by Research Services Ltd., which showed that 82.8 per cent of members never attended business meetings (only 5.4 per cent did so regularly), and that most of those who did attend regularly were aged over 45.[54] The Mass-Observation report concluded that:

there is a tendency among those who have been members of Friendly Societies for some considerable period to look back with regret to the time when the Society was very much more than a useful vehicle for 'a rainy day', when, through the provision of opportunities for social contacts it built up for itself a 'group' loyalty.[55]

The post-war stagnation of membership of ordinary and affiliated accumulating and dividing societies shown in Tables 3.1 and 3.2 suggests that there was a gradual abandonment of those aspects of mutuality and fellowship that had been the hallmark of friendly societies in Victorian Britain. But this does not mean that the idea of independent thrift was itself on the wane. Centralized societies like the Hearts of Oak which ran an impersonal insurance business continued to expand, as did another type of society listed in Table 3.2, the deposit society. This was a half-way house between the centralized society and the savings bank, involving no element of mutuality and very little in the way of risk-sharing. This group of societies was dominated by the National Deposit Friendly Society, the membership of which grew from under 50,000 in 1899 to 1.2m. in 1933.[56] It is worth quoting at length Brabrook's description of the working of the society:

Out of each member's payment, which he is encouraged to make as large as he can, a certain sum is taken towards the benefit funds of the

[53] Mass-Observation Report on The Friendly Societies in Lord Beveridge and A. F. Wells (eds.), *The Evidence for Voluntary Action* (London, 1949), p. 20.

[54] Research Services Report, ibid., p. 76.

[55] Mass-Observation Report, ibid., p. 18.

[56] Report of the Chief Registrar of Friendly Societies for 1900, part A, p. 87; ibid. for 1934, part 2, p. 42 (HMSO, 1935).

society, the remainder being credited to him as his own bank or deposit. When he falls ill, a certain proportion of the sick pay fixed when he becomes a member, upon a scale varying with his age and other circumstances, is taken out of the benefit fund, the remainder he can draw from his own account. When his own account is exhausted, the allowance from the benefit fund also ceases, subject to a provision for a limited allowance of grace pay out of a special fund. ... The element of insurance in the contract is so small that there is no fear of insolvency, and no necessity for valuation; on the other hand, a member who suffers from prolonged sickness may find the relief of the society fail him through the exhaustion of his own bank at a time when he most wants it.[57]

The National Deposit operated by post from its headquarters in Buckingham Palace Road, and its members were quite unknown to each other. The society did not even have cause to use investigators to check on malingerers, as did other centralized societies, since malingering involved nothing more than the drawing upon personal savings. The society could not be harmed by a preponderance of 'bad risks'.

It appears that the members of centralized societies, and even more so of deposit societies, took to heart the frequently-echoed appeals to the virtue of self-help, and eschewed the fraternal bonds of mutuality. But it is not clear whether this represents a change in the behaviour of friendly society members or whether the friendly society population itself changed over time. The shortage of information about the occupation of members of different sorts of friendly societies makes it impossible to resolve the question of whether skilled workers shifted from, say, the Oddfellows to the National Deposit Friendly Society after the First World War. The impressionistic evidence suggests that unskilled workers generally could not afford membership of sickness societies, which were the preserve of skilled workers, and that clerks favoured centralized or deposit societies, where fellowship was non-existent and mutuality at a minimum. The inter-war decline of most of the accumulating societies, which came about not through increased lapsing but rather through an absence of new members, might.be ascribed to the provision of sickness insurance for the majority of manual

[57] Brabrook, *Provident Societies*, p. 68.

workers through the National Insurance system, or a change in
the nature of community esteem which placed less value upon
the cachet of friendly society membership, or some combina-
tion of the two. It should be noted, however, that accumulating
society membership was stagnating in the Edwardian years,
and was bolstered from 1911 by the extra private business
attracted to the societies through their working of the National
Insurance Act. Sickness insurance seemed to be almost fully
extended by the end of Victoria's reign, and it is not true to say
that National Insurance served to kill off otherwise flourishing
private sickness insurance societies.[58] The overall impact of
state welfare on working-class self-help will be returned to in
chapter 7.

The other types of friendly society that had substantial membership in the years before the Second World War were those
devoted to the provision of medical or institutional care without any sort of sickness pay. It is difficult to give any precise
indication of the numbers covered by this sort of insurance as
many clubs were informal affairs, lacking any proper friendly
society rules and regulations. Medical attendance insurance
was variously available from registered and unregistered
friendly societies, companies like the National Medical Aid Co.
Ltd., schemes set up by private individuals, and schemes operated by a doctor or group of doctors themselves.[59] The normal
pattern was that of weekly subscriptions of 1*d.* per person paid
to secure the services of a doctor, either at the doctor's dispensary or, in serious cases, at the insured's home. It was, therefore,
part insurance, part payment by instalment, and involved no
social contact with other members, except in the dispensary
queue. Because of the need to collect monies week by week,
some schemes were linked to the collection of burial insurance
payments. This could be a formal arrangement, as at East-
bourne and Northampton between the Liverpool Victoria and
the National Medical Aid Co., or the system worked in Nott-

---

[58] This is the implication in Gilbert, *Evolution of National Insurance*, pp. 427–8, and in
Stephen Yeo, 'Working-class association, private capital, welfare and the state in the
late nineteenth and twentieth centuries' in Noel Parry, Michael Rustin, and Carole
Satyamurti (eds.), *Social Work, Welfare and the State* (London, 1979).

[59] *Lancet, The Battle of the Clubs* (London, 1896), pp. 97–8, 103–4.

ingham by the London and Manchester Insurance Company, though it was something often done as an unofficial sideline by insurance agents against the wishes of their company.[60] According to the Special Commissioner to the *Lancet*, who made an investigation of medical clubs in 1895–6, their coverage was broad. In Leicester he found that '75 per cent. of the entire population belong to medical aid organizations of one sort or another', in Walsall 'two thirds, if not three-quarters, of the population of the town are members of some sort of medical aid society or else become hospital patients', and the level of membership was alleged to be much the same in rural and mining districts.[61]

Of course, estimates from such a prejudiced source should not be taken at face value. The whole point of the *Lancet* enquiry was to demonstrate the extent to which doctors were exploited by clubs and societies which enrolled not only low-paid workers, but many artisans and shopkeepers who, in the view of the profession, could well afford private treatment. There are many references to prosperous members of Odd-fellows lodges receiving medical attention via the club doctor or, even worse, through some semi-charitable dispensary, and driving out genuine private practice from small towns and villages. It has been estimated that by 1913, half of Britain's 20,000 GPs were engaged in contract practice of one form or another.[62] Part of the complaint, also, was against the out-patient departments of private and Poor Law infirmaries, which were used rather like a free GP service, especially in London.[63] The figures in Table 3.2, col. 5, certainly understate the number of people covered by clubs or societies providing medical insurance, but the pattern of membership in these registered societies is instructive. The introduction of state medical services for one-third of the population through National Health Insurance panel doctors induced a fall of over 50 per cent in the number of registered medical society members. This consequence was quite deliberate; the liberation of

[60] *Lancet, The Battle of the Clubs*, pp. 18–28, 99–100, 159–67, 182.
[61] Ibid., pp. 117, 123, 180.
[62] Frank Honigsbaum, *The Division in British Medicine* (London, 1979), p. 13.
[63] Brian Abel-Smith, *The Hospitals 1800–1948* (London, 1964), chs. 7 and 20.

doctors from the 'sweating' of contract practice was one of the
British Medical Association's aims in its negotiations with the
government over the NHI scheme, particularly in its attempts
to fix an income limit of £2 a week to be applied to those receiving medical benefit.[64]

Insurance for institutional care is likewise difficult to estimate with confidence because of the multiplicity of bodies offering this sort of benefit. The officially registered friendly societies
providing solely for the payment of hospital fees show a notable
increase in the inter-war years (Table 3.2, col. 6), an increase
perhaps not surprising given the absence of any such benefit
from the state scheme, excepting the provision of sanatoria care
for tuberculosis patients. But there were a number of other
ways to avoid paying hospital fees. The Hospital Saturday
Fund was a voluntary contributory scheme organized at the
workplace, which collected small weekly sums from workers
and in exchange gave tickets to contributors which allowed
them to nominate deserving cases or escape registration fees.[65]
This essentially philanthropic pattern of hospital contribution
remained popular in the north of England until the early 1930s
at least,[66] but elsewhere, especially in London, contributory
schemes stressed much more the benefits offered to contributors
and dependants. In London, the Hospital Savings Association,
which grew from 62,000 contributors in 1924 to 1.9m. in 1938,
offered hospital care without either a means test or other payment for 3*d*. per week per family, although this was extended as
a privilege rather than a right in order to avoid any contractual
liability.[67] The best estimates of these contributory schemes,
Hospital Saturday Funds, and organized workmen's collections
put the national membership at 6.2m. in 1933 and 10.3m. in
1938, with annual collections at £3m. and £5m. respectively,
equivalent to a weekly contribution of 2¼*d*. per member.[68]

[64] On the contract scheme, see Noel and Jose Parry, *The Rise of the Medical Profession*
(London, 1976), pp. 147–54, 188–95; Honigsbaum, *Division*, pp. 12–21.

[65] Abel-Smith, *The Hospitals*, pp. 135–6; Sampson Gamgee, *The Origin of Hospital
Saturday* (Birmingham, 1882), pp. 9–14.

[66] *The Hospitals Yearbook 1931*, p. 69.

[67] Abel-Smith, *The Hospitals*, p. 327. See also Hospital Almoners' Association, *The
Hospital Almoner* (London, 1935), appendix B; Constance Braithwaite, *The Voluntary
Citizen* (London, 1938), pp. 143–50.

[68] *The Hospitals Yearbook 1935*, pp. 245–52; *The Hospitals Yearbook 1940*, pp. 289–300.
See also Robert Pinker, *English Hospital Statistics 1861–1938* (London, 1966), section iv.

Although such types of medical insurance had been in existence since the middle of the nineteenth century, it was only since the First World War that they had become a generally recognized source of financial support for hospitals.[69] This was partly due to the general growth of hospital treatment during this period, partly because of the development of a system of partial payment in voluntary hospitals, and also due to the encouragement given to some sort of hospital insurance by the release of funds that insured workers had hitherto directed towards the primary type of medical care, the general practitioner. Also important, though, was the idea of status preservation.

The Medical Relief Disqualification Removal Act of 1885 gave the sick pauper the vote, but it did not free Poor Law medical care from all stigma. In the 1920s it was still necessary for every patient entering a Poor Law infirmary to obtain an admission order signed by the relieving officer, so in London patients would wait months for a place in a voluntary hospital even though the Poor Law could provide equivalent facilities immediately.[70] The transfer of the hospital functions of the Poor Law to local authorities by the 1929 Local Government Act removed the element of pauperization, but it did not do away with the means test. Local authorities had an obligation to charge for treatment in general hospitals, and were able to make husbands liable for wives, parents for children under 21.[71] Free treatment was given only to members of contributory schemes, or to those investigated and found in need by the Lady Almoners, and not everyone was willing to submit to this investigation. As a junior civil servant explained in January, 1939, 'Once, before I got onto the Hospital Maintenance Fund idea, we had a bad break. We lost a five months baby and my wife nearly went under. An operation was immediately necessary and our 'status' so called prevented access to Lady Almoners and all that.'[72]

[69] *The Hospitals Yearbook 1931*, p. 65.
[70] Abel-Smith, *The Hospitals*, pp. 356, 358.
[71] Ibid., p. 374.
[72] M-O, Directive Replies, Jan. 1939, Observer 118.

The use of medical clubs could also affect status. In societies providing sick pay as well as medical attendance, the well-off member, 'jealous of his good reputation', often forsook his right to financial benefit which would be noted in the society's accounts, but readily accepted the services of the club doctor which went unrecorded.[73] Even the poorest members of medical clubs could derive some kudos from them by offering a glass of club medicine to any friends who called by—hence the great demand for thick, dark, strong-tasting draughts.[74] Although the point should not be pushed too far, it is important to note that, despite the lack of any element of mutuality, membership of medical and hospital insurance schemes could confer social as well as economic advantages, both in the negative sense of avoiding pauperism, and in the positive sense of permitting some display of the totems of membership.

UNEMPLOYMENT

In 1911, Lloyd George thought that 'not a tenth of the working classes have made any provision at all' for insurance against unemployment. Only those 1.4m. workmen who were members of the 100 principal registered trade unions appeared to have purchased security against loss of earnings due to fluctuations of trade. Although certain groups of workers like railwaymen and agricultural labourers were perhaps less affected by cyclical unemployment, Lloyd George concluded that 'taking the precarious trades affected by unemployment, I do not believe more than one-third or one-quarter of the people engaged in them are insured against unemployment'.[75]

The affect of unemployment on the income and standard of living of unprotected households is by no means clear, because accurate information on the extent and duration of unemployment before the First World War is not available. National rates of unemployment prior to 1914 are estimated from trade union returns, and whilst they probably give a fair reflection of trends, there is little good reason to suppose that well-organized

[73] *Lancet, Battle of the Clubs*, p. 125.
[74] Ibid., p. 120.
[75] Hansard, 5th ser., vol. xxv, cols. 610–11 (4 May 1911).

and generally well-paid trades experienced unemployment
rates that were representative of all occupations. In the late
1860s Leone Levi estimated that the average worker under 60
could expect to be idle for four weeks in the calendar year, but
Dudley Baxter, taking a more pessimistic view, thought that 20
per cent should be deducted from nominal full-time wages to
account for loss of work.[76] Clearly such estimates depend
crucially both on the occupations considered and on the movement of the trade cycle; the economic consequences for households could range from the awkward to the disastrous.

It is not intended here to embark on a detailed study of either
unemployment or unemployment insurance, but a brief review
is necessary in order to gain a balanced picture of working-class
insurance saving. State unemployment benefit became available on 15 January 1913 for those $2\frac{1}{4}$m. insured workers in the
'precarious' trades of building, shipbuilding, mechanical
engineering, ironfounding, sawmilling, and vehicles, and during the war the scheme was extended to cover munitions
workers. By the Unemployment Insurance Act of 1920 practically all manual and low-paid non-manual workers—12m. in
all—were brought into the state unemployment insurance system.[77] The subsequent financial collapse of the insurance fund
principle under the weight of inter-war unemployment is well
known, but despite increased dependence on Public Assistance
in the early 1930s and despite the introduction of expedients
like 'transitional' and UAB means-tested benefits, almost all
unemployed workmen had more financial security in inter-war
Britain than before 1914. State unemployment benefit did not
provide enough money for a family to live on—the weekly benefits were fixed in 1920 at 15s. for a man and 12s. for a woman,
with half rates for young people—but it did ameliorate the
immediate financial crisis of unemployment and allowed scope
for financial planning and the adoption of long-term expenditure such as hire-purchase.

Private unemployment insurance was the exclusive preserve
of trade unions, and in many unions it was coupled with other
types of friendly benefit. As Table 3.5 shows, the obviously
non-trade benefits for sickness, accident, burial, and

---

[76] James H. Treble, *Urban Poverty in Britain, 1830–1914* (London, 1979), p. 53.
[77] Percy Cohen, *The British System of Social Insurance* (London, 1932), pp. 114–16.

Table 3.5. Expenditure of registered trade unions by type of benefit

	Expenditure per member (*s. d.*)									
	Unemployment	Dispute	Sickness and accident	Superannuation	Funeral	Other benefits	Grants to Feds. etc.	Political fund	Working expenses	Number of members (000)
1892	7. 1	8. 4¾	4. 7¼	2. 3	1. 6¾	7¼	1. 1½		5. 7½	909
1893	10. 0½	12. 10¼	5. 3¼	2. 5½	1. 7¾	9	2. 0		5. 6¼	914
1894	9. 10	3. 6½	4. 11½	2. 7¾	1. 6	1. 1¾	1. 10		5. 5¾	928
1895	9. 2¼	4. 4½	5. 8¾	2. 10½	1. 8	6¾	5½		5. 5¾	917
1896	5. 5¾	3. 7	5. 1¼	2. 11½	1. 6¾	8	7¾		5. 7½	964
1897	6. 2¼	12. 2	5. 0½	2. 10¼	1. 6	5½	1. 8¼		5. 8¾	1,065
1898	4. 7½	6. 0½	5. 4¼	3. 1¾	1. 7¼	6¾	1. 4¾		5. 10½	1,043
1899										
1900										
1901	5. 4	3. 5½	5. 4½	3. 3	1. 6¾	1. 7¾[c]			6. 3¾	1,215
1902	7. 1	3. 7½	5. 7½	3. 7	1. 6¾	1. 6¾			6. 7½	1,212
1903	8. 7¼	2. 11¼	6. 0¾	3. 11½	1. 6½	1. 7			7. 3¼	1,201
1904	10. 11¼	1. 11½	6. 5¾	4. 5¼	1. 7¼	1. 8			7. 0¾	1,196
1905	8. 7½	3. 6	6. 7½	4. 8½	1. 7¼	1. 10¾			7. 0½	1,214
1906	6. 6½	2. 4¼	6. 4½	4. 8½	1. 6¼	1. 7			7. 1	1,299
1907	6. 4	1. 10¼	5. 11¼	4. 5¾	1. 5	1. 6¼			6. 7	1,461
1908	13. 11¾	8. 6¾	6. 5¾	4. 11¾	1. 5¾	1. 10¾			7. 4	1,437
1909	13. 3	2. 2¼	6. 2	5. 3¼	1. 6	2. 0			7. 4	1,425
1910[a]	9. 6¼	4. 10¼	5. 8¾	5. 6¼	1. 5	1. 10¼			7. 0¾	1,459
1910	6. 10	5. 4	4. 10	4. 11	1. 2½		1. 2½		6. 10½	1,981
1911	4. 1½	5. 2	4. 4	4. 4	1. 1		2. 0		6. 4	2,321
1912	4. 11	13. 0	4. 0	4. 1	1. 1		1. 3		7. 2	2,546
1913[b]	2. 6[b]	2. 9½	4. 4½	3. 3	1. 0		1. 3½	0½	7. 0	3,205
1914	4. 5	4. 1½	4. 2½	3. 4	1. 0		1. 2½	1½	7. 4½	3,199
1915	1. 0	6	3. 5½	3. 0	1. 2		1. 0½	2½	7. 6	3,388
1916	6	6	3. 0	2. 9	1. 3		10½	2	7. 3	3,649
1917	11½	7½	2. 5	2. 6	1. 3		1. 3	2	7. 3	4,361
1918	1. 1	1. 1½	2. 6	2. 1½	1. 0		1. 6	6	8. 1	5,259

Year										Members
1919	2.10	6. 6½	2. 1	2. 0	11		2. 0	4	9. 4	6,516
1920	4. 0	9. 3½	2. 2	2. 0	10		4.10	6½	12. 4	6,928
1921	26.10	12. 6	3. 7	3. 1	1. 2		2. 0	7	16. 1	5,453
1922	12. 4	5. 9	3. 8	2. 7	1. 3	8	2. 0	1. 1	14. 5	4,505
1923	5. 3	3. 3	3. 6	3. 4	1. 3	10	1.10	1. 0	14. 3	4,368
1924	5. 1	5. 5	3. 8	3. 8	1. 5	9	3. 0	1. 0	14. 5	4,458
1925	6. 7	1. 5	3. 7	3.11	1. 5	10	1. 7	6	14. 1	4,447
1926	8.11	26. 2	3. 9	4. 3	1. 6	1. 1	2. 1	6	14. 2	4,147
1927	5. 5	11	3.10	4. 8	1. 8	11	1. 2	8	14. 2	3,903
1928	6. 4	8	3.10	4.10	1. 8	1. 4	1. 5	7	14. 6	3,764
1929	5. 5	2. 1	4. 2	4.10	1.11	1. 5	1. 7	11	14.11	3,778
1930	9. 9	1. 8	3. 8	5. 3	1. 9	1. 4	1. 5	6	14.10	3,764
1931	11. 4	11	3. 9	5. 8	1.10	1. 6	1. 6	11	15. 1	3,577
1932	9. 9	1. 6	3. 8	6. 2	1.11	1. 7	1. 6	6	15. 2	3,405
1933	6. 6	1. 2	3. 8	6. 3	1.11	1.10	1. 3	7	14. 6	3,346
1934	4.11	7	3. 3	6. 2	2.11	1.10	1. 9	7	14. 6	3,513
1935	3.10	1. 3	3. 2	5.10	1.10	1.11	1. 3	11	14. 3	3,795
1936	2.11	1. 0	3. 1	5. 5	1.10	1.10	3. 0	6	13.11	4,214
1937										4,695
1938										4,867
1939										5,019

Notes

ᵃ For the period 1892–1910, the figures refer to 100 principal trade unions. For the years from 1910, they refer to all registered trade unions in Great Britain.

ᵇ From 1913 the trade unions received income from the Ministry of Labour to pay the national unemployment insurance benefits due to members. This income has been deducted from the total of unemployment expenditure in order to give as close an approximation as possible to the unemployment expenditure met from the unions' own income and reserve funds.

ᶜ From 1901 to 1910 other benefits to members and grants to federations, trades councils, etc., were classified together. From 1910 to 1922, other benefits to members are classified with superannuation benefit; thereafter they are listed separately.

Sources

1892–8: Abstract of Labour Statistics, PP 1900 lxxxiii, pp. 6–7.
1901–10: Ibid., PP 1912–13 cvii, pp. 212–13.
1910–22: Ibid., PP 1926 xxix, pp. 180–1.
1922–35: Ibid., PP 1936–7 xxvi, pp. 144–5.
1936: Report of the Chief Registrar of Friendly Societies for 1937, part 4, p. 9 (HMSO, 1938).

superannuation took on average about the same percentage of union expenditure as did the trade benefits of unemployment and dispute pay, although these trade benefits fluctuated much more widely from year to year. The welfare policies of trade unions have not received the attention they deserve from labour historians; the student who looks through the standard histories will find little information aside from the accurate but unenlightening generalization that the 'new' unions paid '"fighting" benefits only', whilst the old craft unions were dismissed by their more radical confrères as 'coffin clubs'.[78] There has been some discussion about the relative importance of the welfare and trade protection functions of craft unions in the 1870s,[79] but the evidence comes solely from union leaders, so it gives little or no indication of the way in which the mass of union members valued the different benefits their unions offered. The welfare function of trade unions was keenly observed by some contemporaries; one wrote:

It will be readily understood that the offer of tangible benefits in case of accident, sickness, superannuation, or burial is a powerful magnet whereby to induce men to join the Unions; and also secures the continuance of their membership when they have once joined. The disciplinary powers which the benefits afford are also considerable and may, indeed, be open to abuse. A man is unlikely to oppose the will of his society, when such opposition would reap expulsion and the loss of prospective out-of-work and sick pay, for which he may have contributed for years.[80]

However, any generalization on this matter is sure to be misleading because, as Table 3.6 shows, rates of contribution and benefit varied enormously between industrial sectors, with the established craft unions in printing, engineering, and building levying high membership fees but offering generous welfare benefits. In 1935 the Boilermakers, Amalgamated Engineers, and London Compositors, who together accounted for less than

[78] H. A. Clegg, Alan Fox, and A. F. Thomson, *A History of British Trade Unions since 1889, Volume I, 1889–1910* (Oxford, 1964), p. 94; E. H. Hunt, *British Labour History 1815–1914* (London, 1981), p. 306.
[79] C. G. Hanson, 'Craft Unions, Welfare Benefits, and the case for Trade Union law reform, 1867–75', *Economic History Review*, 2nd ser., xxviii (1975), pp. 243–59, and comment by Pat Thane, ibid., xxix (1976), pp. 617–25.
[80] M. F. Robinson, *The Spirit of Association* (London, 1913), p. 289.

Table 3.6. *Expenditure of registered trade unions in 1935 by class of union and type of benefit*

	Per cent of total membership	Expenditure per member (s. d.)									Contribution per member (s. d.)
		Unemployment	Dispute	Sickness and accident	Funeral	Superannuation	Other benefits	Political fund	Grants to Federations	Working expenses	
Fishing	0.08	—	—	10. 8	1. 6	—	1. 0	—	5	24. 7	35. 8
Agriculture	0.83	—	—	5	5	—	5	7	3	10. 6	13. 2
Mining, quarrying	15.01	2. 6	4. 11	2	1. 10	2. 5	1. 10	4	11	8. 11	24. 0
Bricks, pottery, glass	0.41	7. 4	—	3	2	10	4	9	1. 8	10. 3	28. 5
Chemicals	0.16	1. 10	1. 6	—	3	—	—	—	—	5. 7	8. 10
Metals, machines	15.36	29. 7	11	4. 2	2. 6	16. 10	8	5	1. 9	13. 7	54. 4
Textiles	4.53	44. 8	6	2. 7	1. 3	4. 6	8	6	3. 11	9. 7	31. 5
Fur, leather	0.14	47. 10	1	10	1. 4	—	10	—	6	15. 10	25. 11
Clothing	3.95	38. 11	2	6. 1	10	3	1	7	6	11. 11	29. 7
Food, drink, tobacco	0.68	18. 2	1	6. 1	1. 11	1. 1	1. 0	1. 4	6	18. 5	45. 7
Wood	1.31	31. 5	3. 9	4. 6	9	2. 9	1. 4	1	1. 7	16. 4	47. 9
Paper, printing	3.33	37. 10	2	1. 6	4. 0	41. 11	2. 8	5	1. 7	16. 10	117. 3
Building	7.09	32. 0	3	8. 5	2. 7	10. 3	10	6	2. 0	14. 3	54. 7
Transport and general	34.05	1. 0	7	1. 10	1. 7	10	2. 11	1. 7	7	15. 3	28. 6
Commerce, finance	7.69	2. 3	1	4. 1	5	—	6	1. 3	7	18. 6	30. 9
Public admin.	2.77	—	—	7	10	1.	1. 2	4	9	14. 8	20. 3
Professions	0.17	2	—	—	—	—	—	—	2	23. 4	20. 0
Entertainment	0.61	—	—	—	1. 2	—	1. 5	—	2	17. 10	22. 3
Miscellaneous	1.81	1. 7	4	12. 11	3. 0	2	1. 0	—	4. 5	14. 8	32. 2

Note

a Unemployment pay includes national insurance benefits paid through trade unions. Figures in this column, therefore, are not compatible with those in the same column in Table 3.5.

Source

Abstract of Labour Statistics for 1936. PP 1936–7 xxvi, 146–7.

8 per cent of total union membership, paid over 40 per cent of all trade union superannuation pay. Transport and general workers' unions, on the other hand, paid out practically no superannuation benefit, and spent over half of each member's low subscription on administration.[81]

The impact of union and state welfare benefits on both union policy and membership allegiance deserves more study.[82] A glance at Table 3.5 does not reveal any obvious changes in union expenditure patterns subsequent to the introduction of state pensions and health and unemployment insurance. Dispute pay and union-funded unemployment pay vary as widely and abruptly after 1918 as before. Sickness, burial, and pension payments per member all reach a trough in 1919–20 when union membership is at its peak—an indication that the general unions, which rose and fell rapidly in the decade from 1914, paid few friendly benefits to members. Whether the greater apparent loyalty in the inter-war years of members of expensive craft unions was due to strong political commitment, a general ability to maintain subscription payments, or a desire to preserve long-term friendly benefit rights must for the moment remain an open question.

Most historical studies of trade unions have concentrated on organization, leadership, and political orientation. The figures put forward here suggest that for many members, especially in craft unions, friendly benefits could have been as important a consideration of membership as trade protection. To say more on such sketchy evidence would be to descend into vulgar economism, but to suggest that the interests of a large number of members bore little in common with the stated aims of union leaders and congresses does not seem a priori absurd. Just such a disparity between the interests of leaders and led in the Co-operative movement will be examined in chapter 5.

OLD AGE

The fourth spectre that haunted the working population was

---

[81] Report of the Chief Registrar of Friendly Societies for 1936, part 4, p. 9 (HMSO, 1937).

[82] This subject has recently received attention from Noel Whiteside, 'Wages and Welfare: trade union benefits and industrial bargaining before the first world war' (unpublished paper, Dec. 1983).

old age. In a memorandum to the Royal Commission on the Aged Poor, Charles Booth concluded: 'it may be fairly said that, apart from exceptional conditions or very exceptional administration, pauperism of some kind is the probable fate of 30 per cent. of our old people'.[83] The majority report went on to point out that if due allowance were made for those 'classes which are not likely at any time of their lives to be in want of relief', then the percentage of the working-class relieved must be 'greatly increased'.[84]

The Commissioners dismissed the view that most aged paupers were wantonly profligate. Able-bodied paupers over 65 were but a fraction of the aged workhouse population; most old people in Poor Law institutions were there because of infirmity, not immorality. There was general support for Chamberlain's view that 'as regards the great bulk of the working classes, during their working lives, they are fairly provident, fairly thrifty, fairly industrious, and fairly temperate'.[85] There also seemed to be a consensus that dependence on Poor Law assistance was loathed by the majority of beneficiaries. According to a Liverpool iron-turner and ASE branch secretary, there existed among the aged poor:

a deep-rooted and bitter objection to entering a workhouse, and my experience is that this is owing, in the first place, to what may be termed an independent spirit usually found in those workers who have during the greater part of their lifetime been struggling to save and lay up something as a provision for hard times. Another reason is that the name of pauper is looked upon as a lowering of the manhood and womanhood of those unfortunate enough to require assistance in this form, and a strong feeling exists in many people that death would be preferable to life in a workhouse.[86]

Charles Booth's broad investigation of aged pauperism led him to the same conclusion: 'The aversion to the "House" is absolutely universal, and privation will be endured by the people rather than go into it.'[87]

If hatred of the Poor Law, and especially of the workhouse,

[83] Aberdare Cmmn., Report, cviii.
[84] Ibid., xiv.
[85] Ibid., xv.
[86] Ibid., Evidence, q. 17592.
[87] Charles Booth, *The Aged Poor in England and Wales* (London, 1894), p. 330.

was so widespread, why was recourse to it so common? Clearly many working people failed to make adequate financial provision for old age—and this, it seems, for reasons economic and psychological. In 1870 a spokesman for the IOOFMU thought that to secure an annuity of £13 a year at 60 would require a contribution of 1s. 6d. a week, 'which is more than a labouring man can pay'. The secretary of the Rational Sick and Burial Association felt the same: 'the contribution would be too great for the majority'.[88] Some friendly societies introduced old-age annuity schemes, but most gave them up because of a lack of enthusiasm on the part of the members. In 1882 the IOOFMU started a deferred annuity scheme, but by 1893 only 530 members had joined.[89] Undoubtedly one reason for the lack of enthusiasm was the extent to which societies gave reduced sick pay to aged members incapable of work. This was financially debilitating for the societies, which had not accounted for it in their actuarial calculations, but self-interested members were loathe to abolish it.

Even when income was sufficient to make specific provision for old-age annuities, many people were dissuaded from doing so by their expectations. 'Working men do not believe in deferred benefits', claimed a director of the IOOFMU in 1885, 'they do not think they will live long enough to receive them.'[90] There was good reason to be of this belief; in the nineteenth century less than half of all 20-year-olds could expect to survive to the age of 65.[91] But it was not so much fine calculation as instinctive reaction that guided people, and not just working people. In a discussion of old-age provision, Sir Edward Brabrook said:

Generally, the thing is so much encompassed with contingency, that I fancy no person in any class of life bothers himself very much to buy a deferred annuity . . . I do not know why we should expect the working

---

[88] Northcote Cmmn., Second Report, qq. 201, 17550.
[89] Maxwell Cttee., 1886 xi (208), q. 696; Aberdare Cmmn., q. 11561.
[90] Maxwell Cttee., 1884–5 x (270), q. 771.
[91] Michael Anderson, 'The Impact on the Family Relationships of the Elderly of Changes Since Victorian Times in Governmental Income-Maintenance Provision' in Ethel Shanas and Marvin B. Sussman (eds.), *Family, Bureaucracy and the Elderly* (Durham, NC, 1977), p. 39.

classes to look at these things from any different point of view to that from which we look at them ourselves.[92]

The real distinction was that whereas middle-class people could accumulate sufficient capital to keep themselves in old age by *ad hoc* saving during their lifetimes, workers could not. Their low income prevented any large and lumpy saving—a significant sum could be built up only by small, regular, and frequent contributions accumulated over many years. Saving for a deferred annuity had to begin early if weekly contributions were to be kept reasonably small, and retirement was not uppermost in the minds of most 20-year-olds. Canon Blackley's scheme for National Provident Insurance rested on enforced saving for all people between 18 and 21, but as J. M. Ludlow said:

a young man from 18 to 21, who wants to do the best he can for himself and for others in life, has much better uses to put his money to than by providing for himself on the contingency of his reaching 60 or 70 years of age. I think that later on, when he marries and when he has got children about him, he still has much better purposes to which he can apply his money.[93]

Advocates of mutuality agreed that buying pension rights was far from being an essential element of working-class saving; according to Henry Broadhurst, expenditure on food, clothing, shelter, trade unions and benefit clubs, and children's education should come first, and there was strong agreement from leading friendly society members.[94] Education was particularly stressed as being a worthwhile form of thrift; this was not surprising given the common view before 1909 that 'the most important institution ... for the maintenance of old age is the natural and legal provision made through the family'.[95]

The state had attempted to encourage private provision for old age by establishing a scheme of government annuities in 1864, but it had as little success as the government life assurance experiment. In the nineteen years from 1875 to 1893 only

---

[92] Hamilton Cmmn., app., vol. iii, q. 35217.
[93] Maxwell Cttee., 1884–5 x (270), q. 1458.
[94] Aberdare Cmmn., Report, xcix; *Oddfellows' Magazine* xxxv, no. 345 (Sept. 1903), pp. 420–2.
[95] Helen Bosanquet, *The Strength of the People* (London, 1902), p. 241.

1681 deferred annuity contracts were granted by the government.[96] The reason for the lack of success of any such contributory scheme, according to Lloyd George, was that 'the majority of working men are unable to deflect from their weekly earnings a sufficient sum of money to make adequate provision for old age in addition to that whch they are now making for sickness, infirmity and unemployment'.[97] On these grounds he argued for a non-contributory old-age pension scheme; this was introduced on 1 January 1909. It did not cause the abandonment of those few private pension schemes that working-class people subscribed to, as the details of craft union superannuation make clear. By 1905–7, thirty-nine unions were providing superannuation benefits to 15,604 pensioners.[98] A few employers, particularly railway and gas companies, established superannuation schemes for manual workers; by 1908 railway companies were paying pensions to 5,675 manual employees. Other employers made *ad hominem* pension grants to selected ex-employees, but the numbers receiving this sort of old-age support are inestimable. Although occupational pension schemes expanded rapidly in the inter-war years, they were aimed mainly at salaried employees who did not qualify for state old-age pensions, and by the late 1930s no more than 250,000 manual workers were members of occupational pension schemes; the number receiving pensions was, of course, only a fraction of this. Whether state pensions increased independent working-class saving for old age by guaranteeing a basic level of security which could be topped up by individual effort, or whether they reduced it by removing the necessity for private thrift, was an issue of heated debate among contemporaries, and it will be returned to for more thorough discussion in chapter 7.

Contractual saving in an insurance scheme for a benefit in addition to funeral money was the rule rather than the exception for working-class households in Edwardian and inter-war

---

[96]   Aberdare Cmmn., appendix viii, p. 987.

[97]   Hansard, 4th ser., vol. cxc, col. 568 (15 June 1908).

[98]   The details of superannuation schemes given in this paragraph were provided by Prof. Leslie Hannah. They come from his preliminary investigation into the history of occupational pension schemes.

Britain. There was an obvious hierarchy to this insurance, with medical attendance being the cheapest and most widespread form, and with hospital insurance growing rapidly after 1918, partly because national health insurance freed funds for hospital care, partly because more hospitals were being driven by financial necessity to charge poor patients, and possibly because the state insurance scheme made people more aware of their medical needs. Private insurance for old-age pensions was always a small-scale affair, in part because of the remoteness of benefit, but mainly because of its very high cost, and cost seems also to have been the major limit to private unemployment insurance; low-paid transport and general workers could afford only small union subscriptions, and in consequence gained only minimal unemployment pay. Before the introduction of the state insurance scheme, unemployment pay had practically been limited to skilled workers. Expensive affiliated and ordinary friendly societies were likewise restricted to the better-paid, but dividing societies (registered and unregistered) were cheaper and more extensive.

All these forms of insurance saving had the common characteristics of compulsion through small weekly or monthly subscription, and restriction in terms of the safeguarding of funds until needed for some specific purpose. This was not abstract saving for some undefined future goal, but rather payment by instalment for a service that would definitely be needed sooner or later. The inability of all workers to adopt all the various sorts of contingency insurance available to them stemmed not from thirftlessness or lack of character, but from the economic constraints of a low income. The choice between competing types of insurance was determined in part by financial considerations, and partly by the social characteristics of working-class life. Although the preference for sickness insurance over old-age annuities came about largely because of cost, it was the social forces of community esteem and public display that led 1*d.* a week burial insurance to be purchased much more widely than 1*d.* a week medical attendance insurance. This was something that most middle-class investigators of working-class lifestyles could not understand; they pointed out that if the burial insurance money were spent on a doctor's services, then many of the premature deaths might be avoided. But this logic took

no account of working-class customs. Funerals were public
events, and the ways they were conducted reflected on the status and esteem of the family. Sickness, on the other hand, was a
private suffering, and medical attention was a private benefit
(though a social cost when provided by a stigmatized Poor
Law), so medical insurance had a lower position on the list of
insurance expenditure priorities. For the more prosperous and
financially more secure households, other forms of insurance
were available, notably the payment of benefit during sickness,
but with this essentially private benefit was linked a panoply of
public events—lodge meetings, feasts, parades, outings, and
conferences—all designed to bolster the sense of exclusive fra-
ternity within the societies, and to proclaim publicly the economic strength of the members. The relatively small sums
involved in all the various forms of working-class insurance saving meant that this was not a path to self-betterment through
capital accumulation and social mobility. But the money was
important for avoiding some of the more predictable financial
crises, and the parading and social display were essential for the
maintenance of social position in a society in which almost no
fellow-workers had real economic security.

4

Cash Accumulation

INSURANCE did not exhaust either the scope for or the supply of working-class savings; it would be odd indeed for any group to concentrate its thrift on contingency insurance to the exclusion of any more readily accessible or liquid forms of accumulation. This chapter will look at the variety of cash accumulation practised by workers and their families from 1870. Cash accumulation is here taken to mean saving that extended beyond the cycle from pay-day to pay-day. To the extent to which weekly income is 'lumpier' than daily expenditure, there must be some saving and dissaving during the week. This budget management was the responsibility of the housewife; many would keep cash in a purse or drawer until needed, although, as will be shown in chapter 6, a complex network of credit facilities could be resorted to in order to assist the housewife in her budgetary tasks.

One sort of saving which obviously is inestimable from any institutional records is private hoarding. In so far as hoarded funds may at some time be placed with a financial institution, most likely a savings bank, then they will be included in estimates of working-class thrift, but the extent of this sort of formal deposit is quite unknown. The introduction of 'Home Safes' by the Post Office and Trustee Savings Banks around 1911 provided one means of institutionalizing domestic accumulation,[1] but even in 1939 more casual methods appear to have been prominent. A Huddersfield textile worker reported that his wife 'has her own way of saving with little boxes all over the house', and a Hampshire worker explained that he and his wife 'have evolved a system using labelled Oxo

---

[1] 'Home Safes', lockable boxes for the accumulation of small change, were introduced to post offices in the London Postal District on 11 December 1911, and extended to the whole of the UK on 1 May 1912. For details see PRO NSC 13/19. The first trustee savings bank to introduce home safes was the Belfast bank in 1906. By 1909, twenty-one trustee banks were issuing them. See Horne, *Savings Banks*, p. 289.

tins. On Friday my wages are divided up into these tins for rent (monthly), insurance (monthly and quarterly), clothes (3/-), hospital scheme, doctors club, garden (seeds). The balance goes into "our tin" from which we help ourselves for the luxuries.'[2]

More substantial working-class hoarding undoubtedly did take place in stockings and under mattresses and floorboards. Charles Madge's survey of wartime saving revealed that 'after Glasgow was blitzed, the Glasgow Savings Bank had a spell of abnormal business, with workers bringing bundles and suitcases full of ancient, crumpled notes, the savings of a lifetime', but little other information was forthcoming. As Madge himself realized, few families were willing to tell a complete stranger if they were hoarding large sums, but when a sample of Glaswegian working-class families was asked not whether they hoarded, but whether they kept money by for an emergency, about one-quarter said they did, although only one in twenty-five admitted to holding more than £2.[3] A similar working-class saving survey conducted in Coventry in November 1941 found about 15 per cent of working-class homes held over £5 cash-in-hand, less than 1 per cent had over £20, though it was felt that both these percentages had been inflated by the high level of wartime earnings.[4] These snippets of information on domestic accumulation, when linked with the accounts already given of the difficulty of preventing recurrent raids on money kept at home, all point to an insignificant amount of aggregate working-class hoarding.

Instead, use was made of four types of savings institution— savings banks, building societies, co-operative societies, and savings clubs. Since co-operative societies and savings clubs were so often linked to specific forms of expenditure, and commonly involved the advance of credit, discussion of them will be deferred to chapters 5 and 6 respectively, and this chapter will concentrate on the other two.

In terms both of the number of savers and of funds accumu-

---

[2] M-O, Directive Replies, Jan. 1939, Observers 1257 and 1161.
[3] Madge, *War-time pattern of saving*, pp. 47–8.
[4] M-O, File Report 1053, Feb. 1942, 'A Savings Survey (Working Class), by Mass-Observation', p. 58.

lated, savings banks were the most important of these institutions. Several specialized savings banks existed—for soldiers, sailors, railway employees, and for the citizens of Birmingham[5]—but the general ones, the Trustee Savings Banks (TSBs) and the Post Office Savings Bank (POSB), accounted for the bulk of savings bank business. Although quite separate institutions, the TSBs and the POSB performed the same function—of taking small deposits and paying around 2.5 per cent p.a. interest. In fact, the POSB, which began business in 1861, was established by the government with the express purpose of promoting working-class thrift by providing a secure alternative to TSBs which offered a limited service, often open only a few hours a week, and which had been subject to a number of financial scandals involving the defalcations of officers. This direct competition led to a fall in the number of independent TSBs in the UK from a peak of 645 in 1861 to 99 in 1939, a fall particularly sharp after 1888.

The POSB paid a standard $2\frac{1}{2}$ per cent p.a. on every whole £1 deposited—a rate that did not alter at all in the period under study. The TSBs, however, earned $3\frac{1}{4}$ per cent on their investments with the Commissioners for the Reduction of the National Debt until 1880, 3 per cent to 1888, and $2\frac{3}{4}$ per cent thereafter. Efficient banks which needed only $\frac{1}{4}$ per cent for management expenses could therefore offer rates marginally above those offered by the Post Office until 1888. The sharp decline at this date in the number of TSB banks and depositors gives the appearance of a high degree of interest rate sensitivity among TSB depositors, but this is probably illusory. Extensive frauds by the actuary of the Cardiff TSB came to light in 1886, something which gained wide publicity a year later when a government commissioner, Lyulph Stanley, was appointed to investigate. The potential liability of trustees and managers for the losses due to embezzlement by paid officials prompted a large number of banks to transfer business to the Post Office. In 1888 twenty TSBs closed in England and Wales, including the Bristol bank which had deposits totalling over £500,000.

[5] On naval and military savings banks, see Horne, *Savings Banks*, pp. 142–3; on railway savings banks, see P. H. J. H. Gosden, *Self-Help* (London, 1973), pp. 254–8; on the Birmingham Municipal Savings Bank, see J. P. Hinton, *Britain's First Municipal Savings Bank* (London, 1927), *passim*.

Twenty-six more banks closed in 1889, followed by seventeen in 1890.[6]

Given the almost identical trading conditions of TSBs and the POSB, and the high degree of transfer in the nineteenth century from the TSBs to the Post Office, it is not unreasonable to aggregate the statistics of membership and funds. Table 4.1 (cols. 1 and 5) shows that the number of savings bank depositors rose from 2.5m. in 1870 to 11m. in 1914 and 14m. in 1939. In terms of average balance per depositor, there was an increase (in constant 1913 prices from £19.5s. in 1870 to £21.18s. in 1914 and £26.16s. in 1939.[7] These are surprisingly large sums compared with the estimate of average wealth-holding of the bottom 90 per cent of the population referred to in chapter 2,[8] This, however, is because the aggregate statistics of savings banks conceal as much about the patterns of working-class thrift as they reveal; in particular they give an inflated impression of the scale of cash accumulation.

One feature that aggregation of POSB and TSB accounts conceals is a marked difference in the average size of deposit. In the years from 1870 to 1908 TSB depositors had on average twice as much in their accounts as POSB depositors—around £28 in the Trustee banks, £14 in the Post Office. One explanation proffered for this was that Trustee banks were concentrated in rural areas which, according to Samuel Smiles's observations, lodged more money per caput in savings banks than did industrial districts, where life assurance and friendly society membership was more prevalent.[9] But an analysis of the regional distribution of POSB and TSB accounts in 1889-90 shows no clear evidence of a rural/urban divide. What it does show is that in every county in England in 1889-90 the average deposit per account was higher in the Trustee banks.[10] This difference was partly a reflection of the weight of dormant

---

[6] *Horne, Savings Banks*, pp. 236–45; Interim Report of the Commissioner appointed to inquire into the affairs of the Trustee Savings Bank in Cardiff, PP 1888 xliv (C. 5287).

[7] Using the retail price index in C. H. Feinstein, *National Income, Expenditure and Output of the U.K., 1855–1965* (Cambridge, 1972), Table 65.

[8] Chapter 2, p. 13.

[9] Samuel Smiles, *Workmen's Earnings, Strikes and Savings* (London, 1861), pp. 31–2.

[10] Johnson, 'Credit and Thrift', p. 101.

Table 4.1. Membership and funds of the National Savings Movement

	(1) POSB (000)	(2) POSB £m.	(3) POSB stock (000)	(4) POSB stock £m.	(5) TSB (000)	(6) TSB £m.	(7) TSB stock (000)	(8) TSB stock £m.	(9) TSB SID (000)	(10) TSB SID £m.	(11) NSC £m.
1870	1,183	15			1,384	37				0.3	
1871	1,303	17			1,404	38				0.4	
1872	1,442	19			1,425	39				0.5	
1873	1,556	21			1,445	40				0.6	
1874	1,668	23			1,464	41				0.8	
1875	1,777	25			1,479	42				1.0	
1876	1,702	26			1,493	43				1.2	
1877	1,791	28			1,509	44				1.4	
1878	1,892	30			1,515	44				1.6	
1879	1,988	32			1,506	43				1.8	
1880	2,184	33	2	0.1	1,519	43				2.0	
1881	2,607	36	11	0.7	1,532	44		0.1		2.2	
1882	2,858	39	16	1.1	1,552	44		0.2		2.5	
1883	3,105	41	20	1.5	1,566	44		0.3		2.8	
1884	3,333	44	24	1.9	1,582	45		0.4		3.0	
1885	3,535	47	30	2.5	1,592	46		0.6		3.3	
1886	3,731	50	35	2.8	1,590	46		0.8		3.6	
1887	3,951	53	40	3.3	1,604	47		0.9		3.8	
1888	4,220	58	43	3.7	1,579	46		1.0		4.0	
1889	4,507	62	46	4.1	1,551	44		1.1		4.2	
1890	4,827	67	51	4.6	1,535	43		1.2		4.3	
1891	5,118	71	55	5.0	1,510	42		1.2		4.0	
1892	5,452	75	60	5.5	1,501	42		1.2		4.3	
1893	5,748	80	69	6.3	1,470	42		1.3		4.5	
1894	6,108	89	71	7.0	1,470	43		1.3		4.6	
1895	6,453	97	68	6.9	1,516	45		1.2		4.7	
1896	6,862	102	68	6.8	1,495	46		1.0		4.7	

Table 4.1 (continued)

	(1) POSB (000)	(2) POSB £m.	(3) POSB stock (000)	(4) POSB stock £m.	(5) TSB (000)	(6) TSB £m.	(7) TSB stock (000)	(8) TSB stock £m.	(9) TSB SID (000)	(10) TSB SID £m.	(11) NSC £m.
1897	7,239	115	69		1,527	48		1.0		4.5	
1898	7,630	123	72		1,563	49		1.0		4.5	
1899	8,046	130	78	7.0	1,601	51		1.1		4.6	
1900	8,439	135	93	7.4	1,625	51		1.3		4.5	
1901	8,787	140	109	8.3	1,647	51		1.6		4.5	
1902	9,133	144	118	10.4	1,670	52		1.8		4.5	
1903	9,403	146	131	12	1,687	52		2.0		4.6	
1904	9,673	148	138	14	1,702	52		2.2		4.8	
1905	9,963	152	139	16	1,730	52		2.3		5.5	
1906	10,332	155	145	17	1,759	53		2.3		6.4	
1907	10,692	157	154	17	1,780	52		2.4		7.0	
1908	11,018	160	153	18	1,785	51		2.4		8.2	
1909	7,913[b]	164	157	20	1,804	52		2.5		9.7	
1910	8,371	168	165	21	1,827	52		2.5		10.9	
1911	8,453	176	176	23	1,849	53		2.6		12	
1912	8,868	182	182	24	1,870	53		2.7		13	
1913	9,180	187	183	26	1,912	54	17	2.7	94	14	
1914	9,281	190	181	26[a]	1,917	53		2.6		15	
1915	9,971	186	1,245	75[a]	1,966	51		6.3		15	
1916	10,555	196	2,389[a]	100[a]	2,015	53		8.9		14	1
1917	10,987	203	3,533	150	2,046	52	242	18	91	14	74
1918	11,665	234	4,495	185	2,128	60	300	22	89	14	137
1919	12,829	266	4,770	215	2,220	71	324	25	88	14	226
1920	12,741	266	4,256	204	2,266	75	321	27	92	16	273
1921	10,526[c]	264	4,073	209	2,230	73	317	29	105	19	284
1922	10,636	268	3,532	206	2,231	75	289	30	116	22	341
1923	10,544	273	3,172	202	2,251	79	266	30	116	23	353

1924	10,670	280	2,910	197	2,295	82	256	30	120	24	366
1925	10,672	285	2,557	183	2,340	83	234	31	128	27	368
1926	10,427	283	2,454	184	2,354	82	233	34	135	28	375
1927	9,985	284	2,134	188	2,412	81	221	36	151	32	371
1928	9,783	288	1,953	191	2,460	81	209	38	177	38	362
1929	9,834	284	1,800	190	2,492	79	208	37	203	45	361
1930	9,855	290	1,704	188	2,345	79	205	39	237	54	358
1931	9,781	289	1,653	191	1,972	77	204	40	272	65	371
1932	9,482	305	1,448	194	1,982	79	199	40	290	74	378
1933	9,030	326	1,360	186	2,024	88	167	37	304	82	383
1934	9,322	354	1,277	175	2,076	94	160	36	312	87	389
1935	9,702	390	1,215	169	2,142	107	154	35	313	89	393
1936	10,148	432	1,162	165	2,221	120	150	35	316	91	391
1937	10,631	470	1,126	165	2,319	131	150	37	321	93	390
1938	11,116	509	1,095	165	2,420	142	150	38	329	96	385
1939	11,608	551		165	2,489	152	150	40		99	381

Notes

POSB stock   Government stock purchased through the POSB.

TSB stock   Government stock purchased through the TSB.

a Gaps in the series have been estimated from adjacent observations.

b In 1909, 3,491,273 POSB accounts were transferred to the dormant ledger.

c 2,159,050 POSB accounts which became dormant during the war were transferred to the dormant ledger in 1921.

Sources

Cols. 1, 2, 5, 6, 8, and 10: Horne, *Savings Banks*, pp. 388–92.

Col. 3 (1880–4): Thirty-first Report of the Postmaster-General, PP 1884–5 xxii (C. 4480), p. 41.
(1885–94): Forty-first Report of the Postmaster-General, PP 1895 xxvi (C. 7852), p. 81.
(1895–1904): Fifty-first Report of the Postmaster-General, PP 1905 xxiv (Cd. 2634), p. 72.
(1905–14): Report of the Postmaster-General for 1914–15, PP 1914–16 xxxii (Cd. 7955), p. 77.
(1915): Report of the Postmaster-General for 1915–16, PP 1916 xiv (Cd. 8424), p. 30.

Col. 3 (1917–38) and cols. 7, 9, and 11: Seventy-fifth Statistical Abstract, PP 1931–2 xxiv (Cmd. 3767), pp. 232–6; Eighty-third Statistical Abstract, PP 1939–40 x (Cmd. 6232), pp. 263–8.

accounts—those with no recorded transactions for at least five years and less than £1 on deposit—in the POSB. After these were removed from the 'active' ledger in 1909 the average value of Post Office accounts always stood at something over two-thirds the average value of TSB accounts, but some difference remained up to the Second World War. In 1874 the lower average deposit in the POSB was taken to imply that it carried 'provident habits into a lower stratum of society than that reached by the ordinary savings banks',[11] but this assertion was by no means obvious, since the average account size could be forced up by a small number of large and quite unrepresentative holdings.

The maximum sum that could be deposited in any savings bank, Trustee or Post Office, was limited by statute to £150 until 1893, £200 to 1915, and thereafter was without restriction. There was also a limit to the amount that could be deposited annually; £30 to 1893, £50 to 1915, with no restriction during the war, but a reimposition of a maximum annual deposit in 1923 of £500.[12] The aim of these limits was twofold; to prevent the middle classes taking advantage of preferential interest rates, and to avoid competing for large private deposits with joint-stock banks. Although it was never possible to make a thorough analysis of the occupations of all savings bank depositors, a survey of the stated occupations of depositors opening POSB accounts in the thirteen weeks up to 31 December 1896 was taken to imply that 90 per cent of them were working-class. Table 4.2 reproduces the classifications used in the survey, and shows the dubious way in which they were aggregated, with commercial clerks, shopkeepers, women, and children all being classified as 'belonging to the working classes generally'. A similar survey of accounts opened between 21 October and 20 November 1931 showed no fundamental change in the distribution of occupations, but concluded that the 1896 classification 'provides a fallacious basis for the rough figures of 90% Working Class and 10% Professional'.[13]

---

[11] Northcote Cmmn., Fourth Report, PP 1874 xxiii pt. 1 (C. 961), appendix 1, p. 14.
[12] Horne, *Savings Banks*, pp. 225, 265, 309, 327.
[13] Letter from Col. T. M. Banks (POSB) to G. Ismay (Treasury), PRO NSC 9/264/7.

Table 4.2. *Classification by occupation of new depositors in the POSB in 1896 and 1931*

1896

Belonging to the Working Classes Generally:	%	Professional, Official, Commercial, Independent:	%
Artisans and Mechanics	11.83	Agents, Managers, Travellers	0.77
Children and Scholars	20.93	Army and Navy Officers	0.02
Commercial Clerks	2.65	Artists, Actors, Musicians	0.41
Farm Labourers, etc.	1.13	Authors, Journalists, Analysts	0.06
Fishermen, Trawlermen	0.08	Bankers, Brokers, Merchants, Manufacturers	0.34
Hospital Nurses	0.05		
Labourers and Boys	5.20	Barristers, Solicitors	0.13
Miners	1.40	Civil Service Clerks	0.15
Miscellaneous, incl. Hawkers	0.37	Doctors, Physicians, Surgeons	0.08
Postmen, Telegraph messengers	0.58	Electricians, Engineers, Surveyors, Draughtsmen	0.59
Police, Prison and Workhouse Officials	0.30	Farmers, Cattle Dealers	0.62
Railway Servants, Carmen,		Independent and no occupation	2.98
Sailors (non-RN), Lightermen	2.96	Insurance Agents	0.13
Schoolboard Officers	0.02	Religious Ministers	0.23
Servants (male). Coachmen, etc.	0.96	Rate Collectors	0.01
Servants (female). Domestic, etc.	7.64	Sanitary Inspectors	0.00
Sextons, Vergers	0.01	Schoolmasters, Teachers	0.99
Shopkeepers and Assistants	8.14	TOTAL	7.51
Soldiers, Sailors, Marines	1.75		
Women (Married)	13.86		
Women (Widows)	1.76		
Women (Spinsters)	10.87		
TOTAL	92.49		

1931

Wage Earning Classes:	%	Salaried and equivalent:	%
Soldiers, Sailors, Marines	2.57	Teachers	0.85
Farm Labourers	1.69	Clerks, Agents, Travellers	4.74
Fishermen, Trawlermen	0.09	Civil servants, Naval and Military Officers, Local Govt. Officials	0.58
Labourers and Boys	3.25	Clergy, Legal, Medical, Artistic	0.70
Shop Assistants, Milliners, Dressmakers	4.49	Bankers, Brokers, Merchants	0.94
Servants (male and female)	6.80	Farmers, Cattle Dealers	0.26
Nurses, Hospital Employees	0.89	Shopkeepers	1.28
Hawkers, etc.	0.81	Managers	0.20
Postmen, Police, Firemen, wage-earning Local Govt. Employees	0.96	TOTAL	9.55
Artisans, Mechanics, Printers	10.47	Other:	
Miners	1.70	Married Women, Widows, Spinsters	28.80
Cabmen, Drivers, Engine Drivers	1.07	Children, Infants and Scholars	21.52
Railway Servants, Seamen (non-RN)	1.29	Independent and no occupation	4.05
TOTAL	36.08	TOTAL	54.37

Sources

For 1896: PRO NSC 9/264/1.
For 1931: PRO NSC 9/264/7.

Reflecting on the 1931 survey, a POSB statistician, Miss Curtis, wrote:

> It seems fair to say that only about one third of our accounts are held by weekly wage earners, though many more are no doubt held by their wives and children. I do not think it would be safe to say that the same proportion of the married women etc., or the chidren's group belong to the wage earning 'class'. If we could make this assumption the classification is 71% wage earners, 29% other classes . . . I should say that children of the 'independent means' class and the salaried class are depositors in a far higher proportion than their parents, and no doubt a large proportion of the spinster depositors have independent means.[14]

More information on the status of new depositors comes from the annual reports of the Aberdeen Savings Bank which classified new accounts according to the depositors' occupations and listed the amount standing to the credit of each class at the end of the accounting year. In 1913, for instance, students and scholars comprised almost 20 per cent of new depositors, with an average of £1.6s.5d. credited to each account, whilst widows comprised 4.14 per cent of the total number, with accounts averaging £22.16s. at the end of the first year. Of wage-earning groups, clerks had the largest accounts, at £13.9s., female factory workers the lowest at £4.8s.8d., but most of the occupational categories are so broad as to give little indication of the relative representation of wage-earning and non-wage-earning groups.[15] Furthermore, the level of initial deposit is possibly a poor indicator of the way in which funds were or were not accumulated over time. Because of the different categorization, it is not possible to say whether the Aberdeen Trustee Bank attracted a higher class of depositor than the POSB; what is clear, however, is that the number of unskilled labourers with savings bank accounts was low relative to skilled trades. In Table 4.2 artisans have more than twice the representation of unskilled labourers, which might suggest that in the hierarchy of thrift institutions, savings banks came above the 'necessities' of burial insurance and some sort of sickness provision. For the poorest families, cash accumulation was an unattainable lux-

---

[14] Letter from Miss Curtis to Col. Banks (21 Jan. 1932), PRO NSC 9/264/7.
[15] Report of the Aberdeen Savings Bank for 1913.

ury; assets were so scarce that they had to be used immediately and constantly, not put out to earn interest.

For this low-income group, the barrier to using the POSB was financial, not psychological. If funds could be accumulated, they gave a feeling of independence; as a 65-year-old unemployed spinner who had long since exhausted his POSB account wistfully remarked, 'You've always got summit to look back to, you feel bigger when you've got somethg. in your pocket. You're not frightened to meet anyone else.'[16] Only with ready cash at hand could you meet friends on equal terms in the pub or club.[17] There was, however, little sense among most working-class savers that some forms of accumulation were better value than others. In fact, thrift was very much in the eye of the beholder; a survey of working-class saving conducted at the end of 1941 found that popular notions of saving varied widely. It was found that 'Building Society, Superannuation Funds, etc. were sometimes regarded as forms of saving and sometimes not. Life insurance was seldom considered, by those participating in it, to be a form of saving', and this confusion over appropriate definitions was compounded by the fact that 'the various available methods of saving are not fully understood, appreciated and separated in the working class mind'.[18] The report went on to say:

it has been abundantly borne in on us in this investigation that a large number of people are barely aware that one form of saving is any more advantageous than another. There is a strong tendency, especially among [the unskilled] to think of saving as a way of putting aside a cash sum. The interest rate is a subsidiary matter, and the differences in rate, so important and evident to officials and economists, are often only very vaguely understood by the savers, especially womenfolk. Therefore while there is a strong feeling of personal advantage in saving, only a minority of working people make that a prime consideration in deciding between different sorts of saving.[19]

[16] M-O, Worktown Survey. Box W, file A, 'South Lancashire Survey: Savings'. 'Worktown' was the pseudonym Mass-Observation investigators gave to Bolton.

[17] Mass-Observation, *The Pub and the People*, pp. 176–9. For an expression of exactly the same sentiments in a mining community in the 1950s see Norman Dennis, Fernando Henriques, and Clifford Slaughter, *Coal is Our Life* (London, 1956), p. 152.

[18] M-O, File Report 1053, 'A Savings Survey (Working Class)', pp. 5–6. This survey was undertaken at the behest of six advertising agencies dealing with National Savings Committee propaganda.

[19] Ibid., pp. 18–19.

While it would be true to say that all working-class people recognized the need for some financial security in the face of fluctuations of income and expenditure, and most recognized that cash accumulation was one route to financial security, it is far from clear that most working-class people used savings banks, or used them regularly.

Little information exists regarding the patterns of use of savings bank accounts—details of the average size of account give no hint of whether deposits in most accounts rose over time, or whether individual accounts rose and fell in line with some poverty cycle, or how long accounts remained open. The POSB, however, did conduct two rather narrow surveys that give some hints as to the pattern of use of accounts. An analysis of 1,462 accounts closed on one day in July 1930 showed that 432 of these accounts had been used for five transactions or less, 96 for over one hundred transactions. Almost 50 per cent of the accounts recorded less than eleven transactions, and only 25 per cent had been used more than thirty times for deposits or withdrawal.[20] Another survey of accounts opened in a sample of POSB districts during twelve days between 8 February and 3 March 1937 showed that 20 per cent of them were closed by 31 December of that year. According to L. Simon, the Controller of the POSB, this was very much an underestimate of the total amount of short-term saving in the Post Office as, 'apart from these short-lived accounts, there is, of course, a great deal of short-term saving in accounts which last longer'.[21] These two surveys suggest, but cannot prove, that many POSB accounts were little used and often closed, a suggestion that itself indicates a great deal of short-term saving of less than a year's duration, abandoned possibly because of apathy, but possibly also because the saving programmes were always conceived of as means to fairly immediate ends like summer holidays.

Some savings banks even collaborated with railway companies to organize holiday saving schemes,[22] and the short-term objective of paying for holidays in the summer and

---

[20] Classification of accounts according to number of transactions, PRO NSC 9/265.
[21] Letter from L. Simon to Prof. John Hilton (24 Sept. 1938), PRO NSC 9/264/9.
[22] Holiday Savings Schemes, PRO NSC 9/665.

festivities at Christmas seem to have dominated working-class cash accumulation. In the late 1930s, Mass-Observation investigators found that money for Bolton Wakes week was 'strenuously accumulated' and, according to Bowley and Hogg, amounted in 1924 to almost £250,000.[23] There was a public aspect to this enormous expenditure on private indulgence, and this was so because most people took their holiday in the same place:

The Worktown holiday is a communal affair. In the last week in June, all mills and factories are closed, and a mass migration follows, a large proportion of it to Blackpool where Worktowners recognize in pubs and on promenades the faces that they have been seeing during the working year. So what they have saved together in the Mills Savings Clubs they now spend together on the simple pleasures of holiday week.[24]

The Mass-Observation surveyors saw this as a continuation of the social aspects of nineteenth-century working-class organizations like friendly societies, but in a new, less formal guise: 'The pageantry and conviviality is still a feature of some of the manifestations of club saving, but now Blackpool provides the colour.'[25]

Holiday saving was closely linked to income levels. The postwar survey of voluntarism conducted by Mass-Observation for William Beveridge found that '61 per cent of the working class, 51 per cent of the artisan, but only 14 per cent of the middle class, said they save up [for holidays] during the year'. The report goes on to make the important point that 'people tend to save because they haven't enough money to budget for a holiday without saving, not because they can spare enough money to save'.[26] Working-class saving involved the conscious commitment of funds to some specific end—club or society subscription, premium payment, the purchase of a durable good, or the preparation for a holiday. Middle-class saving involved the accumulation of an unspent residual; as a clerk, one of the

---

[23] A. L. Bowley and Margaret Hogg, *Has Poverty Diminished?* (London, 1925), p. 166.
[24] M-O, 'Motives for Saving', p. 42.
[25] Ibid., p. 41.
[26] Beveridge and Wells, *Evidence for Voluntary Action*, p. 64.

panel of Mass-Observers, explained, 'I look at my bank balance and cash in hand at the end of every month and decide how much if any I can save.'[27] It seems likely, then, that whereas middle-class savings bank depositors would keep accounts running for a long period, working-class depositors would tend to build up funds over a relatively short period, and then withdraw all the cash and close the account when the time came for spending.

The high rate of account closure in the POSB in the 1930s was part of a well-established pattern. In 1870, 236,000 accounts were closed, equivalent to about 20 per cent of all accounts open at the start of the year, and in the period from 1913 to 1930 closures averaged well over 1m. per year, an annual rate of over 10 per cent.[28] This probably means that the proportion of people who used a savings bank at some stage of their lives was considerably higher than that using it at any one time—children especially were encouraged to learn the habit of thrift at an early age through school savings banks and penny banks linked to the POSB or local TSBs.[29] As there was no cost to either opening or closing a savings bank account, the large transfer into and out of this particular form of saving was perhaps not surprising.

In many ways the most revealing picture of the use made of savings banks comes from breakdowns of POSB accounts by size of balance. Table 4.3 presents the figures for 1894, 1899, 1913, and 1929. The categories vary slightly between years, and the 1929 numbers are estimates based on a sample survey of ten POSB divisions claimed to be representative in terms of average size of balance and distribution of balances, but the general pattern is a remarkably consistent one. In all the years surveyed the great majority of accounts were in the lowest category—about 83 per cent of accounts held balances of under £25 in the 1890s, and this fell slowly to around 75 per cent in 1929. The average balance in these accounts stood at just over £4, a figure clearly influenced by accounts in the higher range

[27] M-O, Directive Replies, Jan. 1939, Observer 1207.

[28] Return relating to Post Office Savings Banks, PP 1871 xxxvii (280), p. 63; Annual Abstract of Statistics, PP 1931–2 xxiv, p. 215.

[29] Horne, *Savings Banks*, pp. 196–7; Roberts, *Ragged Schooling*, p. 148.

Table 4.3. Classification of POSB accounts by size of balance

	No. of accounts	% of accounts	Value of accounts £m.	% of value	Average value per account £
For 1894					
Under £50	5,570,759	91.2	33.87	38.0	6
£50–100	323,610	5.3	22.37	25.0	69
£100–150	123,697	2.0	14.99	16.8	121
£150–200	71,458	1.2	12.46	14.0	174
Over £200	19,239	0.3	5.56	6.2	289
TOTAL	6,108,853	100.0	89.25	100.0	15
For 1899					
Under £25	5,518,275	83.1	22.24	17.2	4
£25–50	551,305	6.9	20.13	15.5	36
£50–75	298,904	3.7	18.06	13.9	62
£75–100	146,065	1.8	12.71	9.8	87
£100–125	121,365	1.5	13.47	10.3	111
£125–150	66,409	0.8	9.13	7.0	137
£150–175	58,002	0.7	9.41	7.2	162
£175–200	62,410	0.8	11.85	9.1	190
Over £200	52,281	0.7	13.01	10.0	249
TOTAL	6,893,577	100.0	130.11	100.0	19
For 1913					
Under £25	6,664,632	77.9	29.25	16.2	4.4
£25–50	746,833	8.7	27.13	15.0	36
£50–75	406,653	4.8	24.58	13.6	60
£75–100	209,633	2.4	18.17	10.0	86
£100–125	168,654	2.0	18.74	10.3	111
£125–150	97,144	1.1	13.30	7.3	137
£150–175	79,724	0.9	12.90	7.1	162
£175–200	80,927	1.0	15.32	8.5	189
Over £200	102,734	1.2	21.77	12.0	212
TOTAL	8,556,934	100.0	181.16	100.0	21
For 1929					
Under £20	6,440,000	71.7	21.8	7.6	3.4
£20–25	283,000	3.1	6.3	2.2	22
£25–30	199,000	2.2	5.5	1.9	27
£30–40	319,000	3.6	11.1	3.9	34
£40–50	242,000	2.7	10.9	3.8	45
£50–100	685,000	7.6	48.6	17.0	70
£100–200	493,000	5.5	68.8	24.1	140
£200–500	283,000	3.1	82.4	28.8	291
Over £500	43,000	0.5	30.4	10.7	707
TOTAL	8,987,000	100.0	285.8	100.0	32

Notes
Dormant accounts are excluded for 1899, 1913, and 1929.
Society accounts (representing the funds of friendly societies, co-operative societies, and trade unions, and generally allowed to exceed the personal account maximum) are excluded for 1913 and 1929.

Source
Classification of POSB accounts according to balance, PRO NSC 9/263.

of this first size category. For 1929 the total for accounts in the range £20–25 can be excluded to show that over 71 per cent of accounts contained balances of less than £20, averaging £3.8*s*. each, and comprising a mere 7.63 per cent of total POSB deposits.

The table also shows that the abolition of a maximum deposit at the end of 1915 allowed a great expansion in the number of large accounts over £200, an expansion which had a disproportionate impact on the average balance of POSB accounts, since the percentage of total deposits contributed by these large accounts rose from 12 per cent in 1913 to 39.5 per cent in 1929. The average balance for all accounts rose from £21.3*s*. in 1913 to £31.16*s*. in 1929; if accounts over £200 are excluded for both years, then there is only a marginal increase from £18.17*s*. to £19.19*s*., even though retail prices were 60 per cent higher in the latter year.

What these figures reveal about trends in working-class savings is a matter for speculative interpretation. It is certainly not the case that all small accounts below £20 were held by manual workers or their dependants. Children, who opened 21 per cent of new accounts in the 1931 survey, might be expected to hold small balances—this was certainly true of the Aberdeen children, and there is no good reason to expect wide variation across the country. On the other hand, if children's accounts were of less than average duration, then their overall proportion among existing accounts would be less than the representation among new accounts. In the absence of any worthwhile indication of what share of small accounts was due to non-working-class depositors, it will simply be assumed in the following discussion that all small accounts belong to the working population, an assumption that involves some obvious degree of exaggeration.

With large accounts some less hesitant conclusions can be drawn. One way to establish a plausible maximum for working-class savings bank deposits is to examine the total wealth-holding of the adult population, available for the years 1911–13, 1924–30 and 1936–8. There are many weaknesses with these estimates, not least that, for low wealth holders, they are balance sheet calculations rather than estate duty calculations, and so here they are being appealed to in order to interpret information that they are in part derived from.[30] Nevertheless, they do provide a general guide to the distribution of capital among the adult population aged over 25 of England and Wales. The estimates for the three periods show that in 1911–13, 88.3 per cent of this population held capital valued at £100 or less, a percentage that fell to 78.6 per cent in 1924–30 and 74.3 per cent in 1936–8.[31] Atkinson and Harrison, in their detailed study of wealth distribution in Britain, feel that these estimates for the earlier periods may be slightly too high, but they reckon that the 1936–8 figure 'does not appear unreasonable'.[32]

These figures are close enough to the percentage of the working population employed in manual jobs (1911: 79.7 per cent, 1920: 76.8 per cent, 1931: 76.5 per cent)[33] to suggest a significant, and not surprising, correspondence between low pay and low wealth. Of course, it was not impossible for a manual worker to accumulate considerably more than £100 of capital, but given the limited financial means this must have been very much of an exception (though readers of Samuel Smiles would be forgiven for thinking otherwise). The aggregate wealth figures include items like co-operative and building society funds, industrial life assurance company capital, government stock purchased through savings banks, and household goods, as well as savings bank deposits. If it is assumed that small wealth holders did not keep more than half their total assets in a savings bank account, then £50 could be considered as an upper limit for most working-class savings bank deposits. If all balances up to £50 are taken to be due to working-class saving, they are seen to account for around 30 per cent of POSB funds and 86.6 per cent of depositors in 1913, figures which fell to 19.4 per cent and 83.3 per cent by 1929.

[30] Since the estimates of the percentage of the population holding assets worth less than £100 are derived from estate duty returns, they will not be affected by the inaccuracies in the balance sheet estimates of the value of assets held.

[31] Kathleen M. Langley, 'The Distribution of Capital in Private Hands in 1936–38 and 1946–47', *Bulletin of the Oxford Institute of Statistics* xii, no. 12 (Dec. 1950), p. 357.

[32] A. B. Atkinson and A. J. Harrison, *Distribution of Personal Wealth in Britain* (Cambridge, 1978), chs. 4 and 6, and particularly appendix vi.

[33] Routh, *Occupation and Pay*, pp. 6–7.

Since much working-class cash saving was for short-run purposes, and so probably related more closely to income than
wealth (particularly once state insurance schemes provided
some long-term financial security), it might be appropriate to
inflate the 1913 figure by some wage index to take into account
general rises in real income. The £50 maximum for 1913 was
arrived at through the estimates of wealth, and in fact represents about half the average annual earnings for a skilled
manual worker at that time; to take about half this same average for the early thirties suggests a working-class deposit limit
of close to £100, which in 1929 represented about 90 per cent of
accounts and 36 per cent of funds.[34]

Any interpretation of the course of working-class accumulation in savings banks during the period studied depends upon
whether either of these estimates is considered worthwhile, and
if so, which. The 'wealth' estimate points to a decline in the real
value of working-class funds in savings banks of over 35 per
cent between 1913 and 1929; the 'income' estimate suggests a
rise of more than 10 per cent.[35] The guesswork involved in
arriving at both estimates is disconcertingly large, but the information gleaned from the PRO records should mean that
these figures are closer to the truth than the hitherto accepted
estimates that two-thirds of POSB and TSB deposits were held
by wage-earners. This number was proposed by R. B. Suthers
in an article on national savings in the *People's Year Book* for
1931,[36] and has subsequently been used by Radice in his 1939
study of savings in Britain,[37] and by Atkinson and Harrison,[38]
but it is not clear how it was arrived at. No such certainty was
offered by T. S. Ashton in a paper on savings bank deposits he
presented in 1930:

It is frequently assumed that the savings banks funds are almost
exclusively the product of working-class thrift . . . That the majority of

---

[34] Figures taken from Table 4.4.
[35] The figures are: 1913: £56.4m.; 1929: £55.6m. ('wealth' estimate), £104.2m.
('income' estimate). Feinstein's retail price index is 1913:100, 1929:161.
[36] R. B. Suthers, 'The Mystery of National Savings and Spendings' in *The People's
Year Book, 1931* (Fourteenth Annual of the English and Scottish Co-operative Wholesale Societies, Manchester, 1931), pp. 260–8.
[37] E. A. Radice, *Savings in Great Britain 1922–1935* (OUP, London, 1939), p. 50.
[38] Atkinson and Harrison, *Distribution of Wealth*, pp. 302–3.

those who enter the doors of Savings Banks are workers is patent even to a casual observer. But that the manual workers control the bulk of the deposits is most unlikely.[39]

The Suthers estimate of the working-class share of POSB funds is obviously excessive, but there are some grounds for believing that the estimates based on the PRO papers are also too high. Because these new calculations assume all small accounts to be working-class, they overestimate the working-class number and amount of deposits. The most generous interpretation of the 1931 occupational survey of POSB depositors showed that only 70 per cent could be put in the working-class category, so some of the small accounts should definitely be excluded from consideration. This implies that an optimistic estimate of the working-class share of POSB funds would be no more than 30 per cent and the actual figure could be substantially lower. Ashton's survey of five Trustee banks suggests much the same pattern of deposit in the TSBs, with the bottom 70 per cent or so of depositors with accounts below £50 contributing around 30 per cent of total funds.[40]

It is just as unlikely that manual workers and their dependants controlled the bulk of the funds in three other asset types connected to the savings banks, these being accounts held with TSB special investment departments, government stock purchased through savings banks by depositors, and money invested in National Savings Certificates. Suthers suggested reasonable numbers would be one-third of funds in the first two categories belonging to wage-earners, one-quarter in the third category, but again some revision of these estimates is required.

TSB special investment departments, authorized under section 16 of the 1863 Savings Bank Act, consisted of funds which trustees were allowed to invest other than with the National Debt Commissioners. Most often these were loans to local authorities and public boards, and they had the advantage of realizing a generally higher rate of interest than that paid on the national debt—especially attractive when open market rates stood well above the $2\frac{1}{2}$ per cent offered on ordinary

[39] T. S. Ashton, 'Fluctuations in Savings Bank Deposits', *Transactions of the Manchester Statistical Society* (1929–30), p. 97.
[40] Ibid., Tables vii to xi, pp. 106–10.

deposits. Another advantage was that the maximum deposit in the special investment departments was substantially higher than in the ordinary department, so it appealed particularly to large-scale depositors. If the Aberdeen Savings Bank was at all representative, then small depositors were debarred from these higher interest rates, as:

deposits are received for Special Investment only from persons who are depositors in the Ordinary Department to the extent of not less than £50. The total deposit allowed by statute is £500, and this amount may be deposited annually or in one sum. The Department is chiefly designed for depositors in the Ordinary Department whose accumulations are approaching the statutory limit of £200.[41]

In 1913 the average deposit in all TSB special investment departments was £152 (compared with £28 in the ordinary department), in 1929 it stood at £221. On the previous assumptions about the size of individual working-class deposits, it would appear that a negligible proportion, say 5 per cent, of special investment department assets were contributed by wage-earners.

The same was true for the purchase of government stock by depositors through either the POSB or TSBs, at least until the beginning of the First World War. This scheme, introduced in 1880, allowed depositors to buy government stock in units of £10 or more, with an initial maximum annual purchase of £100, and maximum total holding of £300, figures which were raised to £200 a year and £500 in total in 1893.[42] As can be seen from Table 4.1 the average amount of stock remaining to the credit of stockholders at the end of each year rose from £63 in 1881 to £144 in 1913, a sum remarkably close to the average in TSB special investment departments and likewise probably held by the non-working-class population. In 1915, however, the number of stock accounts rose over tenfold, the direct consequence of the war savings scheme.

The financial needs of the government during the war forced

[41] Report of the Aberdeen Savings Bank for 1913, p. 3. The same was true in the Perth Savings Bank; see *A Brief Sketch of the History, Aims and Practice of the Savings Bank of the County and City of Perth, 1815–1915* (Perth, 1915), pp. 16–17.
[42] For details see twenty-seventh Report of the Postmaster General, PP 1881 xxix (C. 3006), pp. 5, 26–8.

it to develop a wide range of new opportunities for personal saving which would reduce the inflationary consequences of increased wages at a time when fewer consumer goods were available. The National Organising Committee for War Savings (later the National War Savings Committee) saw that savings propaganda could affect morale as well as national finance:

The appeal to reduce expenditure, in other words to restrict the consumption of things and the employment of services for private ends, so that more things and more services may be available for war purposes by the government, must be addressed to *all* classes of the population, and indeed with special emphasis to the wealthier classes. The well-to-do people, the income receivers as opposed to the wage earners, already have ample machinery for saving at their command, but if the Committee were to confine its propaganda to the small investor classes, for whom we are to provide new machinery for saving, we should deprive ourselves of one of our most effective weapons of appeal—viz. that as the need is national so the effort must be national.[43]

So the war savings campaign really had two goals—one was to involve the maximum number of people, and so required an appeal to wage-earners, the other was to draw on the maximum amount of money, which meant making investments attractive to the top 10 per cent of wealth holders. These different aims led to a conflict of interests as small savers had different needs from large-scale investors, a difference explicitly recognized in 1916 in the report of the Montagu Committee on War Loans for the Small Saver. This committee found that the typical small saver 'does not understand complicated machinery, and he wishes to handle paper as little as possible'. He seeks three things: (i) secure capital value, (ii) withdrawal at short notice, since 'the financial emergencies of life come upon the working man with startling suddenness', (iii) as high an interest rate as the large-scale investor, and of these the first and second points are more important than the third.[44] Compared with large-scale investors, small savers were held to be

[43] National Organising Committee for War Savings, Memoranda for Chairmen (7 Feb. 1916). PRO NSC 1/1.
[44] Report of the Committee on War Loans for the Small Saver [Montagu Cttee.], PP 1916 xv (Cd. 8179), p. 3.

relatively insensitive to interest rate differentials between alternative investment opportunities, but highly sensitive to liquidity.

The twin goals were lost sight of by the War Savings Committee as it came to concentrate its efforts on stimulating working-class savings through savings groups and savings certificates, leaving the large-scale investor to respond through the normal institutional channels to changes in government interest rates. But, as columns 4 and 8 of Table 4.1 show, not all stock accumulation did proceed through the normal institutional channels. War Loan and Exchequer Bonds were available through the Post Office government stock register, and substantial sales were made; for instance, almost £40m. of the June 1915 4.5 per cent War Loan was issued through the Post Office, 7 per cent of the total.[45] The number of holdings on the Post Office government stock register rose rapidly during the war to reach a peak of 4.7m. in 1919, valued at £215m., or £45 per holding, under one-third of the pre-war average. Can this be taken to mean that, contrary to the beliefs of the Montagu Committee, small investors were buying illiquid government stock, albeit in small individual holdings?

There is little evidence to support this; the rapid increase in the number of wartime holdings represents no more than an administrative change. Before 1914, each Post Office stock investor had a single recorded holding of government stock to which he could add or subtract at will. To simplify the issue of War Loan and Exchequer and Treasury Bonds, each depositor had a single holding of each specific bond, so that an individual who had purchased both the 1915 War Loan and the 1916 Exchequer Bond would have two holdings on the stock register. In mid-1917 it was estimated that the $3\frac{1}{4}$m. holdings on the stock register represented about 2m. holders,[46] a degree of double counting that increased with each successive debt issue up to the 1919 4 per cent Victory Bond. Much of the post-war decline in the number of holdings was due to the conversion of different types of government debt into new issues of debt

[45] First Annual Report of the National War Savings Committee, 1917, PP 1917–18 xviii (Cd. 8516), p. 14.
[46] A Report on investment through the Post Office in government stock. PRO NSC 12/32.

which counted as a single holding—this is why the value of stock shows only a very slight fall.

The average amount of stock held by each individual represented on the Post Office government register was clearly much greater than the unadjusted figures indicate at first sight, and this would suggest that working-class holdings were not substantial. On the other hand, the fact that this stock was purchased through the Post Office points to it having been bought by people not used to normal institutional channels. But these people could as well have been clerks, shopkeepers, or the wealthy residents of country areas who did not have direct access to a bank, as workers. If estimates of working-class holding of government stock are to be made, then a negligible holding of 5 per cent by value of the stock might be reasonable, significantly below the figure of one-third of the Post Office stock fund suggested by Suthers.

For the third type of investment, National Savings Certificates (until September 1920, War Savings Certificates), the estimate by Suthers that only one-quarter was held by wage-earners seems somewhat at odds with the view of Sir Bernard Mallet that the introduction of WSCs in February 1916 was 'specially designed to attract the savings of the small investor, a class which had hitherto been ignored in war finance'.[47] These certificates satisfied the needs of the small investor outlined by the Montagu Committee by offering security, liquidity, and a good interest rate. Certificates were issued at 15s.6d., repayable at £1 in five years time, with the accumulated interest being tax-free. The original payment and accumulated interest could be withdrawn at any time, although the interest rate structure was biased towards those who held the certificates to maturity. The income tax exemption was of increasing importance to workers as wartime inflation brought more of them above the income tax threshold of £120, but it was particularly attractive to large taxpayers. To prevent the well-off taking advantage of savings certificates, originally they were confined to people whose total income did not exceed £300 a year. The inability to impose this restriction led to its abandonment in

---

[47] Sir Bernard Mallet and C. Oswald George, *British Budgets, 1913–14 to 1920–21* (London, 1929), p. 356.

June 1916, although individual holdings were restricted to 500 units.[48]

Table 4.4 shows the pattern of issue of certificates between 1916 and 1939 by size of certificate, and it is at once apparent that a considerable proportion of the funds directed into savings certificates came in large investments. Certificates for twenty-five units or less never accounted for more than 55 per cent of investment in any of the seven separately listed issues of savings certificates. The question of who purchased savings certificates was considered by the 1923 Committee of Enquiry into Savings Certificates and Local Loans. Submitting evidence on behalf of the Trustee Savings Banks Association, Sir Thomas Jaffrey, the actuary of the Aberdeen Savings Bank, said:

> the great bulk of the Certificates have been sold by the Joint Stock Banks and the Trustee and Post Office Savings Bank, to people of considerable means, and there can be little doubt—indeed, it is a matter of common experience—that the purchasers of the Certificates have been actuated by a desire to avoid Income Tax. From all sources from which calculation can be made, as well as from my personal experience in dealing both with Depositors and Saving Associations, I would venture the opinion that not more than 50 or 60 millions constitute the share of the total amount derived from the small investor.[49]

This was disputed by the committee, which thought that 'at least half' of all savings certificates had been bought 'by those classes of the community for whom this form of saving was primarily designed'.[50] A better indication of the distribution of certificates comes from a breakdown according to manner of purchase of certificates of the fifth and sixth issues (June 1933–November 1939).

Certificates could be bought by individuals through banks and post offices and through savings groups organized by the National Savings Committee. These groups were usually centred around the workplace, and were based on a system of

---

[48] Horne, *Savings Banks*, pp. 310–11.

[49] Reports of the Committee of Enquiry into Savings Certificates and Local Loans. Outline of Evidence proposed to be submitted on behalf of the TSB Association by Sir Thomas Jaffrey, p. 13. PRO NSC 11/65.

[50] Report of Committee of Enquiry into Savings Certificates, PP 1923 xii pt. ii (Cmd. 1865), appendix p. 25.

Table 4.4. *National Savings Certificates issued 1916–39, by size of certificate*

	Issue dates	Issue value	Issue price
War Savings Certificates	(Feb. 1916–Sept. 1920)	£331.8m.	15s. 6d.
NSC First Issue	(Oct. 1920–Mar. 1922)	£114.2m.	15s. 6d.
NSC Second Issue	(Apr. 1922–Sept. 1923)	£73.7m.	16s.
NSC Third Issue	(Oct. 1923–June 1932)	£347.2m.	16s.
NSC Conversion Issue	(Jan. to April 1932)	£46.8m.	16s.
NSC Fourth Issue	(Aug. 1932–May 1933)	£39.2m.	16s.
NSC Fifth Issue	(June 1933–Feb. 1935)	£54.3m.	16s.
NSC Sixth Issue	(Mar. 1935–Nov. 1939)	£114.7m.	15s.

	£1	£5	£12	£25	£26–499	£500
			(000 of certificates)			
WSC and NSC 1st Issue						
Total units issued: 575.6m.	132,400	27.8	3,936	5,363	1,050	217
% of issue value	23	0.2	8.2	23.2	26.6	18.8
NSC 2nd Issue						
Total units issued: 92.2m.	11,706	–	653	930	237	30.2
% issue value	12.7		8.5	25.2	37.2	16.4

	£1	£5	£10	£25	£50	£100
			(000 of certificates)			
NSC 3rd Issue						
Total units issued: 434.1m.	55,767	5,547	4,935	2,913	2,311	1,128
% of issue value	12.8	6.4	11.4	16.8	26.6	26.0
NSC Conversion Issue						
Total units issued: 58.6m.	644	154	245	155	114	445
% of issue value	1.1	1.4	5.1	6.6	9.8	76.0
NSC 4th Issue						
Total units issued: 49m.	4,483	580	460	253	159	227
% of issue value	9.2	5.9	9.4	12.9	16.2	46.3
NSC 5th Issue						
Total units issued: 68m.	7,989	938	706	351	211	288
% of issue value	11.8	6.9	10.4	12.9	15.6	42.4
Certificates issued through:						
Post Office	4,443	818	604	271	139	137
Bank	234	66	79	71	70	150
Savings Group	3,311	54	23	9	2	1
NSC 6th Issue						
Total units issued: 153m.	17,786	1,962	1,777	615	444	700
% of issue value	11.6	6.4	11.6	10.1	14.5	45.8
Certificates issued through:						
Post Office	9,387	1,661	1,515	475	299	337
Bank	624	164	205	123	140	339
Savings Group	7,774	136	55	16	4	3

Source

National Savings Certificate Accounts, PRO NSC 11/365.

voluntary deduction from the weekly wage packet—an early version of save-as-you-earn. It seems reasonable to suggest that certificates bought through these groups represented the savings of working people, certificates bought through banks represented the savings of non-wage earning groups, with those bought through the Post Office split between the two groups. If we assume that purchases through the Post Office for up to twenty-five units were from wage-earners, those for fifty and 100 units were from others, then we find that about 37 per cent of National Savings Certificates purchased in these six years were held by workers, 63 per cent by the rest of the population.

The fund of capital represented by savings certificates might be distributed in a slightly different way from that suggested by the purchase figures since working-class certificate-holders were more likely to be forced by circumstances to request early redemption than were large-scale holders.[51] This would bias the capital fund figures in favour of middle-class holdings, so an overall estimate of the working-class share of NSC capital of about one-third would seem to be a more reasonable and accurate figure than Suther's suggestion of one-quarter. The results of this extended exercise in assumption and interpretation show that it would be wrong to consider funds accumulated in supposedly working-class savings institutions as belonging wholly, or even mainly, to the manual labour group. While it is reasonable to assume that friendly societies and industrial assurance companies were class-specific, it is clearly not the case with the savings banks and funds considered here.

Of course, the fact that working-class people deposited only a minority of funds in savings banks does not mean that these banks were unimportant agencies for working-class thrift. As Ashton noted, the majority of those who crossed the savings bank threshold were workers, and some indication of how they used the banks can be derived from the statistics of deposits and withdrawals. The average amount deposited in each transac-

[51] The departmental Committee on the system of issuing National Savings Certificates [Bunbury Cttee.] found in 1921 that the percentage of certificates repaid to those issued up to 30 April 1921 was: 500 units—14.1 per cent, 26–499 units—17 per cent, 25 units—19.7 per cent, 12 units—21.2 per cent, 5 units—57.5 per cent, 1 unit—25.6 per cent. PRO NSC 11/64.

tion with the POSB between 1870 and 1914 varied between £2 and £3, the average size of each withdrawal varying between £4.10s. and £7. But these averages are just as distorted by large deposits and withdrawals as are average account estimates by large balances. An estimate of the distribution of deposits by size was made by the POSB for the year 1879, and this is reproduced in Table 4.5. The amount deposited within each of the

Table 4.5. Estimated number of deposits in the POSB of the undermentioned amounts in 1879

Amount of deposit	No. of deposits (000)	Estimated value (£000)	% of number of deposits	% of value of deposits
1s.	168	8.4	5.03	0.09
2s.	208	20.8	6.22	0.23
3s.	133	20.0	4.00	0.22
4s.	98	19.6	2.93	0.22
5s.	257	64.2	7.68	0.71
6s.	77	23.1	2.30	0.26
7s.	53	18.8	1.60	0.21
8s.	54	21.7	1.62	0.24
9s.	17	8.0	0.53	0.09
10s.	353	176.6	10.55	1.96
11s. to 15s.	152	99.4	4.57	1.10
16s. to £1	424	360.7	12.68	4.01
£1. 1s. to £5	913	2,741.4	27.30	30.47
£5. 1s. to £10	249	1,871.6	7.46	20.80
£10. 1s. to £20	118	1,784.4	3.56	19.83
£20. 1s. to £30	62	1,550.3	1.85	17.23
Over £30	4	208.7	0.12	2.32
Total estimated value of deposits		8,997.2		
Actual value of deposits		9,887.1		

Note

The value of deposits has been estimated by taking the mid-point of each deposit range. This underestimates the total value of deposits by about 9 per cent, biasing downwards the value of the larger deposits.

Source

Statement showing estimated number of Deposits in the Post Office Savings Banks of the undermentioned Amounts for the year 1879. PP 1880 xl (342 Sess. 2).

higher deposit classes has been estimated by taking the mid-point of the class, an arbitrary method that clearly understates the total sum deposited, but it is enough to give a rough and ready guide to the distribution. Deposits of £1 and under accounted for 60 per cent of deposit transactions and only 10 per cent of the value of deposits; 60 per cent of the total value of deposits came in sums over £5, accounting for only 13 per cent of transactions. The same was true for the Manchester and Salford TSB in 1897—56 per cent of deposits were for £1 or less, and these comprised about 8 per cent of the total sum deposited.[52] A survey of deposit transactions with the Glasgow Savings Bank carried out in 1935 showed a similar picture; despite much higher wage levels than in the nineteenth century, deposits for £1 or less accounted for 43 per cent of the total number.[53] It is probable that most child depositors made deposits of less than £1, but the figures suggest that there was a significant number of other small depositors.

No similar analysis of withdrawals was carried out by the POSB, but some approximation can be made for the period 1905–14 because of a change in the system of withdrawal. The normal way to withdraw funds from the POSB was to present the deposit book at a post office conducting POSB business. The post office forwarded the book by post to the ledger department in London where the depositor's book was checked with the central records, the sum required for withdrawal was deducted from both, the deposit book was posted back to the initiating office, and the book and money requested would then be handed over to the patient depositor.[54] The whole operation usually took about a week and obviously greatly reduced the attractiveness of the POSB to those families who had low asset reserves and so placed a high premium on liquidity. In 1893 a telegraphic withdrawal system was introduced; for 1s.3d., the cost of a reply-paid telegram, withdrawal requests would be telegraphed to London and sanction returned the same day.

[52] Derived from figures in George H. Pownall, *Savings Banks and their Relations to National Finance* (London, 1903), p. 7.

[53] Thomas Henderson, *The Savings Bank of Glasgow: One Hundred Years of Thrift* (Glasgow, 1936), p. 27.

[54] Short history of the POSB. PRO NSC 9/758.

Although this gave a much greater degree of liquidity, it imposed a high service charge on the small account holder. On 3 July 1905 the POSB introduced a withdrawal-on-demand system for sums not exceeding £1. There was no extra charge to the depositor for this service; any sum up to £1 could be withdrawn by presenting a POSB deposit book at any post office, providing that after withdrawal at least 1s. was left in the account.[55]

This new system was introduced in order to save costs in the ledger department, not to provide an improved service to the depositors, but intentions and results were quite at odds. In the first full year of operation of this scheme it accounted for 55 per cent of withdrawals, representing 7 per cent of total funds withdrawn, and by 1913 65 per cent of the 11m. withdrawals were made on demand for sums under £1.[56] As early as September 1908 the Treasury was pressing for the abolition of this innovation because its popularity, far from reducing administrative costs, had increased them substantially, a pressure successfully resisted by the POSB controller who believed that 'the new facilities have added to the popularity of the Savings Banks, and have been a contributory cause of growth'.[57]

The use made of this withdrawal-on-demand facility shows that many POSB depositors had cause to draw upon their small savings at short notice; for the poorest families, struggling with a hand-to-mouth existence, this immediate access to money saved made the POSB for the first time an attractive repository for funds. Yet putting money in a savings bank was not as

[55] Withdrawal-on-Demand. PRO NSC 9/1021.

[56] Ibid.; Report of the Postmaster-General for 1914–15, PP 1914–15 xxxii (Cd. 7955) appendix J, p. 76.

1.1m. of the 7.4m. small withdrawals in 1913 were made from 'coupon accounts'. The coupon system, introduced in January 1912, was an early version of the national saving stamp scheme. New accounts which were opened with an initial deposit of less than 10s. were not entered in the central POSB ledgers. Deposits and withdrawals were represented by the addition or subtraction of coupons to the depositor's book. Only when coupons to the value of £1 were affixed would the account be registered in the ledger department and given an account number. Details can be found in PRO NSC 15/14.

[57] Fifty-second Report of the Postmaster-General, PP 1906 xxvii (Cd. 3114), p. 12. For the views of the Treasury, see the correspondence in PRO NSC 9/1021.

immediately attractive as other, more communal, forms of thrift, since it did not combine security with sociability. A savings bank deposit book could not be flaunted in the same way as a friendly society banner paraded to church on a Sunday or a piano placed in the front parlour. Savings banks do not appear to have been much used for long-run accumulation; working-class cash saving was of a short-term kind, done with some specific expenditure in mind. These specific expenditures were often quite small, and the sums deposited even smaller, so the opportunities savings banks gave for small deposits and withdrawals made them much more popular among working-class savers than the other, larger-scale, forms of accumulation offered by the Post Office and Trustee banks. But the rough occupational analyses of savings bank depositors suggest that unskilled workers could seldom afford to make even the small cash deposits necessary; savings banks tended to be patronized more by the slightly better-off workers who had sufficient income to afford both insurance and cash accumulation. Saving was not always easy, even for this better-off group of workers, and the POSB could be used to protect funds from any impetuous desire to spend. As one working-class interviewee explained, 'when I get any spare money I put it in the post office. Then its easy to get out if you really want it, but ordinary times its out of your reach. Out of sight, out of mind!'[58] Although the bulk of account-holders were wage-labourers or their dependants, it is clear that the bulk of funds in these savings institutions were the property of people who were not working class.

BUILDING SOCIETIES

In 1939 the draft report of the Treasury Committee on Small Savings noted that:

such bodies as the Building Societies and the Co-operative Movement are at present offering rates of interest which in the case of Building Societies, range as high as 3.5% tax free with facilities for easy withdrawal, and ... these forms of investment have, in general, come to be

[58] M-O, 'A Savings Survey (Working Class)', p. 20.

regarded by the public as without risk. They have undoubtedly provided a most attractive form of investment to the small man and the funds of the institutions which offer them have shown a continuous and rapid increase.[59]

Exactly who the 'small saver' was, and how much he invested in these institutions was not made clear by the committee; in fact there are good grounds for believing that, in the inter-war years, building societies appealed mainly to middle-class rather than working-class investors.

The mythology of building societies tells a glorious story of the facilities advanced by these self-governing groups of working-class capitalists for the erection or purchase of private residential accommodation. The benefits of home-ownership, according to the managing director of the Abbey Road Building Society in 1927, were ethical and moral as well as material:

The man who has something to protect and improve—a stake of some sort in the country—naturally turns his thoughts in the direction of sane, ordered and perforce economical government. The thrifty man is seldom or never an extremist agitator. To him revolution is anathema; and as in the earliest days Building Societies acted as a stabilising force, so today they stand, in the words of the Rt. Hon. G. N. Barnes, as 'a bulwark against Bolshevism and all that Bolshevism stands for'.[60]

But neither in the early years, nor during the period of rapid expansion between the wars, do the societies seem to have made a major appeal to workers, whether agitators or respectable artisans.

The early nineteenth-century building clubs and freehold land societies of Birmingham catered mainly for the middle classes, since 'their subscription rates clearly excluded all but those whose incomes consistently allowed a comfortable margin above subsistence'.[61] In 1850 a trustee of a building society established to promote working-class property ownership told

[59] Draft Report of the Committee on Small Savings appointed by Treasury, minute of 24 June 1939, p. 2. PRO NSC 7/4.
[60] Sir Harold Bellman, *The Building Society Movement* (London, 1927), p. 54.
[61] S. D. Chapman and J. N. Bartlett, 'The Contribution of Building Clubs and Freehold Land Societies to Working-Class housing in Birmingham' in S. D. Chapman (ed.), *The History of Working-Class Housing: A Symposium* (Newton Abbot, 1971), pp. 236–7.

the Select Committee on the Savings of the Middle and Working Classes that 'the punctuality of payments, the fines, and those arrangements which are essential to the proper working of a society, acting upon men who are occasionally thrown out of employment, and without means altogether, have compelled them to withdraw'.[62] At this time, fines for lapses from regular payments were imposed on borrowers and lenders alike, so building societies were not attractive repositories for occasional savings. In the early 1870s the Northcote Commission heard conflicting evidence of building society membership. In Birmingham, it was claimed, members 'mostly belong to the working population of the town', whereas in Newcastle, 'really and truly the bulk of the money, whether as shareholders or as investors, is the money of the middle classes'.[63] Whatever the true financial and social position of their members, societies had a vested interest in presenting a working-class visage to the Commissioners, since they could thereby secure certain stamp duty and registration privileges. Where workers were members, they were depositing rather than borrowing members; most loans were made to builders and salaried people.

Until 1914 the effect of building societies on the housing market was slight; perhaps 10 per cent of houses were owner-occupied at the outbreak of the First World War, and a negligible proportion of these were owned by manual workers.[64] Table 4.6 shows the development of the societies from 1880, a development that was attenuated by the failures of the 'Liberator' building society in 1892 and of the 'Birkbeck' in 1911.[65] The inter-war years saw an enormous expansion of building society activity—the value of share accounts increased twelvefold, deposits almost tenfold, and there was a threefold increase in the average sum credited to each share account. The average size of a building society share account was at all times considerably greater than the average value of a deposit account in

[62] Select Committee on Investments for the Savings of the Middle and Working Classes, PP 1850 xix (508), q. 507.

[63] Northcote Cmmn., First Report, PP 1871 xxv (C. 452), qq. 3652, 8199. See also qq. 3537, 4291, 4384–5, 5125–6, 5258–62, 5628, 5892–4, 6685–9, 7728–30.

[64] Martin Boddy, *The Building Societies* (London, 1980), p. 154; John Burnett, *A Social History of Housing 1815–1970* (London, 1980), p. 145.

[65] Details are given in chapters 8 and 9 of the standard history by E. J. Cleary, *The Building Society Movement* (London, 1965).

Table 4.6. *Membership and capital of building societies and retail co-operative societies*

	BUILDING SOCIETIES				CO-OPERATIVE SOCIETIES			
	Share capital £m.	Loan capital £m.	Membership (000)	Share capital per member (£)	Share capital £m.	Loan capital £m.	Membership (000)	Share capital per member (£)
1880	27.1	25.7						
1881	31.6	25.7						
1882	36.0	28.4						
1883	38.2	28.2			6.4	0.7	627	10.2
1884	39.5	27.2			6.7	0.8	696	9.6
1885	41.0	26.7			7.5	0.8	746	10.0
1886	41.5	26.4			7.9	1.0	774	10.2
1887	42.7	26.0			8.6	1.0	828	10.3
1888	42.5	25.3			8.9	1.0	867	10.3
1889	42.1	25.3			9.5	1.0	932	10.2
1890	41.6	25.3			10.3	1.1	961	10.7
1891	40.2	25.2	646	62	11.3	1.2	1,044	10.8
1892	39.5	22.1	639	61	12.2	1.3	1,126	10.8
1893[a]	36.5	18.9	588	62	12.5	1.4	1,169	10.7
1894	35.9	18.0	570	62	13.2	1.3	1,212	10.9
1895	34.4	17.5	631	54	14.1	1.6	1,274	11.1
1896	34.4	18.9	622	55	15.4	1.5	1,355	11.3
1897	34.0	19.9	605	56	16.3	2.0	1,465	11.1
1898	34.0	21.3	599	56	17.4	2.3	1,535	11.3
1899	34.5	22.3	589	58	18.9	2.5	1,613	11.7
1900	35.0	21.6	584	59	20.6	3.0	1,707	12.0
1901	35.4	22.1	577	61	22.0	3.3	1,793	12.2

Table 4.6 (continued)

	BUILDING SOCIETIES				CO-OPERATIVE SOCIETIES			
	Share capital £m.	Loan capital £m.	Member- ship (000)	Share capital per member (£)	Share capital £m.	Loan capital £m.	Member- ship (000)	Share capital per member (£)
1902	36.4	22.8	581	62	23.2	3.5	1,892	12.2
1903	37.5	23.9	588	63	24.2	3.8	1,987	12.2
1904	38.5	24.5	597	64	25.1	4.0	2,078	12.1
1905	39.8	25.4	602	66	26.1	4.2	2,153	12.1
1906	41.2	25.8	607	67	27.3	4.3	2,222	12.3
1907	42.3	25.6	614	68	29.0	4.3	2,323	12.5
1908	43.6	25.3	616	70	30.0	4.6	2,404	12.5
1909	44.6	26.0	624	71	30.8	4.8	2,469	12.5
1910	45.6	25.9	626	72	31.6	4.8	2,541	12.4
1911b	43.9	16.0	602	72	33.2	5.8	2,640	12.6
1912	44.5	15.9	607	73	35.3	7.0	2,749	12.6
1913	45.6	16.0	617	73	37.8	8.0	2,881	12.9
1914	46.5	15.9	627	74	40.1	8.3	3,046	13.0
1915	46.4	15.3	626	74	43.7	9.0	3,276	13.2
1916	46.7	14.4	620	75	47.8	9.6	3,520	13.4
1917	46.6	13.6	612	76	49.1	9.9	3,786	13.0
1918	50.1	14.1	625	80	54.7	11.6	3,862	14.0
1919	56.6	16.2	672	84	66.1	13.4	4,062	15.9
1920	63.9	16.1	747	85	76.3	15.1	4,443	16.9
1921	70.9	17.2	789	89	75.5	15.7	4,531	16.4
1922	80.4	19.3	826	97	73.5	16.4	4,471	16.2
1923	93.5	21.8	895	105	75.8	17.2	4,531	16.5

1924	109.0	24.5	1,000	109	80.5	18.8	4,662	17.1
1925	127.8	27.3	1,129	113	85.9	20.7	4,859	17.4
1926	147.7	30.5	1,257	117	88.1	22.2	5,146	16.9
1927	172.8	33.4	1,416	122	92.0	24.1	5,532	16.5
1928	213.2	36.0	1,130c	188	99.3	26.5	5,844	16.9
1929	250.2	38.9	1,265	197	106.3	28.4	6,128	17.3
1930	302.8	44.6	1,449	208	112.6	30.3	6,366	17.6
1931	341.8	50.4	1,577	216	117.6	32.1	6,557	17.9
1932	380.8	61.5	1,692	225	120.8	34.1	6,722	17.9
1933	395.5	75.5	1,747	226	124.0	36.1	6,882	17.9
1934	424.3	97.3	1,857	228	128.2	37.5	7,151	17.9
1935	447.2	114.8	1,938	230	135.1	40.6	7,435	18.1
1936	480.7	128.4	2,010	239	184.8		7,766	
1937	517.5	143.3	2,083	248	193.0		8,023	
1938	548.3	155.7	2,152	254	199.9		8,338	
1939	559.4	152.0						

Notes

 a Fall in building society capital and membership due to failure of the Liberator Building Society.
 b Fall in building society capital and membership due to failure of the Birkbeck Building Society.
 c Share investors only in this and the following years. In previous years borrowers who were not also share investors were included.

Sources

Building societies: share and deposit capital—David K. Sheppard, *The Growth and Role of U.K. Financial Institutions 1880–1962* (London, 1971), pp. 150–2.
membership—Friendly Societies Report for 1938, part 5 (HMSO, 1939), p. 16.
Co-operative societies: share and deposit capital—Abstract of Labour Statistics PP 1900 lxxxiii, 26; ibid. PP 1912–13 cvii, 232; ibid. PP 1926 xxix, 192; ibid. PP 1936–7 xxvi, 152; eighty-third Statistical Abstract PP 1930–40 x, 269
membership—J. A. Hough, *Dividend on Co-operative Purchases* (Manchester, 1936), pp. 183–4.

the POSB or TSB, and an analysis of share accounts by size of balance in the Abbey Road Building Society (Table 4.7) points to large and increasing middle-class investment. As with savings banks, the majority of accounts were for sums of less than

Table 4.7. Distribution by size of share accounts in the Abbey Road Building Society for 1913 and 1932

| | 1913 | | 1932 | Adjusted | |
	% no. of accounts	% value of accounts	% no. of accounts	% no. of accounts[a]	% value of accounts
Up to £50	64.6	8.9	58.4	33.8	3.07
£50–100	13.2	12.9	8.3	13.2	3.7
£100–150	6.7	10.5	6.2[b]	9.8	4.5
£150–200	4.85	11.1	4.2[b]	6.7	4.4
£200–500	8.6	33.6	13.6	21.6	26.1
£500–1,000	1.7	15.3	6.2	10.0	25.9
Over £1,000	0.35	7.7	3.1	4.8	32.33

Notes

[a] In 1932, 51,885 of the 138,591 share accounts were valued at less than £1. Many of these represented the holdings of borrowers who under the rules of the society were required to qualify as members by opening a partly-paid share account and paying 1s. per £100 advanced. To overcome the downward bias that this places on the average size of share account, all accounts of £1 and under have been excluded from the 'adjusted' figures.

[b] In the original table, the membership figures for the £100–150 category and the £150–200 category are transposed.

Source

Sir Harold Bellman, 'Building Societies—some economic aspects', *Economic Journal*, xliii (Mar. 1933), pp. 14–17.

£50, but the majority of capital was held in accounts of £200 or more. There was a significant growth of large accounts in the Abbey Road between 1913 and 1932, particularly for sums over £1,000, but even in 1913 there was a much greater emphasis on accounts over £100 than was the case in the POSB. Using the same criteria for estimating the capital held by the working-class population as was adopted with savings banks suggests about 9 per cent of building society funds in 1913, and between 3 per cent and 7 per cent in 1932. A generous estimate would put the working-class share of building society funds at one-tenth. It is not possible to establish whether the distribution of loan capital followed the same pattern as share capital. In 1930 there were over 400,000 depositors, with an average balance of £118,[66] well below the average for share accounts. However, many deposit accounts were opened by shareholders who had reached the financial limit on share account, a limit often strictly adhered to in the 1930s when the societies had surplus funds, so the lower average balance need not imply a greater representation of small savers among depositors.[67]

The reason for the increased popularity of building societies in the inter-war years, particularly for large depositors and shareholders, was the attractive interest rate. Throughout the 1930s the societies were offering interest on share accounts that was higher than the yield on Consols.[68] But this was not the only attraction; income tax on receipts from building society accounts under £5,000 was paid at source at a reduced rate, and so the income was effectively tax-free for investors.[69] The interest rate advantage of building societies increased markedly over other assets from 1931, and this probably raised the pro-portionate share of building society assets owned by the non-working-class group.[70] As *The Economist* explained in 1936, 'The rapid fall in interest rates from 1931 onwards led directly to the "bad money" problem, since many investors faced with the conversion of War Loan placed large amounts with the building societies to earn over 4 per cent. tax free on shares and 3¾ per cent. on deposits.'[71] It seems unlikely that many work-ing-class savers responded to the interest rate advantage of building societies. A direct question to a sample of Bolton workers in 1939 asking them why they saved revealed that none of them was affected by the interest rate,[72] whereas for many

[66] *The Building Societies Yearbook*, 1932, p. 34.
[67] George Elkington, *The National Building Society 1849–1934* (Cambridge, 1935), pp. 55–8.
[68] Cleary, *Building Society Movement*, p. 190.
[69] Up to 1931, one-quarter of the standard rate was paid at source, thereafter two-fifths was paid.
[70] Cleary, *Building Society Movement*, p. 190; Radice, *Savings in Great Britain*, pp. 50–1.
[71] *The Economist*, Building Societies Special Survey (11 Apr. 1936), p. 16.
[72] M-O, 'Motives for Saving', p. 3.

middle-class members of the Mass-Observation panel it was an important factor. One of them, a retail chemist, explained, 'The Building Society I use as a means of saving because interest is at a higher rate than bank interest ... I pay the most of my savings into the Building Society, keeping about £20 in the bank as an easily negociable (sic) account. When the figure approaches £30 I make a contribution to the Building Society.'[73]

The placement of funds with building societies through share or deposit accounts is only one way of looking at savings channelled into this sector. An alternative is to consider mortgage repayments, and it is possible that this will encompass a larger share of working-class savings since the inter-war years saw a great expansion of home-ownership 'well down into the lower middle class and even into the upper levels of the working class'.[74] It seems clear that some borrowers were manual workers; the development of 90 per cent mortgages to assist the purchaser who could not afford the usual 25 per cent deposit may be a sign of this,[75] as also the fact that in 1932 the Abbey Road society claimed that 37 per cent of its borrowers were 'wage earners'. However, only 5 per cent of the number of mortgage advances made by this society in 1932 were for £400 or less, and few manual workers would have been granted more given the general rule of building societies that mortgage repayments and rates should not exceed 25 per cent of income.[76] Although many workers did experience a change of housing tenure during the inter-war period, it was largely a move from private rented accommodation to council housing rather than home-ownership. Neither in terms of savings invested nor in terms of loans repaid can building societies properly be described as working-class financial institutions.

The rapid growth of institutions for the small saver, particularly the growth of the POSB, shows there was considerable demand for some safe repository for funds, but the low value of

[73] M-O, Directive Replies, Jan. 1939, Observer 1194.
[74] Burnett, *Social History of Housing*, pp. 245–6.
[75] H. C. Heales and C. H. Kirby, *Housing Finance in Great Britain* (London, 1938), pp. 26–8.
[76] Sir Harold Bellman, 'Building Societies—some economic aspects', *Economic Journal* xliii (Mar. 1933), pp. 14–17.

most accounts, the small average number of transactions, and
the high annual rate of account closure all point to the facility
being used primarily for short-run protection of savings rather
than long-run accumulation—saving to spend rather than
'thrift'. The only really popular form of long-term accumulation was the purchase of life assurance, particularly after the
First World War, in the form of endowment assurances. None
of these forms of accumulation responded to changes in interest
rates. Working-class savers were not speculators; they preferred
to place their bets on the backs of horses rather than financiers.

5

Co-operative Societies

RETAIL co-operative societies were without doubt primarily working-class institutions. Although middle-class patronage and leadership was accepted, particularly during the nineteenth century, the movement was one of small-scale consumers and savers. It was also a major provider of credit to working-class customers, and this dual role gives it an odd position in the hierarchy of thrift. The extension of retail credit by co-operative societies was constantly denied, criticized, or under-emphasized by co-operative activists and propagandists who felt that dependence on credit was incompatible with both co-operative idealism and respectable behaviour. The way in which the dual function of savings bank and loan office were differentially portrayed by co-operative leaders gives a good insight into contemporary attitudes towards credit and thrift, and into the way the views of rank and file could be ignored or misrepresented by delegates and spokesmen.

The savings side to co-operation rested on the dividend. The essence of retail co-operation was the division of surplus among trading members at the end of each accounting period in proportion to the amount purchased at the store; for many members the savings bank was an automatic one, since quarterly dividends were often left to accumulate in share accounts for quite long periods. The sums involved were small when compared with building society and savings bank accumulation (see Table 4.6); in 1932 the average annual sales per co-operative society member stood at just under £30, share capital at just under £18.[1] The average share capital per member was less heavily influenced by very large shareholdings than was the case with building societies, since the legal maximum for a share account was £200, and owing to the superabundance of capital within the co-operative movement from the early years

---

[1] J. A. Hough, *Dividend on Co-operative Purchases* (Manchester, 1936), p. 106.

of the twentieth century many societies imposed further restrictions on shareholdings to prevent them being used for investment purposes.[2]

The holdings of deposit capital were perhaps more likely to be concentrated, particularly among members whose accumulated dividends exceeded the share limit. Unfortunately no detailed evidence of the distribution by size of share and deposit accounts in the co-op is available, so definitive statements cannot be made. It is true, however, that few co-operators made use of the deposit banking facilities offered by the CWS Bank to individual members from 1910 onwards. The 2,472 depositors in 1912 had risen to only 20,657, with an average balance of £262, by 1938. It was felt that the minimum deposit of £10 (later reduced to £5) was the great hindrance to the growth of personal banking among members.[3]

The accumulation of capital in co-operative societies was heartily praised by middle-class observers, not just because it promoted economic self-sufficiency among workers, but because the co-operative ideal provided a moral training akin to that proffered by the affiliated friendly societies. In 1898 Dr Creighton, the Bishop of London, declared that co-operative distribution was 'valuable as a means of intellectual and moral education'. It induced 'an intelligence of economic principles' and 'a power of economic restraint' which together promoted stability in the social order.[4] For Samuel Smiles, who advocated a widely-publicized blend of associationism and self-help, co-operative societies induced a healthy independence quite divorced from the damaging sectional interests of trade unionism. He went so far as to say, 'the secret of social development is to be found in co-operation.'[5]

The mass of the members were more interested in money than in social development; it was the dividend, and the use to which it could be put in managing a family's finances, that was the real inducement to co-operate. One respondent to a government inquiry into working-class expenditure in 1889

---

[2] Arnold Bonner, *British Co-operation* (Manchester, 1970), p. 166.
[3] Percy Redfern, *The New History of the C.W.S.* (London, 1938), p. 404.
[4] Thirtieth Co-operative Congress, Peterborough, 1898, *Report*, p. 8.
[5] Smiles, *Thrift*, pp. 97–107.

explained, 'I am a member in a co-operative provision store which I find to be a great advantage. I receive as dividend about £5. 10s. per annum, paid half yearly, which comes in very handy at rent time.'[6] But quarterly rent payments could only be met in part by dividends, and other ways of putting-by had to be used as well. In the household of an Edinburgh labourer studied by Paton *et al.*:

the dividend received from the store pays the rent for those two quarters. The yearly society ... 'breaks' in February, and the 1s. a week deposit is returned then, £2 12s. in all (also a dividend averaging about 5s.), and this pays the February rent. The only rent troublesome to meet is the August rent, and this is met by money put into the children's savings bank at Sunday School.[7]

Spending at the co-op could be part of a system of quite de- liberate financial planning,[8] and the dividend was therefore of vital importance to many co-operators. As a felt-hat maker wrote to the Women's Co-operative Guild in 1931, 'At our work we had many debates over Co-operation, and one thing always struck me; it was the poorest people in the room that were the most loyal. Ideals had nothing to do with it, it was the "divi" that was so useful.'[9]

Because the dividend was so important to many members they sometimes resisted a reduction in payment. The history of the Failsworth (Manchester) society records that:

In the balance sheet for the quarter ending July 1st, 1873, the pay- ment of dividend of 1s. 6d. in the pound was recommended, but the members at the quarterly meeting decided that the dividend be 1s. 8d. There were no surplus profits which would permit this increase, and such action was therefore illegal. The difference was charged to the next quarter's trade account. The previous quarter's dividend was 1s. 10d., and the members did not like the idea of going back to 1s. 6d.[10]

This sort of behaviour was deeply offensive to co-operative idealists who felt that the movement was 'being slowly and

---

[6] Returns of Expenditure by Working Men, PP 1889 lxxxiv (C. 5861), p. 15.
[7] Paton, Dunlop, and Inglis, *Diet*, p. 26.
[8] Hough, *Dividend on Co-operative Purchases*, p. 151.
[9] Margaret Llewelyn Davies (ed.), *Life as we have known it* (London, 1977 reprint), p. 91.
[10] J. H. Ogden, *Failsworth Industrial Society Ltd. Jubilee History 1859–1909* (Manches- ter, 1909), pp. 57–8.

incessantly broken on the wheel of self-interest'.[11] G. J. Holyoake, the grand old man of the co-operative movement, was less prosaic:

Co-operation, like the corn-laden caravan of merchants in the desert, is seized upon by marauding bands who carry off treasures intended for honest sale. Now it is discerned that co-operation creates wealth, swarms of mere mercenaries swoop down upon it, to avail themselves of it as a means of gain—caring nothing for the social education and equality it was intended to promote, and can and should promote.[12]

Even Beatrice Potter, who had many differences with the idealists over the true direction of co-operation, agreed that the dividend was misused by some societies. Its real significance, she said, was not as an automatic savings bank, but as an advertisement of a principle 'which powerfully but silently promotes the spread of the spirit of association'.[13] Thirty years later, and now in formidable partnership with Sidney Webb, she reiterated these views:

We do not regard Co-operation particularly as a method by which poor men make savings and advance their own position in the world, nor yet as a philanthropic device for eking out wages and producing contentment. To us the social and political significance of the Co-operative Movement lies in the fact that it provides a means by which, in substitution for the Capitalist System, the operations of industry may be (and are increasingly being) carried on under democratic control without the incentive of profiteering, or the stimulus of pecuniary gain.[14]

As the conservative political economist W. A. S. Hewins pointed out, these descriptions seemed to bear little relation to practical co-operative trading. 'The merest acquaintance with the average co-operator', wrote Hewins, 'reveals the keen interest which he takes in the quarterly dividend', and as a prominent university extension lecturer in northern England, he was in good position to know.[15] 'It is evident', he concluded, 'that

[11] V. Nash, *The Relation of Co-operative to Competitive Trading* (Manchester, n.d., c.1887), p. 4.
[12] Press cutting of C. J. Holyoake's paper to the London Co-operative Board, n.d., Holyoake Papers, no. 4281. Co-operative Union Library, Manchester.
[13] B. Potter, *The Co-operative Movement in Great Britain* (London, 1891), pp. 71–2.
[14] S. and B. Webb, *The Consumers' Co-operative Movement* (London, 1921), p. vi.
[15] W. A. S. Hewins, *Apologia of an Imperialist* (London, 1929), i. 19–23.

it is the financial advantages of Co-operation which make it "go".[16]

For the members, dividends were good, and large dividends were best. Idealists opposed high dividends gained at the expense of inflated prices, particularly when the dividend to the consumer prevented any distribution of profit to the co-operative workers.[17] The Women's Co-operative Guild felt that the craze for high profits kept prices artificially high, and thereby prevented the extension of co-operative stores in poor neighbourhoods, though a survey it conducted in 1902 showed that the relation between high dividends and high prices was not a simple and obvious one.[18] A study of co-operative dividend policy published in 1936 showed that the median dividend had fallen from the range 2s. 6¼d.–3s. in 1895 to 1s. 6¼d.–2s. in 1932, and that there were broad regional variations, with the highest in Scotland, the lowest in Ireland, and with the northern half of the country having higher dividends and slightly higher prices than the south. However, it was reported that 'in no individual instance was the margin of difference between co-operative prices and private trade prices in a selected area found to be equal to the rate of dividend per £ of sales paid by the co-operative society operating in that area.'[19] The dividend variation was more due to the fact that in the north of England co-operative societies dominated the grocery trade in many towns and villages, and therefore could set the market price, whereas in the south, especially in London, keen competition from other retailers kept market prices low.[20] These high-dividend societies were in the heartland of co-operation, the area where the co-operative ideal had taken root most firmly, yet they were the societies that most obviously served the economic self-interest of the member, by providing a system of automatic accumulation.

[16] W. A. S. Hewins, 'The Co-operative Movement', *Economic Review* i (1891), p. 541.

[17] E. V. Neale, *The Economic Aspect of Co-operation* (Manchester, n.d., c.1884), p. 5; Nash, *Relation*, p. 10.

[18] Women's Co-operative Guild, *The Extension of Co-operation to the Poor* (Manchester, 1902), p. 15.

[19] Hough, *Dividend on Co-operative Purchases*, pp. 78, 106, 112.

[20] Ernest Aves, *Co-operative Industry* (London, 1907), p. 51. For an account of the difficulty of establishing co-operation in London see W. Henry Brown, *A Century of London Co-operation* (London, 1928), pp. 114–51.

Economic self-interest was not confined to self-denial through saving; it also embraced self-indulgence through credit trading, and this, too, was readily condemned by co-operative spokesmen and supporters. Rule 21 of the Rochdale Pioneers, the founding fathers of consumers' co-operation, stated that all goods bought and sold by the society should be paid for in cash.[21] This regulation was designed in part to prevent the accumulation of bad debts which might threaten the financial security of the society, but as William Cooper, one of the original Pioneers, quite clearly explained in a letter to Professor Fawcett in 1866, it was also to make members more thoughtful in expenditure, to 'foster a spirit of saving', and to improve habits among the masses in order to raise them from a state of general indebtedness.[22] Two of the most widely read books on co-operation, the *Manual for Co-operators* written by Thomas Hughes and E. V. Neale in 1881, and *Working Men Co-operators* by Arthur Dyke Acland and Ben Jones, first published in 1884, both stress the crucial importance of cash trading. 'Many people', wrote Acland and Jones, 'hardly realise how fatal an evil is the credit system. Many speak very lightly of debt who have a horror of drink, but it has been said with truth, "the credit system of this country is only second in its demoralising influence to the drinking customs of the people".'[23] If co-operators could not pay with cash for the goods they want, then, according to these books, they should be turned away.

Co-operative leaders objected to indebtedness among working men not solely because it was costly and limited the outgrowth of individualism, but also because it prevented the development of mutuality in trading. A paper read to the 1889 co-operative congress declared the credit system to be:

wrong in principle and opposed to true co-operation. All who have joined a co-operative store have done so for the purpose of working together for mutual advantage and good, not to try how much one can make out of the other, and it is a decided injustice to those

---

[21] Bonner, *British Co-operation*, appendix v, p. 523.

[22] Ibid., appendix iv, p. 521.

[23] A. H. D. Acland and Ben Jones, *Working Men Co-operators* (London, 1884), p. 13. The reference is to a speech by Joseph Cowen at the 1873 Co-operative Congress. See Fifth Co-operative Congress, Newcastle, 1873, *Report*, p. 4.

members who are doing their business on a ready-money basis if others are trading on credit.[24]

However, the paper goes on to point out that credit trading causes more general social harm, particularly extravagance and unthriftiness, and, as with much co-operative criticism of the credit system, it is difficult to isolate the chief cause of complaint.

There were, it seems, two principal objections to credit trading. One was that giving credit to members of a co-operative society was dangerous, in so far as a store with a small capital might not be able to cover bad debts, unfair in that such debts could only be paid for by raising prices for ready-cash customers who would in effect be subsidizing the deliberate breach of co-operative principles, and uneconomic, since the capital used to cover debts could be better employed in the expansion of the co-operative movement. The other objection to retail credit was that it was used by private traders to tie customers to a particular shop at which they would be sold inferior goods at inflated prices. The customers could not object or the tick book would be closed and they would face the twin spectres of starvation and the debtors' court.

More often than not these two reasons for objection were conflated, so it was believed that, by denying co-operative customers credit facilities, the evils of the quite unrelated small-shopkeeper credit would be eradicated. In 1872 Thomas Hughes expressed just this belief when he wrote, 'By giving no credit our associations have rescued hundreds of thousands of working people from the thraldom in which they were held to shopkeepers, and from the recklessness, intemperance and improvidence which arose out of that thraldom.'[25] In fact, the denial of credit facilities to customers was an enormous block to co-operative progress, since, as will be explained more fully in chapter 6, credit was such an important and necessary part of working-class economic life. A co-operative store that deprived a man (or more often a woman) of essential provisions in times

[24] Twenty-first Co-operative Congress, Ipswich, 1889, Mr Swallow's paper on 'The Credit System', *Report*, p. 15.
[25] Fourth Co-operative Congress, Bolton, 1872. Inaugural Address by Thomas Hughes, *Report*, p. 2.

of distress would not find it easy to attract his or her loyalty in times of plenty. Sidney Webb argued that if co-operation was to gain ground in areas of low membership, 'it must come in the shape of something more attractive than a new shop which gives no credit in even the cruellest winter'.[26] This it could easily have done, but 'no credit' continued to be held as one of the 'essential points' of co-operation,[27] and many working-class people who could not be sure of a regular income were excluded from the movement on grounds of economy.

This problem of irregular income was recognized by some co-operators, especially by the Women's Co-operative Guild, and various plans were floated for local societies to establish loan funds to assist members in exceptional distress.[28] But the plans, thought up at Congress meetings, seldom filtered their way through the co-operative democracy to give any benefit to the members in need. The movement away from the rigid stance of 'no credit' came from the grass roots, as one local society after another decided to extend credit facilities to customers. From 1886 to 1911 the drift can be traced easily, since during this period the Chief Registrar of Friendly Societies published in his annual report details of which co-operative societies allowed credit. In 1886, 511 of the 946 registered industrial and provident societies in England admitted to giving credit; by 1911 this had risen to 1168 out of 1426—an increase in percentage terms from 54 to 82.[29] These figures came as a great shock to many co-operative leaders,[30] who believed in the truth not only of what they said about the evils of credit, but also of their statement that co-operative societies did not give credit in any circumstances.

[26] S. Webb, *The best means of bringing co-operation within the reach of the poorest of the population* (Manchester, 1891), p. 7.

[27] See Acland and Jones, *Working Men Co-operators* (6th edn., revised by Julia P. Madams, Manchester, 1932), p. 32.

[28] M. C. Spooner, *Emergency Funds and their Application* (London, n.d., *c.*1910), *passim*; W. H. Elliot, *Reflections on Credit Trading* (Manchester, 1909), p. 7; John Ormorod to G. J. Holyoake (5 Dec. 1864), Holyoake Papers, no. 1566; 'Co-operation for the Poor', *Co-operative News* (27 Oct. 1900), pp. 1211–12.

[29] See Annual Reports of the Chief Registrar of Friendly Societies from PP 1887 lxxvii to PP 1912–13 lxxxii.

[30] See discussion of the Registrar's returns at the twentieth Co-operative Congress, Dewsbury, 1888, *Report*, pp. 1–2.

A rearguard action was immediately launched against this threat to the movement's principles. The year after the publication of the Registrar's figures, a paper was read to the co-operative congress which described the giving of credit by co-operative societies as 'malicious' and 'dishonest', and J. C. Gray, who in 1891 was to become secretary to the Co-operative Union, published an analysis of the Registrar's returns of credit-giving societies, in which he condemned all but one of the reasons advanced by societies for the extension of credit facilities to members. A Co-operative Union questionnaire drew replies from 224 credit-giving societies in England and Wales, of which 72 claimed to give credit because of sickness, distress, and temporary want of employment in the district, 90 because wages were locally paid at too great an interval to permit cash payments, 106 gave it for the convenience of members living at a distance from the store, and 76 gave credit either because it was the local custom or in order to compete with local shopkeepers who were offering easy terms.[31] The majority of societies put some limitation on the extent of credit advanced, most commonly by restricting it to some proportion of the member's share capital or by imposing a fixed time for repayment, but 16 per cent of credit-giving societies imposed no limit at all.[32] The results of this survey were used by Gray to demonstrate that nearly all the credit given was unnecessary. The only reason he admitted as valid was that of allowing credit during a period of temporary distress, but even this he saw as dangerous to co-operative principles and individual morals, and better dealt with by a loan fund. It is, he concluded,

a well-known practice with many people to be always a week or two behind in the world. Habit has become in their case second nature. So long as left to their own resources they could not throw it off however they were to try. It is here where co-operation should step in and give them the backbone to resist the temptation and make a new start in

[31] J. C. Gray, *The System of Credit as Practised by Co-operative Societies* (Manchester, 1889), *passim*.

[32] For England, Gray lists 488 retail societies giving credit, the extent of which was unlimited in 79, limited by time for repayment in 113, restricted to some fixed sum per member in 77, limited to some proportion or amount of share capital in 168, and confined to certain articles with a specified time for repayment in 51 societies.

life. This is part of our duty as co-operators, and we should not shirk it.[33]

After these outbursts by co-operative leaders, and the strongest possible restatement of the 'no credit' principle, the issue drifted from public view, or, as one co-operator put it, was dropped like a hot iron because the Registrar's returns were such a disturbing revelation of the true state of co-operative trade.[34]

Agitation among some co-operators induced the congress to return to the subject of credit in 1902, carrying with only a few dissentients a motion 'that this congress views with alarm the increase of "credit trading" by retail co-operative societies, believing that such a system of trading is opposed to the principles of co-operation, and is calculated to retard the growth of the movement'.[35] Two years later, all but two delegates voted in support of a resolution 'that this congress desires once again to place on record its emphatic condemnation of the system of credit trading, which appears to be growing in the movement, and calls upon all societies to use their utmost efforts to abolish the credit system and to substitute cash payments for all goods sold in their shops'.[36] But it would take more than a congress resolution to break the trend. Between 1900 and 1905, for instance, membership of English co-operative societies rose from 1.44m. to 1.8m. people, sales increased from £59m. to £72m., and the number of credit-giving societies rose from 880 to 1039, or from 69.1 per cent to 75.5 per cent of the total.[37] It was far from obvious that credit trading was retarding the growth of the co-operative movement.

Nevertheless, an established principle of co-operation was being undermined, and this prompted the Central Board of the Co-operative Union to report to the 1906 congress that:

The growth of credit trading in the movement is such as to cause serious anxiety to those who have its best interests at heart. We have

---

[33] Gray, *System of Credit*, pp. 26–7.

[34] Mr D. E. Gerrard at the Thirty-sixth Co-operative Congress, Stratford (London), 1904, *Report*, p. 325.

[35] Thirty-fourth Co-operative Congress, Exeter, 1902, *Report*, pp. 162–3.

[36] Thirty-sixth Co-operative Congress, Stratford, 1904, *Report*, p. 324.

[37] Reports of the Chief Registrar of Friendly Societies, PP 1901 lxxii and PP 1906 cxii.

on many occasions called attention to this growing evil, and the practice has been condemned over and over again by the Congress. Unfortunately, however, as in many other matters, the spirit of the movement and the ideas of Congress do not always actuate and guide societies in the conduct of their business, and many of them anxious to maintain trade and extend their business, follow on the line of their competitors, and sacrifice principle for gain.[38]

In an attempt to arrest this 'growing evil', a sub-committee of the Central Board was established to investigate credit trading and, until its dissolution in 1913, this committee detailed the progress of credit in the co-operative movement. The first report of the committee in 1907 revealed that 'the total indebtedness of members of distributive societies was £857,419, and, averaged out, each member was a week behind in payments'.[39] By 1911 the total debt of distributive societies' members was £1,099,287. Only a small part of this was due to draw clubs or hire-purchase; book debts for general shop goods accounted for 93.9 per cent of the total, and 79 per cent of societies were found to be giving credit to their members in this form.[40] It is likely that the true extent of credit was even greater than that revealed by the official returns, since many societies did not record it either because the committee deliberately hid it under the head of stocks, or because shopmen allowed it unofficially to customers without the committee's sanction.[41]

The efforts of the Anti-Credit Committee in trying to induce societies to withdraw credit facilities, or at least establish them on sound and strictly limited principles, had almost no success,[42] and the committee was dissolved in 1913 so that the whole subject of credit trading could be allowed to fade from co-operative memory. Meanwhile the extent of co-operative credit trading continued to grow, with debts outstanding at the

---

[38] Thirty-eighth Co-operative Congress, Birmingham, 1906, *Report*, pp. 138–9.

[39] Thirty-ninth Co-operative Congress, Preston, 1907, *Report*, p. 115.

[40] Forty-third Co-operative Congress, Bradford, 1911, *Report*, pp. 77–9.

[41] James Deans, *Credit Trading in Co-operative Societies* (Glasgow, 1903), p. 4; fortieth Co-operative Congress, Newport, 1908, *Report*, pp. 389–90.

[42] For the suggestions and recommendations of the committee see the Report of the Sub-Committee on Credit Trading, which can be found at section 24 of the Central Board Report to each annual congress from 1909 to 1913. See also Joint Anti-Credit Committee, *Suggestions for the control and limitation of credit trading in Co-operative societies* (Manchester, 1912), *passim*.

end of 1929 totalling over £5m.[43] Part of this increase was caused by the growth of organized credit in the form of club trading or hire-purchase, systems of trading that had to be introduced by co-operative stores in order to compete with American retailing methods brought to the English high street by aggressive chain stores.[44] The effect of introducing 'mutuality' or credit clubs into co-operative retailing could be dramatic. In the London Co-operative Society the sales of clothes, fabrics, and furnishings in 1923, the year before mutuality club trading was introduced, totalled £210,866. By 1927 this had risen to £985,211, of which £535,173 was done on a credit basis.[45] Even so, some of the old co-operators objected to this move. In 1929, in his inaugural address to the congress, H. J. May, Secretary of the International Co-operative Alliance and former Co-operative Party parliamentary candidate, criticized the extension of mutuality club trading among co-operators:

The use of the word 'Mutuality' in such a connection is a gross abuse of the term which, in reality, connotes not only a fundamental instinct of humanity, but the spirit of co-operation itself. Considered economically, this new method of credit trading places a premium on thriftlessness and puts the loyal co-operator at a discount ... 'Mutuality' clubs correspond to no true principles of Co-operation, but are rather a device to increase trade.[46]

The defeat for the co-operative movement's leadership on the question of credit trading was in no way due to a deliberately organized opposition. There was no pro-credit campaign, and very few voices in congress willing to concede that the problem might not be as serious as most speeches and writings on the subject claimed. The pressure for credit facilities came entirely from the store members, and societies individually had to yield to this pressure in order to retain the custom of established members and gain that of new entrants to the movement.

Some examples of the way in which members responded to attempts to control credit are illuminating for the insights they

[43] Hough, *Dividend on Co-operative Purchases*, p. 100.

[44] F. S. Smith, *Credit Trading in Retail Co-operative Societies* (Manchester, 1928), p. 2.

[45] Brown, *Century of London Co-operation*, p. 160.

[46] Sixty-first Co-operative Congress, Torquay, 1929, *Report*, p. 360.

give into the workings of co-operative democracy. The committee of St Cuthbert's (Edinburgh) society, the largest in Scotland with a membership of 1,310 in 1878, decided in that year to control the amount of credit taken by members, and proposed to prohibit the payment of interest on the share capital of members in debt to the society. The society history reports that 'fair as the proposition of the committee was, the members rejected it'.[47] A proposal in 1879 to terminate the credit system was lost by 122 to 74 votes. Exactly the same could happen in small societies. At Cainscross in Gloucestershire (membership in 1873: 129) it was resolved:

that a list of members' debts be laid upon the table for the inspection of members at every Quarterly Meeting; but at first this was not effective, for there was no reduction in the debts for many years. Another suggestion ... was that 'all members who pay ready money have a larger dividend than those who take credit'. There were, however, too many 'credit' members for such a proposal to be accepted.[48]

Financial advantage was a topic that could induce members to attend meetings, but even in this small society apathy seems to have been the rule, at least by the turn of the century. Of six society meetings held in 1904–5, two had to be abandoned for lack of a quorum of ten, out of a membership by then over 2,500.[49]

It seems likely that much of the credit was given to assist members through times of hardship and so had an important part to play in the economic management of a working-class household's budget. There is no evidence to suggest that credit advanced within the co-operative movement led to the prodigality and vice that its opponents attributed to it when allowed by private traders. Writing in 1942, with conclusions based on a broad survey of contemporary practice and histori-

---

[47] William Maxwell (ed.), *First Fifty Years of St. Cuthbert's Co-operative Association Ltd., 1859–1909* (Edinburgh, 1909), pp. 115–17; Report of the Chief Registrar of Friendly Societies for 1879, part 1 (B), appendix (E), PP 1880 lxviii (373), p. 40.

[48] Bramwell Hudson, *History of Co-operation in Cainscross and District* (Manchester, n.d., *c.*1913), pp. 55–6.

[49] Ibid., p. 136.

cal experience in the co-operative movement, A. M. Carr-Saunders noted: 'In general it appears that a working class emergency—either a strike or a trade depression—leads to an increase in ordinary credit.'[50] During the Durham mining strike in 1892, the Bishop of Auckland Co-operative Society gave generous credit to miners, established a special fund to relieve the needy, and paid out almost £50,000 to shareholders who needed to withdraw their funds.[51]

The effect of credit trading on the co-operative movement as a whole is difficult to assess. The amount owing to distributive societies at the end of the year averaged about 3 per cent of share and loan capital and 1.4 per cent of retail trade between 1881 and 1925, rose to over 2 per cent of trade in the year of the General Strike, and continued at this higher level through the late twenties and thirties,[52] but it is not clear how much trade was financed by credit, as the period of repayment cannot be estimated. Since it was most unlikely that credit would be extended for a twelve-month period (even clubs seldom worked beyond a twenty-six-week cycle), the annual credit trade was sure to be greater than the total amount of credit outstanding at any one time. But of primary interest here is the impact of credit trading not on the organization, but on the members. Despite strong and persistent congress resolutions against credit trade, it spread throughout the co-operative movement, and could seldom be resisted even by determined local committees; it seems that the members were not prepared to follow their leaders.

Was it because of dire financial need? Few needy members seem to have benefited from the loan funds proposed by the Women's Co-operative Guild, but then few co-operators were really needy, at least, not before the period of rapid inter-war growth. At the 1896 co-operative congress it was stated that the pursuit of high dividends had compelled 'the lowest paid workman, to whom co-operation should be an especial blessing, to

[50] A. M. Carr-Saunders *et al.*, *Consumers' Co-operation in Great Britain* (Revised edn., London, 1942), p. 122.
[51] T. Readshaw, *History of the Bishop Auckland Industrial Co-operative Flour and Provision Society Ltd. 1860–1910* (Manchester, 1910), p. 224.
[52] Figures based on the statistical appendices of the co-operative congresses for 1889, 1895, 1900, 1905, 1910, 1914, 1920, 1926, and on Hough, *Dividend*, p. 100.

go to the private trader, on account of his inability to purchase our higher priced goods',[53] and in 1902 J. C. Gray felt that 'the Co-operative movement belongs to the well-to-do artisan class'.[54] Some co-operators thought the absence of the poorest workers from co-operative membership was partly a moral problem, related to their inability to look to the future. Ernest Aves, a strong advocate of co-operation through production rather than retailing, wrote:

since the financial basis of the society has been the possession of at least a small margin of reserve capital by the individual member, even if this was only represented by the shilling paid on application for membership, and by the willingness to let subsequent dividends accumulate to the price of the qualifying paid-up share, the constitution of the society has been unable to appeal to those to whom the idea of even the smallest margin of reserve is quite alien, and who, moreover, in spending habitually think only of the return of the moment, and whose minds therefore never, and whose purses perhaps not very often, are able to reach out to the idea, or the acquisition, of a deferred advantage.[55]

Miss Llewelyn Davies had no doubt that the economic explanation was the right one. A desire for high dividends kept up prices, whilst the poorest went elsewhere in search 'of low prices, small quantities and inferior goods'.[56]

The enthusiasm of these well-to-do artisans for high dividends and co-operative credit shows three things. First, that even this relatively well-paid regularly-employed group faced temporary fluctuations of income that they could not or would not cover by drawing on cash reserves. Second, that they deliberately accumulated funds in co-operative societies in the full knowledge and expectation that they could draw on these funds at times of need. Third, that they supported a form of forced saving, with high prices allowing the payment of high

[53] Twenty-eighth Co-operative Congress, Woolwich, 1896, *Report*, p. 74, quoted in Joseph Ackland, 'The Failure of Co-operation', *Economic Review* vii (1897), p. 346. See also *Reading Co-operative Record*, Jan. 1899, p. 9, quoted in Stephen Yeo, *Religion and Voluntary Organisations in Crisis* (London, 1976), p. 286.

[54] Quoted in H. W. Woolf, 'Co-operation and the Poor', *Economic Review* xiii (1903), p. 25.

[55] E. Aves, *Co-operative Industry* (London, 1907), p. 111.

[56] Margaret Llewelyn Davies, *Co-operation in Poor Neighbourhoods* (Women's Co-operative Guild, Manchester, 1899), p. 7; Butler, *Oxford*, p. 122.

dividends. This confirms the views presented earlier that almost no manual workers were free of financial worries, and that to ensure some degree of saving out of a relatively low income they imposed upon themselves various systems of forced or contractual saving.

Because co-operative credit was costless, with no interest payments or dividend penalties, and because many members might want access to it at particularly difficult times, there was strong support for credit facilities among members even though activists in congress persistently condemned it. Although the principle of cash trading was adhered to by some mid-Victorian co-operators,[57] it was by no means universal, and this discrepancy between what the leaders were saying and the members doing is an indication of where real power lay in the co-operative movement.

The apparent hypocrisy of repeated congress resolutions against credit and high dividends being treated with complete indifference by local societies requires some explanation. It was undoubtedly in part the result of the odd and unrepresentative composition of the congress. Ben Jones explained that:

By the rules, societies of a fair size have power to send more representatives than they will usually bear the expense of sending. But there are a number of enthusiasts desirous of ventilating their ideas, and of people wishing to enjoy a co-operative holiday, who are willing to pay their own expenses; and these people find no difficulty in obtaining appointments under such conditions. It is asserted that it is by the votes of these honorary representatives that resolutions in favour of profit-sharing have been carried; and as the congresses are not legislative, but only propagandist assemblies, whose resolutions have no binding force, the decisions recorded there are not acted upon, unless the respective societies agree with them.[58]

Hewins thought the problem might simply be that local society members refused to accept congress decisions that hurt their own interests, a view that some of the society histories tend to confirm;[59] Beatrice Potter blamed it all on the dominance of

[57] Crossick, *Artisan Elite*, p. 169.
[58] Ben Jones, 'Co-operation and Profit-Sharing', *Economic Journal* ii (1892), p. 617. Societies could send one congress delegate for every 500 members. See Potter, *Co-operative Movement*, p. 175.
[59] Hewins, *Economic Review* (1891), p. 542.

Christian Socialist idealists within the Co-operative Union.[60] Congress rhetoric was often at odds with co-operative practice, and the spending power of the masses was ultimately more important than the idealism of the leaders.

This was true in the inter-war years, too, when much of the late nineteenth-century idealism had been sacrificed to professional management, and much of the social exclusiveness of co-operative membership had been diluted by the influx of members and amalgamation of societies.[61] This shift in the social importance of co-operation is well shown by changes at the annual co-operative congress. In the nineteenth century the inaugural address to congress was an opportunity to bring co-operators into contact with notables like the Earl of Derby and Professor Alfred Marshall and to indulge in the same sort of jamborees as the major friendly societies. The annual congress reports give full details; here is just one example, from the Ipswich congress of 1889:

At two o'clock the members of the board and the reception committee were entertained to a substantial and well-served luncheon in the Co-operative Hall, by the Committee of the Ipswich Society ... The company then formed a procession, and headed by a local volunteer band, proceeded to the Drill Hall to take part in the ceremony of opening the industrial exhibition.[62]

The elements of feasting and festivity declined as twentieth century congresses became more an annual business meeting. Idealism withered as no one could be found to take on the mantle of people like Hughes, Neale, and Holyoake. Prestige declined as well; a society of shopkeepers did not attract the patronage that a society of community-builders had drawn in Victorian times. This fall was confirmed at the 1937 congress at Bath, where the town council felt the co-operators unworthy of the hitherto traditional civic reception, and instead of meeting on municipal premises, the delegates were forced to hire the Forum Cinema for use as a conference hall.[63]

[60] Potter, *Co-operative Movement*, pp. 176–80.
[61] Between 1918 and 1935 the number of retail societies fell from 1,364 to 1,118 while the membership rose from 3.8m. to 7.4m.
[62] Twenty-first Co-operative Congress, *Report*, p. 2.
[63] Sixty-ninth Co-operative Congress, Bath, 1937, *Report*, p. 391.

An understanding of how and why members made use of the consumers' co-operative movement provides many important insights into the tension between political ideals, social prestige, and economic advantage, all of which were influences on at least some co-operative members. On two issues that were supposedly fundamental to nineteenth-century co-operative ideals, cash trading and dividend policy, the membership refused to take the path advocated by the co-operative leaders. In the mid-Victorian period some local societies were guided by activists who did put principles above economic advantage, but the number of such societies seems to have declined as membership rose. As co-operative societies grew in membership and coverage, extending well beyond the geographical spread of each small working-class community (in 1925, 36 per cent of co-operators were in 44 societies with over 20,000 members, 6.5 per cent in 650 societies with under 1,000 members),[64] so the social importance of co-operation diminished, and this was reflected in a change in the nature of co-operative congresses. The real success of consumers' co-operation rested on its dual nature as a saving and as a credit institution, thereby serving the twin financial requirements of working-class households— providing a repository for funds and allowing access to these funds (through credit purchases) at times of need. Because saving in the co-operative movement was compulsory for all members, disguised in the form of a mark-up on the price of food and other household necessities, it did not take on the appearance of a barely-afforded deduction from the weekly housekeeping money which, as we have seen, was one reason why working-class people found cash saving so difficult. The 'divi' was an automatic savings bank, and for most members it was the most valued part of co-operation. Ideals were all very well, but they were too costly for most co-operators to take too seriously.

[64] Sydney R. Elliott, *Co-operative Store-keeping* (London, 1925), p. 59.

6

Credit

THE preceding chapters have surveyed the leading forms of thrift practised by working-class families, and they have suggested that much of the saving was directed towards specific problems of household budgeting—problems caused by death, sickness, and unemployment. The unpredictable timing and extent of such crises meant that financial provisions were not always adequate for those households that made them; for families with less income or prudence, some other financial expedient was essential to tide over periods of want without some recourse to the parish. The common action of a family without funds of its own was to use someone else's money—that is, to obtain credit.

There was a multiplicity of credit instruments available to working-class households throughout the period in question—it is quite wrong to think of the inter-war development of hire-purchase as the birth of 'never-never' trading—and the extent and variety of credit is itself indicative of widespread demand. In financial terms, working-class credit was a world away from the large-scale loans and mortgages advanced by joint-stock banks and building societies, but in its basic forms it was similar. In an essay written in 1896, Mrs Bosanquet identified these forms as (i) 'not paying', (ii) pawning, (iii) borrowing, and these distinctions will be followed in this chapter.[1]

'NOT PAYING'

The acquisition of goods or services without immediate payment covered a wide range of credit facilities, from the formality of a hire-purchase contract to the unlawful expedient of

---

[1] Helen Bosanquet, 'The Burden of Small Debts', *Economic Journal* vi (1896), pp. 212–25.

doing a 'moonlight flit' before rent-day,[2] but almost certainly the most common was shop credit advanced by local retailers. The extent of the retail credit trade cannot be stated with any precision, but the evidence available suggests that it was large. Shop credit for working-class customers was likely to come from small family shops; multiple shops and department stores tended to demand cash from customers, especially for food and household goods which were the main items of expenditure for working-class families. In 1931, despite the inter-war development of department stores and multiples which by then accounted for about 25 per cent of retail trade, something between one-half and two-thirds of the 750,000 retail outlets in Great Britain were family shops, employing no assistants.[3] Some of these shops were undoubtedly specialized, but many would have been general dealers serving a very small area. The horizons of local communities were narrow, and for day-to-day purchases nearby shops were used. According to Jerry White's study, at Rothschild Buildings, an East End tenement block built in 1887 for Jewish immigrants, the residents did most of their daily shopping in the four neighbouring streets, despite being only two minutes walk from 'the paramount marketplace for the whole of the Jewish East End'. They did so because the local shopkeepers gave credit, sold in small quantities, stayed open late, and knew their customers.[4] This sense of and knowledge of community was important for both buyers and sellers. Robert Roberts, writing from the corner-shop perspective, pointed out that 'if bankruptcy . . . was to be avoided, one had to assess with careful judgement the honesty, class standing and financial resources of all tick customers'.[5] The 'careful judgement' could only be made after long acquaintance, so for the

---

[2] See Paul Thompson and Gina Haskell, *The Edwardians in photographs* (London, 1979), p. 30, for a brief comment on flitting. The authors point out that the family shown in the photograph was not at the lowest level, since it had a table, chair, and clock piled on the handcart. This seems to miss the point that it was these possessions that made the flit necessary. The aim was to keep household goods out of the hands of the landlord's bailiffs.

[3] These figures are taken from the estimates in Lawrence E. Neal, *Retailing and the Public* (London, 1932), pp. 5–6, 19–20, 29, 39–40, and in Henry Smith, *Retail Distribution* (OUP, London, 1937), p. 35.

[4] Jerry White, *Rothschild Buildings* (London, 1980), p. 105.

[5] Robert Roberts, *The Classic Slum* (Harmondsworth, 1973), p. 18; Bosanquet, 'Small Debts', p. 219.

credit seeker 'being known' in a district was important. Gareth
Stedman Jones has identified 'tick' as one cause of labour
immobility in London: 'Credit arrangements which had been
built up in one neighbourhood over a period of time could not
immediately be transferred to another.'[6] This was not a pecu-
liarly urban phenomenon. In rural districts the village shopkeeper had in his hands the fate of the labourers in time of
depression—more so than in a city where different sources of
supply might be tapped—and the natural action for the retailer
was to advance credit only 'where he knows that there is an
honest endeavour to pay on the part of the customer'.[7] The
problem of raising credit in villages where there were few
traders forced hard-pressed housewives to spend much time
and effort searching for tick. As one woman with debts of over
£10 said, 'we have to go where any one will give us a bit of
credit. They won't let it run here in the village—I go miles
sometimes.'[8]

In both cities and villages the local shop did not just revolve
around the cash (or credit) nexus; it functioned as a sort of
community centre, providing aid, advice, information, and a
meeting place. The role of the 'community' shop in the 1950s
has been analysed by Young and Willmott in their study of
Bethnal Green,[9] but a picture of life in the corner shop is more
vividly painted in Francie Nichol's description of the general
dealer's shop that she ran in a poor area of South Shields from
1935 until the war:

... poor people make good customers. They can't always pay on the
dot, but they're honest if ye trust them. And they can never be
bothered to shop around. If they know where they can get all they
want handy then that's where they'll go. They like a place where they
can come in drunk and know you'll give them the stuff they want
even if they've forgotten what they've come in for ... They want a
place they can come in with their curlers in or in their slippers and

[6] Gareth Stedman Jones, *Outcast London* (Oxford, 1971), p. 88.
[7] F. G. Heath, *Peasant Life in the West of England* (London, 1880), pp. 315–16.
[8] Rowntree, *How the Labourer Lives*, study iv, p. 60. See also study vii, p. 77; study
xviii, p. 146.
[9] Michael Young and Peter Willmott, *Family and Kinship in East London* (Harmondsworth, 1962), p. 153.

dressin' gowns. They know ye aren't goin' to diddle them by bamboozlin' their little bairns if they send them in with a message.[10]

The relationship of knowledge, trust, and familiarity between shopkeeper and customers was reciprocal, but the underlying bond was an economic one. In prosperous times customers would continue to trade at their local shop, even though lower prices could often be obtained elsewhere, partly for reasons of convenience and habit, but also as a form of insurance. The unwritten rule was that a good cash customer would deserve generous credit if she came upon hard times.[11]

The shopkeepers were not guided by altruism, but by competition, though financial success was far from guaranteed. As the son of a Kent shopkeeper put it, 'if you didn't give any credit you never got any trade; if you did give credit, you often did not get it back'.[12] Credit facilities attracted customers from cheaper competitors such as branch stores and cash grocers like Liptons, and then committed them to future trading on account of accumulated debts. In a survey of life in a poor district written in 1899, Miss Llewelyn Davies reported that:

The kind of shops you notice are first of all small general shops, where the trade is almost entirely a 'booking' one. The terrible debt burden is round the necks of most of the people, and the object of the small shopkeeper is to fasten it securely there. Not only are high prices (that is, compared to the quality) charged, as is natural and inevitable, but the accounts are often falsified—the 1*d.* slipping into the 1*s.* column—and the customers are often so ignorant and helpless that such things escape notice.[13]

Whether customers were quite as ignorant as she declares is not certain. Illiteracy was no barrier to financial rectitude; a Bolton woman recalled that, although neither her mother nor the woman who kept the local shop could read or write, 'they had their own symbols for reckoning up the score which later was

[10] Joe Robinson, *The Life and Times of Francie Nichol of South Shields* (London, paperback edn. 1977), p. 140. For another description, see Rose Gamble, *Chelsea Child* (London, 1979), p. 31.
[11] Economic Club, *Family Budgets: Being the income and expenses of twenty-eight British households 1891–1894* (London, 1896), p. 30.
[12] Quoted in John Benson, *The Penny Capitalists* (Dublin, 1983), p. 124.
[13] Llewelyn Davies, *Co-operation*, pp. 10–11. See also Albert Paul, *Poverty—Hardship but Happiness* (Brighton, 1974), p. 37.

chalked up on the door leading into the living room'.[14] The imaginative accounting of grocer Garfinkle was well known to the inhabitants of Rothschild Buildings, and it caused many arguments and sometimes led to long-lasting hostility, but financial necessity forced most people to keep on speaking and trading terms with him.[15] The mutual dependency of credit givers and credit takers was sharply described by Frank Bullen, a small trader who was himself driven into the Bankruptcy Court by his bad debtors:

Many hundreds of families would come to the workhouse long before they do, especially in hard winters, but for these small tradesmen giving them credit for the bare necessities of life, and thus tiding them over the pinching time. This system of first aid can hardly be called philanthropy, since those who extend it do it for a living, and yet in the multitudinous life of poor London it is a huge and most important factor.[16]

The 'pinching time' might last for just a couple of weeks, but much longer debt cycles were not unknown. According to Charles Booth, irregular labourers in London were as a rule given credit in winter against repayment the following summer,[17] and for some customers the slate would never be wiped clean during a decade or more of child-bearing and rearing.[18] The credit cycle did not, however, follow in a strict way Rowntree's 'poverty cycle', since the advance of credit was itself an acknowledgement by the tradesman of the customer's potential future earnings, and this potential did not exist for the old, the disabled, or the widowed. As Robert Roberts wrote, 'the very poor never fell into debt; nobody allowed them any credit'.[19]

Not so the strikers; their future earnings were likely to be high enough for them to pay off large and rapidly accumulated debts. The only adequate evidence of how retail credit was affected by strikes comes from the co-operative movement,

[14] Alice Foley, *A Bolton Childhood* (Manchester, 1973), p. 19.

[15] White, *Rothschild Buildings*, p. 113.

[16] Frank Bullen, *Confessions of a Tradesman* (London, 1908), pp. 159–60.

[17] Charles Booth, *Life and Labour*, 1st ser., i. 46. See also Norman B. Dearle, *Problems of Unemployment in the London Building Trades* (London, 1908), p. 141.

[18] Roberts, *Ragged Schooling*, pp. 22–3.

[19] Roberts, *Classic Slum*, p. 105.

which published annual statistics of the credit outstanding with each society at the end of December. The coal strike of 1921 pushed the average amount owing per member in the Western Division of the Co-operative Union (covering the South Wales coalfield) from 16s. 5d. at the end of 1920 to £3. 15s. 5d. at the end of 1921.[20]

This sort of spontaneous 'crisis' credit advanced to customers in straitened circumstances was not the only sort of 'accommodation' offered by retailers; they also did a very large and pre-meditated credit trade through clubs. The economic rationale behind patronage of a club was much the same as for weekly insurance payments. As Lady Bell explained, 'the difficulty of paying for anything for which more than a very small sum in ready money is needed explains the eagerness with which the house-wives of the town embrace any system by which they are enabled to buy in small instalments'.[21] Similar behaviour was noted among a group of young mothers living in Lambeth on incomes of between 18s. and 30s. a week:

So much a week regularly paid has a great attraction for them. If the club will, in addition to small regular payments, send someone to call for the amount, the transaction leaves nothing to be desired. A woman who can see her way towards the money by any possibility agrees at once.[22]

Some of the systems were good, others bad. Thirty years after these comments, another social survey reported that:

Nearly every shop in Lambeth runs a club of some kind. In the case of some this is a real help to mothers of families; they can choose the goods they want and are not forced to pay more than the ordinary cash price; in others there is no choice and the goods are very expensive.[23]

As this extract suggests, the development of working-class

---

[20] Figures from the statistical appendices to the Co-operative Congress Annual Reports for 1921 and 1922.

[21] Bell, *At the Works*, p. 70.

[22] Maud Pember Reeves, *Round About a Pound a Week* (London, 1913), p. 63.

[23] Lady Margaret Hall Settlement, *Social Services in North Lambeth and Kennington* (OUP, London, 1939), p. 13. For a comprehensive description of different types of clothing club in a Midland district during the early years of the Second World War, see Women's Group on Public Welfare, *Our Towns, A Close-up* (OUP, London, 1943), appendix vii.

credit facilities could be seen by observers as a legitimate aid to household budgeting, or alternatively as 'a means of foisting cheap luxury articles, which would otherwise be unsaleable, upon people who cannot really afford to buy them, at prices far in excess of the real value of the goods'.[24] These different views depended much on the prejudice of the observer, but also in part on the type of retail credit being looked at. The shop-keeper's club was but one of several ways of buying goods by instalment, and to get a fair picture we must look also at hire-purchase and the tally system.

The one common aspect of all these forms of credit sale is that a fairly large total sum was paid in a number of small, regular (usually weekly) instalments. It is immediately obvious that this sort of credit was fundamentally different from the spontaneous shop credit advanced to carry the customer over hard times. The function of premeditated credit was not to keep body and soul together, but rather to enable special pur-chases to be made. Club, tally, and HP credit was directed towards the purchase of expensive items like clothes and boots, furniture and pianos, and to pay for costly seasonal items like winter coals and Christmas jamborees. In general, the greater the amount of credit advanced, the more formal was the credit agreement—casual club for small items of clothing, HP for an upright piano.

Some of the clubs, it should be stressed, did not advance any credit. Payment was by small regular instalments, but purchase was not allowed until the final sum had been paid—they were nothing more than savings clubs directed towards specific expenditure rather than general accumulation. In 1902, Sidney Dark found many publicans and licensed grocers in working-class areas of London ran goose clubs and Christmas clubs amongst their customers. 'Putting by for Christmas Day', he thought, 'is one of the most popular forms of London Thrift.'[25] Some such clubs were of a semi-philanthropic nature. Church or school clothing and coal clubs were designed to help the poor help themselves, and thereby learn of the vir-tues of thrift. In London schools, children who managed to pay a certain amount into the boot club were rewarded for their

    [24] R. Dallas Brett, *Usury in Britain* (London, 1946), p. 60.
    [25] Dark, 'London Thrift', in Sims, *Living London*, ii. 257–8.

efforts by having the rest paid by the Ragged Schools Union or the Bare Foot Mission.[26] The St Andrew-by-the-Wardrobe with St Anne, Blackfriar Provident Clothing Fund was one such philanthropic club, established to teach providence and planning to the poor, as the rules printed on the reverse of the collecting cards show:

Rule I. The amount deposited on this card can only be received out in the way of Clothing at end of the year.

II. The money deposited is not to be withdrawn, except in case of removal from the parish, or a death in the family.

III. Depositors are recommended to make some payment every week, and it is requested the cards be kept clean.

The reward for such prudence and cleanliness was a bonus of 1*d*. per 1*s*. added at the annual distribution.[27]

Others were genuine self-help affairs, unrecorded except in personal accounts. One such was:

a private concern with seven members at present, formed as the Weather Club. We take the week from Friday to Friday, and each day should it rain during the whole twenty-four hours we pay one penny; for fog we pay two-pence, snow threepence and a thunderstorm fourpence, and this is shared out at the end of the year. It does not come to a very large amount, but it makes a welcome little extra at the time you really need it.[28]

Pub clubs were common among the regulars. They were in part an excuse for social gatherings and homespun entertainment, but they would also commonly provide for a boozy summer outing and a share-out of surplus funds at Christmas.[29] This sort of saving for specific acts of self-indulgence was not considered by moralizing observers to be a valid form of thrift—it

---

[26] White, *Rothschild Buildings*, p. 174.

[27] St Andrew-by-the-Wardrobe with St Anne, Blackfriar Provident Clothing Fund collecting card, attached to the inside cover of the weekly account book for 1896–1921. Guildhall Library, MS 9292.

[28] M-O, Directive Replies, Jan. 1939, Female Observer 1050.

[29] Mass-Observation, *The Pub and the People*, pp. 270–4; Foakes, *Between High Walls*, p. 47.

was all part of that widespread 'self-taxation of the working classes'.[30]

Even worse, from the point of view of 'self-taxation', and at least as common as the saving club, was the credit club. A Women's Co-operative Guild survey of purchasing patterns in poor districts in the winter of 1901–2 found that 'practically every poor person we spoke to, bought boots, drapery and furniture through these clubs',[31] and an article on 'Industrial Credit' in March 1914 reported that 'the bulk of the credit trade with working men is done in wearing apparel and household requisites'.[32] The usual type of club was that which involved the payment of twenty-one instalments of 1*s*. in exchange for £1 worth of goods. If run privately by a group of women, the club would be a 'drawing club', that is, one in which lots would be drawn to decide the order of payment to the twenty members; the surplus money was paid to the treasurer. Sometimes a street draw would be organized on these lines to help a neighbour fallen on hard times—the draw would be fixed to ensure that the unfortunate took the first week's payment.[33] When this sort of club was managed by a trader, the element of credit was usually much more obvious since goods to the value of £1 could normally be obtained on payment of the first week's subscription.

An important development of this system was that known as 'check trading', which involved independent companies selling checks on credit, which could then be redeemed at certain associated stores which were reimbursed by the issuing company. By far the largest of the check traders was the Provident Clothing and Supply Company Ltd., formed in 1881 and still monopolizing the business of check trading.[34] This form of credit sale had clear advantages over private clubs both for the customers, who could shop around for their goods, using any store that had an arrangement with the issuing company, and for the

---

[30] M. Loane, *Neighbours and Friends* (London, 1910), pp. 278–98.

[31] Women's Co-operative Guild, *Extension of Co-operation*, pp. 19–20.

[32] W. H. Whitelock, 'Industrial Credit and Imprisonment for Debt', *Economic Journal* xxiv (Mar. 1914), p. 34.

[33] Roberts, *Classic Slum*, p. 33; Grant, *Farthing Bundles*, p. 90.

[34] Report of the Committee on Consumer Credit [Crowther Cttee.], PP 1970–71 (Cmnd. 4596), pp. 75–6.

retailers, who no longer had to bother with the regular collection of monies. The rate of interest charged seemed reasonable—one shilling in the pound over twenty-one weeks, or a
nominal annual rate of about 25 per cent[35]—but when compared with the costs of collection of industrial insurance premiums, it is clear that it would hardly pay for the check
companies' force of collecting agents. Profits came from the
interest received on funds held after collection from customers
but before redemption payments to traders, and from redeeming checks at 10–15 per cent below their face value—in other
words, the check companies charged the retailers commission
for supplying them with extra trade.

'Toys, chocolate, even face powder' could be bought through
clubs or with checks—almost anything, in fact, except food—
though the most common purchases were clothing, footwear,
and bedding.[36] The trade was much the same as that done by
the Scotch draper or tallyman, whose business 'or round is
worked up by door-to-door canvassing of an intensive nature
over a limited area and the goods offered include every kind of
wearing apparel, bedding, drapery, and soft furnishings'.[37]
Tallymen came in for particular criticism from some quarters,
both for the pressure which their form of doorstep salesmanship
put upon poor housewives who could not really afford the
goods on offer, and for the expensiveness of the items they
sold.[38] Tallymen did not, as a rule, levy specific interest
charges; they covered costs by selling goods at inflated prices,

---

[35] The formula used to calculate the rate of interest is:

$$i = \frac{200md}{p(n+1)+d/3(n-1)}$$

where:

i   is the nominal annual rate of interest;
m   is the total number of instalments per annum;
n   is the total number of instalments;
p   is the amount borrowed;
d   is the total amount repaid as capital and interest less the amount borrowed.

For check trading of the type described in the text m=52, n=21, p=1, d=0.05,
i=23.3 per cent.

This formula is suggested in the Crowther Cttee., Report, vol. ii, appendix iv, p. 584.

[36] Grant, *Farthing Bundles*, p. 90.
[37] Edward C. Warren, *Credit Dealing* (London, 1939), p. 29.
[38] For intance, Bell, *At the Works*, pp. 70–1, 82–3; Llewelyn Davies, *Co-operation*, pp.
11–12.

sometimes supplying goods of inferior quality to the samples originally shown to customers.[39]

Both check trading and the tally trade were most popular in London, the north of England, and Scotland,[40] and they were concentrated in urban centres. Although the tallyman may have been of most use in country districts, where he was 'a very useful link between the customer and the supplier',[41] he usually sought business in areas of high population density, which reduced the time spent travelling between customers. A concentrated clientele also enabled the salesman to make quick, on-the-spot investigations into the financial standing of each prospective new customer by personal enquiry from existing clients.[42] This sort of local knowledge and personal contact was essential if bad debts were to be minimized; doorstep credit retailing is a potentially risky business. Certain individuals, and sometimes whole streets, would be blacklisted for bad debts,[43] and efforts were always made to persuade existing and trusted customers to take on new indebtedness once an item had been paid for. In a good credit district in the 1950s, 80 per cent of customers would renew business at the end of each contract, and it would be surprising if the proportion had been any lower in the first half of the century.[44] Tallymen could bring pressure on customers to renew indebtedness by promising not to foreclose on debts outstanding. Although the nominal rate of repayment was a shilling in the pound per week, 'it doesn't average sixpence', according to a London tallyman speaking in 1876, and the same was true in the late 1930s.[45] But if the rate of repayment fell too far it would jeopardize the tallyman's chances of selling his round for a good price. Rounds would be sold for between 50 per cent and 200 per cent of the face value

[39] E. S. Watkins, *Credit Buying* (London, 1939), p. 71.

[40] L. C. Wright, 'Consumer Credit and the Tally Man', *Three Banks Review* 44 (1959), pp. 19–20; Crowther Cttee., p. 48.

[41] Watkins, *Credit Buying*, p. 71.

[42] Warren, *Credit Dealing*, pp. 33–4. In this respect the business was very similar to Industrial Assurance premium collection, and at least one credit clothing club was founded by a former insurance agent. See *Insurance Mail* 211 (16 May 1908), p. 322.

[43] Whitelock, 'Industrial Credit', p. 35.

[44] Wright, 'Tally Man', p. 20.

[45] James Greenwood, *Low Life Deeps* (London, 1876), p. 262; Warren, *Credit Dealing*, p. 30.

of the book debts, depending on the rate of repayment, area, type of customer, and local employment conditions.[46]

The last major type of working-class credit facility was that known as easy or deferred payments or hire-purchase. Although in law these were two quite distinct types of credit, in common parlance the terms were used synonymously to describe the purchase of fairly expensive articles like furniture, pianos, and sewing machines on an instalment system, with repayments spread over a period usually ranging from one to five years. The legal distinction is that a good bought on hire-purchase remains the property of the dealer until the last payment is made, at which point the period of hire is terminated and the good becomes the absolute property of the customer. The dealer has the right to take back his property if rental payments fall into arrears, and the contract is broken. Easy payment, on the other hand, involves the immediate and outright sale of the good. The customer cannot determine the contract by returning the good, nor can the dealer make good default in payment by repossession; his only remedy is to sue for payments due and payable in the future.[47]

From the traders' point of view, hire-purchase offered much better security, and so was the preferred form of credit device, although not until the decision of the House of Lords in 1895 on the case of *Helby* v. *Matthews* was the title of a good sold on HP finally deemed to be in absolute possession of the dealer up to the moment of payment of the final instalment.[48] Hire-purchase trading, however, was established well before this judgement, and it has been estimated that in 1891 about one million hire-purchase agreements were in existence.[49] Professor Ehrlich reckons that hire-purchase for pianos, known as the 'three year system' as repayment was spread over twelve quarterly or thirty-six monthly instalments, was 'widespread by the 1860s'.[50] For other goods, no special repayment period was standard. According to one trade paper, '"Half a crown a

[46] Wright, 'Tally Man', p. 18.
[47] Warren, *Credit Dealing*, pp. 20–1; Crowther Cttee., pp. 41–5.
[48] *Law Reports* (1895), Appeal Cases, pp. 471–84.
[49] Crowther Cttee., p. 43.
[50] Cyril Ehrlich, *The Piano, A History* (London, 1976), p. 100.

week" is a favourite sum, and one which looks well in an advertisement, but the whole question of the number of instalments
and the amount of each is simply one of agreement between
owner and hirer, or vendor and purchaser.'[51] The sorts of
articles sold on HP can be gauged by looking at the occupations of the founding members of the Hire Traders' Protection
Association. Of the 68 members recorded in the first annual
report in 1892, 32 dealt in sewing-machines, 15 in furniture, 8
in musical instruments, 5 in cycles, and 2 in jewellery.[52]

There is no doubt that many hire-purchase sales were made
not to manual workers, but to lower middle-class white collar
employees like Mr Pooter, whose wife was not above 'practising
the "Sylvia Gavotte" on our new cottage piano (on the three
years' system)'.[53] The Pooters of this world, always keenly conscious of their position in society, needed pianos, because 'to the
Victorians a piano symbolized respectability, achievement and
status'.[54] The same was true for aspirant manual workers, but
some goods available through HP, like sewing-machines, might
be required not so much for status as for the contribution they
could make to the family income by enabling the wife to take in
out-work. It was because of the high cost of these 'useful' goods
that William Booth condemned the Hire System in these
words:

The decent poor man or woman who is anxious to earn an honest
penny ... is charged, in addition to the full market value of his purchase, ten or twenty times the amount of what would be a fair rate of
interest, and more than this if he should at any time, through misfortune, fail in his payment, the total amount already paid will be confis-
cated, the machine seized, and the money lost.[55]

The sharp practice of hire traders in resuming possession of

[51] *The Journal of Domestic Appliances and Sewing Machine Gazette* xii, no. 174 (1 Jan.
1885), p. 9.
[52] *The Hire Traders' Guide and Record* ii, no. 15 (1 Apr. 1892), p. 6.
[53] George and Weedon Grossmith, *The Diary of a Nobody* (Harmondsworth, 1977),
pp. 19–20.
[54] Ehrlich, *The Piano*, p. 97.
[55] 'General' William Booth, *In Darkest England and the Way Out* (London, 1890), p.
217.

goods almost fully paid for was still being reviled for causing 'a multitude of misery' right up to the passing of the Hire Purchase Act in 1938.[56] The solicitor to the Hire Traders' Protection Association responded to these accusations by arguing that 'it is only those parties who break their agreements who object to terms they have deliberately promised to fulfil', and in this he was more or less correct.[57] The dispute was really over how far default was due to unforeseen financial crises like unemployment, and how much due to a wilful deceit, and it was hardly surprising that traders and customers took different views on this; as pointed out above, credit traders could not afford to be philanthropic if they were to prosper in a competitive market.

It was during and after the First World War that the hire-purchase system, already well established, really expanded into the mass market. In 1921 there were over 16m. hire-purchase agreements in force in Britain, with 4m. new agreements being entered into annually. These figures had risen to 24m. and 7m. respectively in 1935, by which time it was estimated that 80 per cent of cars, 90 per cent of sewing-machines, 75 per cent of furniture and 95 per cent of the pianos, wireless sets, and gramophones sold in Britain were bought on HP.[58] It is obvious from this that a large number of working-class households made repeated use of HP by the mid-1930s, extending a pattern of consumption finance that was, for many, learnt during years of wartime prosperity. The 'munitions worker's piano', bought on the instalment system, was a symbol of this prosperity, acquired for reasons of utility, respectability, and for those unused to institutional saving, investment.[59] By the early 1920s, the piano was no longer the preserve of the shopkeeper, publican, or artisan.[60] It is not clear exactly how far or how fast hire-purchase credit expanded in the inter-war years, but a sample of eight hire-purchase finance houses shows an

[56] See Aylmer Vallance, *Hire-Purchase* (London, 1939), pp. 58–90.
[57] *Hire Traders' Guide and Record* ii, no. 17 (1 June 1892), p. 4.
[58] *Hire-Purchase News* no. 27 (12 Mar. 1930), p. 5; *Hire Traders' Guide and Record* xlv, no. 543 (1 Apr. 1936), p. 5.
[59] Ehrlich, *The Piano*, pp. 171–2; Raphael Samuel, *East End Underworld 2: Chapters in the Life of Arthur Harding* (London, 1981), p. 237.
[60] Roberts, *Classic Slum*, p. 228.

increase of HP credit from £2m. in 1925 to £5m. in 1930 and £15m. in 1939.[61]

One result of this growth of HP was a strengthening of those voices raised against the easy availability of retail credit to working-class consumers. In so far as HP credit was usually for a larger sum than alternative types of retail credit, and the repayment period longer, it was seen as a greater evil. A typical criticism was that 'people are persuaded to shoulder staggering debts. They mortgage their future wages and salaries. Every pay-day a collector calls at the door or a payment has to be sent to a shop.' Why was this done? Simply because 'very few people have patience and perseverance. They are willing to sacrifice the Future to the Present. They take short views of life.'[62] This was little different from the comments of Mrs Bosanquet on the poor thirty years earlier: 'their mental horizon tends to be limited to a stretch of seven days'.[63] Credit allowed them to live and consume today and avoid any coherent thought of or planning for the future.

This fairly common view of the effects of retail credit was, for many credit purchases, inappropriate and incorrect. For any durable good which continued to provide services to the purchaser after payment of the final instalment, total expenditure clearly preceded total consumption. Where a lump sum deposit was required at the commencement of the credit contract, expenditure normally preceded consumption of services throughout the entire period of ownership. Professor Seligman made the point very clearly in 1927 when he wrote:

the ordinary purchaser really pays in each periodic instalment for something which he will utilize in the future; and ... this situation persists until the final payment, when he finds himself in possession of a commodity which will still be of value to him for a considerable period. It would therefore not be correct to say that instalment selling provides present enjoyments at the cost of future utilities. On the contrary it is evident that instalment purchases are subtracting from present enjoyments for the sake of storing up future utilities. Instal-

[61] David K. Sheppard, *The Growth and Role of U.K. Financial Institutions 1890–1962* (London, 1971), pp. 168–9.

[62] Herbert N. Casson, *Debts! How to Collect Them* (London, 1930), pp. 99–100.

[63] Helen Bosanquet, 'Wages and Housekeeping', in C. S. Loch (ed.), *Methods of Social Advance* (London, 1904), p. 136.

ment credit, in other words, is in this respect more like cash payment than like credit payable in a lump sum.[64]

The criticisms should have been not of the credit system itself, for this made expenditure on and consumption of services provided by a durable good more nearly synchronous than with cash payment, but against high rates of interest charged, lack of information for customers on the terms of credit, and the provision of shoddy goods which became totally worn out before instalment payments had finished. Instead, the complaints and accusations tended to be general and ideological, like those of the Grimsby Stipendiary Magistrate who, in 1929, described hire-purchase as 'a wretched system by which traders tempt young people to get married on borrowed money'.[65] This temptation credit gave to the young to make early and improvident marriages is a common theme in much of the critical writing on the credit system,[66] something that spilt from the pens of commentators much more easily than any analysis of the real cost of hire-purchase credit.

This is not surprising; even customers seem to have looked at credit as much from a moral as an economic standpoint. As already pointed out, nominal annual interest rates for 'tick', club, and tally trading were often impossible to establish because they were capitalized in the final selling price, and the same was true of hire-purchase. An investigation of HP costs in 1929 found that 'so little standardization of terms appears to exist, that no precise statistical generalizations can safely be made'.[67] More important to credit customers was likely to be the problem of squaring credit purchases with their own conscience and hiding it from the eyes of their neighbours. The writer who thought that the inter-war growth of consumer credit had 'succeeded in removing the stigma hitherto attaching to hire-purchase in many minds' was deceiving himself.[68]

[64] Edwin R. Z. Seligman, *The Economics of Instalment Selling* (New York, 1927), i. 256.
[65] *Hire-Purchase News*, no. 17 (1 Jan. 1930), p. 1.
[66] See, for instance, Whitelock, 'Industrial Credit', p. 36; Mr B. E. Astbury, Asst. Sec. of the COS in *Hire Traders' Record*, no. 543 (Apr. 1936), p. 5.
[67] W. F. Crick, *The Economics of Instalment Trading and Hire-Purchase* (London, 1929), p. 117.
[68] Warren, *Credit Dealing*, p. 14.

The shame of being in debt, or rather of having one's debts known about locally, applied to all forms of working-class credit, but in ways that sometimes appear contradictory. The threat of a public blacklisting in the local shop-window often had the required affect on recalcitrant 'tick' customers, yet, on the other hand, we learn from Robert Roberts that a 'tick book, honoured each week, became an emblem of integrity and a bulwark against hard times'.[69] But this was true only for the poor; in better-off families, 'all goods one saved for, of course, and bought on the nail, or at worst through weekly clubs run by local shops—a method much frowned on'.[70] An inquiry into social conditions in poor working-class areas of certain towns at the start of the Second World War found that 'it is a sure sign of respectability if a family pays cash, living on last Friday's wages rather than next Friday's'.[71] Even where families bought on credit, they might try to deny this to themselves by calling it something else. One East Ender, recalling his mother's reliance on small credit grocers in the 1920s, explained, 'we wouldn't call it tick. In Mulberry street we called it getting things on trust.'[72] Even check credit carried its social opprobrium. One heavy user (8s. per week) of co-op and Provident clothing checks felt them to be a useful service, but:

At the same time I cannot say that we feel quite conscience clear in regard to it. There still lingers a sense of loss of respectability. We feel that the opportunity to buy with cash would be better and more straightforward. We never talk to anybody about our dealing with these clubs. Collectors call, and neighbours notice things like that, still we keep it to ourselves as much as possible.[73]

One way collectors could get money out of clients in arrears was by 'calling slanderous remarks out loudly, so that all the neighbours could hear'.[74]

Furniture dealers were fully conscious of this desire to conceal the method of payment. 'Free delivery in plain vans', ran their advertisements, the unwritten implication being 'so your

[69] Roberts, *Classic Slum*, p. 82.
[70] Ibid., p. 32.
[71] Women's Group on Public Welfare, *Our Towns*, p. 21.
[72] Jim Wolveridge, *'Ain't it Grand'* (London, 1976), p. 46.
[73] M-O, Directive Replies, Jan. 1939, Observer 1148.
[74] *The Times* (28 Jan. 1957), p. 10.

neighbours will not know you have been buying on the instalment system'.[75] The problem with this, as *The Times* pointed out, was that 'in the long residential roads of new building estates everyone has read the same advertisements as her neighbour and knows a plain van when she sees one'.[76] But at least nothing could be proven. The importance of secrecy in credit dealings for most working-class customers was even lost on Ellen Wilkinson, initiator of the 1938 Hire-Purchase legislation. In a speech to the Domestic Appliance Section of the London Chamber of Commerce she stated that:

she could not understand why hire-purchase was considered in this country to be something not quite the thing ... and [she] could not understand the plain van idea. Surely it was better to have a van labelled 'Furniture on Hire-Purchase Terms'; no-one should be ashamed of it, and certainly it would not cause the smiles that arise when a plain van arrives in a respectable suburb.[77]

The reason was that communal knowledge of a household's credit position affected both its community and self-esteem. In the main, dependence on credit was seen to signify reduced financial security, and with it reduced respectability. On the other hand, many of the goods that could be bought on credit— Sunday suits, net curtains, ornaments, pianos—increased financial security and respectability by adding to the observable (and realizable) capital stock of the household. No matter how rational the instalment method might be as a way of making expensive purchases, the aim was to use and display the goods whilst concealing the means of payment.

Respectability was not a concrete attribute, a tangible thing. It was, as Brian Harrison suggests, 'a process, a dialogue with oneself and one's fellows, never a fixed position'.[78] Respectability involved gaining the esteem of one's peers, however mighty or lowly they might be, and this could be achieved by different individuals with actions apparently quite opposed. For the very poor, getting a 'tick' book was a sign of success, of

[75] *Hire-Purchase News*, no. 1 (11 Sept. 1929), p. 10; ibid., no. 17 (1 Jan. 1930), p. 2.
[76] Quoted in *Hire Traders' Record*, no. 544 (May 1936), p. 5.
[77] *Hire-Purchase News*, no. 77 (19 Feb. 1931), pp. 1–2.
[78] Brian Harrison, *Peaceable Kingdom* (Oxford, 1982), p. 161. See also Peter Bailey, '"Will the real Bill Banks please stand up?" Towards a role analysis of mid-Victorian working-class respectability', *Journal of Social History* xii (1979), pp. 336–53.

credit-worthiness; for the regularly employed the use of 'tick' for food and household goods was a sign of bad money management and incurred neighbourly disapproval—if you could not feed and clothe yourself without resort to someone's generosity or trust, you could make little claim to any great independence of action which was a higher form of respectability than basic credit-worthiness. Any sort of premeditated credit, adopted to facilitate the acquisition of luxuries rather than ensure survival, was less damaging than 'crisis' credit, and for expensive items like bedroom suites and pianos it was an indication of a retailer's belief in the customer's ability to pay instalments regularly over several years. So in some circles the very ability to get HP terms put certain individuals above the rest;[79] in more prosperous districts the use of HP was an admission of inadequate funds—hence a desire for delivery in a plain van.

This socially ambiguous aspect of working-class respectability will be returned to in the final chapter. Confining attention here to aggregate trends, is it possible to explain the growth of hire-purchase trading during and after the First World War in part, at least, by changes in the way in which use of credit affected personal social standing? Some stigma continued (and continues to this day) to be attached to the use of consumer credit, but it is not quantifiable. Although the First World War had a great impact on British society, this is difficult to chronicle, let alone analyse. The movement of millions of men away from their local environments and the recruitment of millions of women into new forms of wage-labour may have reduced both the coherence of and the individual need for community esteem; the experience of death and injury, and of wartime inflation, may have prompted people to be less cautious with money, to buy now and pay later. But this is speculation, and there are certainly other factors which contributed to the inter-war expansion of HP, one of the most important of which was the fall in the price of many consumer durables. The average price of furniture and furnishings (including pianos and gramophones) fell by over 25 per cent between 1922 and the

---

[79] Ron Barnes, *Coronation Cups and Jam Jars* (London, 1976), pp. 29–31.

mid-1930s, cars and bicycles by almost 60 per cent, whilst average weekly wage earnings fell by less than 10 per cent.[80] For those in employment, therefore, real incomes increased markedly during this period. Also of importance was the development of specialized institutions known as Finance Houses which arranged the advance of consumer credit and the collection of premiums for retailers. They both enlarged the scale of HP trading, and made it more noticeable by centralizing the administration of credit sales that hitherto had been operated unseen by individual traders.[81] Unemployment insurance may also have been a contributory factor, increasing the willingness to enter into long-term financial commitments by reducing income variance and so lessening the likelihood of default on payment and repossession of goods.

Statistics of default are not available, but those of debtors sued in county courts for sums under £20 are, and they are presented in Table 6.1. Immediately apparent is both the large number and small scale of plaints—around 1m. a year, for an average of about £3—ample testimony to the extent of working-class indebtedness throughout the period. Plaints would be entered for debts incurred to moneylenders and landlords as well as traders, so they do not represent just the result of retail default, and, as already mentioned, because hire-purchase contracts gave traders the right of repossession on default without resort to the courts, the figures are not affected substantially by the inter-war expansion of HP.

Before 1914 several attempts were made to explain the variation in the number of plaints entered annually, with attention being focused on wage rates, strikes, the extension of cash trading by multiple grocery stores, and the general state of trade[82]—none of them was conclusive. The rising trend of plaints from 1870 to 1914 is in line with the increase in population; the ratio of plaints to people remained more or less

---

[80] Richard Stone and D. A. Rowe, *The Measurement of Consumers' Expenditure and Behaviour in the United Kingdom 1920–1938*, Volume 2 (Cambridge, 1966), pp. 26, 59; Feinstein, *National Income*, table 65.

[81] Warren, *Credit Dealing*, ch. 11.

[82] See Judicial Statistics for 1897, PP 1898 civ (C. 8838), pp. 69–72; ibid. for 1911, PP 1912–13 cx (Cd. 2681), pp. 17–18; ibid. for 1912, PP 1914 c (Cd. 7267), pp. 15–17; ibid. for 1913, PP 1914–16 lxxxii (Cd. 7807), pp. 15–16.

Table 6.1. Number of plaints entered in county courts in England and Wales for sums below £20, 1870–1938

	No. of plaints (000)	Average amount per plaint		No. of plaints (000)	Average amount per plaint
		£ s. d.			£ s. d.
1870	898	2. 18. 6	1905	1,325	3. 0. 8
1871	904	2. 18. 3	1906	1,307	3. 1. 0
1872	886	2. 17. 7	1907	1,297	3. 0. 10
1873	850	3. 0. 9	1908	1,330	3. 1. 2
1874	849	3. 2. 5	1909	1,351	2. 19. 0
1875	861	3. 5. 6	1910	1,313	2. 19. 0
1876	930	3. 7. 9	1911	1,259	2. 19. 2
1877	1,007	3. 5. 9	1912	1,214	3. 0. 7
1878	1,014	3. 5. 10	1913	1,207	3. 0. 4
1879	1,028	3. 5. 10	1914	921	not available
1880	1,081	3. 2. 6	1915	721	,,
1881	1,022	3. 1. 9	1916	547	,,
1882	1,009	3. 1. 4	1917	424	,,
1883	991	3. 1. 9	1918	301	,,
1884	940	3. 2. 11	1919	311	,,
1885	948	3. 3. 6	1920	414	,,
1886	966	3. 2. 3	1921	505	,,
1887	1,000	3. 0. 3	1922	683	,,
1888	1,031	2. 18. 8	1923	791	,,
1889	1,022	2. 18. 0	1924	839	,,
1890	978	2. 19. 2	1925	847	,,
1891	1,019	2. 19. 5	1926	792	,,
1892	1,055	3. 1. 1	1927	937	,,
1893	1,055	3. 1. 8	1928	1,013	,,
1894	1,153	3. 0. 5	1929	1,021	,,
1895	1,105	3. 1. 2	1930	1,085	,,
1896	1,095	3. 0. 7	1931	1,128	,,
1897	1,105	3. 0. 4	1932	1,192	,,
1898	1,142	3. 0. 1	1933	1,192	,,
1899	1,137	3. 0. 6	1934	1,115	,,
1900	1,166	3. 0. 8	1935	1,121	,,
1901	1,213	2. 19. 10	1936	1,215	,,
1902	1,266	2. 18. 10	1937	1,052	,,
1903	1,309	2. 19. 1	1938	1,150	,,
1904	1,366	2. 18. 4			

Sources

For 1870–1913: The returns of county courts in successive annual publications of Judicial Statistics for England and Wales. Part II: Common Law, Equity, Civil and Canon Law. PP 1871 lxiv (C. 442) *et seq.*

From 1914: Summary of County Courts, Judicial Statistics PP 1938–9 xxv. (Cmd. 6135), table xxi.

constant at about thirty-seven per thousand, though there was
some regional variation with the north of England appearing to
be more litigious than the south. Drawing a line across the
country from the Wash to the Severn Estuary, the annual
average number of plaints per thousand people in the period
1892–6 was thirty-one south of the line and forty-four north.[83]
One reason for this may be the greater extent of credit and tally
trading that was conducted in northern industrial towns. If we
make the reasonable assumption that most of these small debt
plaints were entered against manual workers and their wives,
and taking the average family size in the 1890s to be five persons, the figures seem to imply that one in five working-class
families in the north of England were sued for debt annually. In
fact bad debtors were likely to face a number of actions simultaneously from landlord, shopkeepers, and tallymen, so the
number of households affected would certainly have been less
than the number of plaints. Even so, being 'county courted' for
debt must have been a common experience in working-class
communities.

PAWNING

Pawning, popping, pledging, or visiting 'Uncle' was even more
common. Information on pawnbroking is more detailed than
that on credit trading as it was collected by the state—a by-
product of the legislation that has regulated the trade in Britain
since the thirteenth-century.[84] The function of the pawnbroker
is to advance small loans against the security of goods and chattels. By the Pawnbrokers Act of 1872, the size of loan was
limited to a maximum of £10, although greater sums could be
loaned according to the conditions of a special contract drawn
up between borrower and lender, which was not subject to the
limitations of the pawnbroking laws. These laws determined
both the rates of interest that could be charged and the conditions of resale of unredeemed goods.[85]

On loans up to £2, the rate of interest was $\frac{1}{2}d.$ in 2s. or in any

[83] Judicial Statistics for 1897, p. 64.
[84] For the early history of pawnbroking in Britain, see A. Hardaker, *Brief History of Pawnbroking* (London, 1892).
[85] 1872 35/36 Vict. C93. The account that follows of the terms and conditions of the pawnbroking trade are taken from this Act.

fraction of 2s. per month, i.e. 25 per cent p.a. For loans over £2
the rate was ½d. per half-crown, or 20 per cent p.a. This interest
was charged for a full month on any part of the first month.
Thereafter, any portion of a month up to fourteen days was
reckoned as half a month for interest charges. The interest was
levied at the time of redemption of the good, but a flat-rate
charge, known as the ticket fee, of ½d. for pledges under 10s.
and 1d. for those above was deducted from the sum advanced
when the pledge was made. Although the legislation fixed the
monthly rate of interest quite clearly, the real rate paid by any
particular customer varied with his or her pawning habits. The
loan on a good worth, say £5, pledged in January and
redeemed twelve months later would have a nominal annual
interest rate of 20 per cent. A loan of 2s. 6d. on a good pawned
and redeemed week by week throughout the year would cost
1d. per week interest, plus ½d. per week ticket fee, or 260 per
cent p.a. It is important to bear this difference in mind; the
degree of 'exploitation' of the pawner depended more on personal decisions about when to pawn than it did on the greed or
power of the pawnbroker.

If goods were not redeemed within twelve months and seven
days by repayment of capital loaned and interest due on the
loan, or if the pledge was not renewed by payment of interest
due, then the goods became the outright property of the pawnbroker. Those items pawned for 10s. or less could be disposed of
by the pawnbroker however he wished. Most pawnshops were
divided into two parts, with a 'sale counter' at the front, for the
disposal of unredeemed goods, usually with other new or
secondhand goods, and a 'pledge counter', often with a separate entrance at the side or rear, where the business of pledging
and redeeming was carried on. Goods deposited for more than
10s. had to be sold by public auction, and were redeemable
until the date of sale. The pawnbroker had to keep a record of
the auction for three years after the event, and at any time during this period the possessor of the pawn ticket could claim any
profit on the sale in excess of the sum loaned, the accumulated
interest, and the auction costs.

These legislative restrictions clearly determined the sorts of
goods pawnbrokers were willing to take as security against
loans. Perishable goods were not pawnable, and items likely to

be out of fashion in a year's time would not receive a good price. The most popular articles were clothing and bedding, watches, jewellery, and ornaments—all easily portable. Furniture and pianos could be pledged, but the pawnbroker offered a low advance to compensate for the cost of storing such bulky goods. One piano that had cost £40 on HP realised £8 at the pawnshop.[86] Some pawnbrokers would not lend above the £10 limit, and this could depress the advance offered on high-value goods, but others, admittedly a small minority, did a considerable trade by special contract on loans over £10. The best-known family of London pawnbrokers, the Attenboroughs, carried on an extensive high-class business, Richard from his shop in Piccadilly, George from 204 Fleet Street. They dealt mainly in jewellery and silver tableware, but would also sometimes take bills of exchange as security, charging 15 per cent p.a.[87]

Most goods pawned, however, were of low value. A survey of the business done in 1869 by thirty of Liverpool's 189 pawnbrokers showed that 702,657 pledges were received for sums of 2s. 6d. or less, 638,477 for sums between 2s. 6d. and 10s., and 74,530 for sums between 10s. and £10.[88] The attempt in 1872 by Archibald Orr-Ewing to introduce an amendment to clause 14 of the Pawnbrokers Bill prohibiting any pledge of less than 2s. in order to remove this 'black spot upon our social system', was vigorously and successfully resisted by the Pawnbrokers Protection Association. They argued that these low pledges did not provide funds to indulge the 'gross passions' of the workers, but supplied instead the temporary finance needed by families to tide them over until pay-day.[89]

Although this amendment found no friends in Parliament, Orr-Ewing was not alone in holding the view that the pawnbroker promoted profligacy and excess. Inevitably Mrs Bosanquet had harsh words to say about pawnbroking. It was the worst means of equalizing income; but for the pawnbroker's

[86] Bullen, *Confessions*, p. 223–4.
[87] Both Richard and George Attenborough gave evidence to the Select Committee on Pawnbrokers [Ayrton Cttee.], PP 1870 viii (377). Two of George Attenborough's receipt books for loans made by special contract, covering the period 1846–50, are deposited with the Guildhall Library, uncatalogued.
[88] Ayrton Cttee., appendix 9.
[89] Hardaker, *History of Pawnbroking*, pp. 262–9.

'untimely assistance, many would have been forced early in life to learn the art of saving for bad times, and would be in a position of independence, who now pass every winter in piling up a burden of debt for the summer'. He encouraged people to take a short view of life, to shirk financial burdens rather than face up to them boldly.[90] A more sympathetic commentator disagreed—abolition of pawnbroking would increase pauperism, not stimulate saving.[91] The pawnbroker was on the one hand the curse of the working class, on the other, the poor man's banker.

Such differences are indicative of sharply divergent attitudes towards the probity of working-class credit, and a look at the patterns of pawning and the interpretation placed on them can reveal much about different class values. The bulk of the trade—95 per cent if the Liverpool figures are representative—was for small sums, almost certainly with working-class customers. In 1870, according to a leading pawnbroker, 50 per cent of pledges were clothes of one sort or another, and a considerable portion of the remainder would have been made up of blankets, sheets, and other household 'soft goods'.[92] The number of these pledges made annually was very large. The average for each of the thirty Liverpool pawnbrokers was 47,175. Estimates made in 1870 and 1902 suggest that London pawnbrokers took an average of 60,000 pledges annually, and provincial brokers 40,000.[93] Table 6.2 gives the number of pawnbrokers' licences granted annually in Great Britain from 1870 to 1939, and when linked with the estimate of pledges suggests that between 1870 and 1914 the total number of pledges per annum rose, in line with the growth of population, from about 150m. to 230m., averaging between five and six per person each year, and thereafter fell to about 120m., or $2\frac{1}{2}$ per person in 1939. In fact the post-1914 decline in pawnbroking was not confined to the number of pawnbrokers, but was also reflected in the trade they did. The *Pawnbrokers' Gazette*, in its

[90] Bosanquet in Loch, *Methods of Social Advance*, p. 137; Bosanquet, 'Small Debts', p. 218.

[91] Bullen, *Confessions*, pp. 74–5.

[92] Hardaker to Ayrton Cttee., q. 421. This same pattern had been observed earlier in the century. See *Meliora* iv, no. 15 (1861), pp. 241–2.

[93] Ayrton Cttee., q. 1862; *Pawnbrokers' Gazette*, no. 1729 (24 Apr. 1871), p. 132; C. A. Cuthbert Keeson, 'Pawnbroking London' in Sims, *Living London*, ii. 36–7.

Table 6.2. *Number of pawnbrokers' licences issued in Great Britain*

1870	3,390	1905	4,727
1871	3,450	1906	4,766
1872	3,537	1907	4,803
1873	3,567	1908	4,914
1874	3,606	1909	4,965
1875	3,663	1910	4,984
1876	3,720	1911	5,026
1877	3,784	1912	5,047
1878	3,814	1913	5,075
1879	3,856	1914	5,087
1880	3,844	1915	5,022
1881	3,928	1916	4,956
1882	3,993	1917	4,821
1883	4,097	1918	4,648
1884	4,172	1919	4,563
1885	4,213	1920	4,559
1886	4,236	1921	4,440
1887	4,273	1922	4,302
1888	4,302	1923	4,200
1889	4,368	1924	4,121
1890	4,433	1925	4,045
1891	4,443	1926	3,973
1892	4,460	1927	3,875
1893	4,471	1928	3,786
1894	4,478	1929	3,702
1895	4,537	1930	3,598
1896	4,556	1931	3,498
1897	4,611	1932	3,384
1898	4,654	1933	3,264
1899	4,675	1934	3,154
1900	4,706	1935	3,065
1901	4,705	1936	2,981
1902	4,744	1937	2,889
1903	4,722	1938	2,777
1904	4,716	1939	2,672

Sources

For 1870–85: Twenty-eighth Report of the Commissioners of Her Majesty's Inland Revenue. PP 1884–5 xxii (C. 4474), p. 188.
For 1886–1909: From the annual Reports of the Inland Revenue.
For 1910–39: From the annual Reports of Customs and Excise.

review of business in 1939, remarked that the sale side rather
than the pledge was now 'the backbone of the business' so the
number of pledges taken in the inter-war years was almost certainly less than the pre-1914 average of 40,000.[94] On the
assumption that 95 per cent of the pledges before 1914 came
from 80 per cent of the population described as working-class,
then the figures suggest that, on average, every working-class
family in Britain made at least one pledge a fortnight, or something over thirty each year.

Again it must be stressed that some families on hard times
would be forced to pledge many goods, others would seldom
pay a visit to 'Uncle', but it would be fair to say that most
working-class households turned to the pawnbroker at some
stage during the low points of the poverty cycle. The Womens'
Co-operative Guild found that 'the deeply-seated habit of
pawning is well known, and similar in all towns',[95] and the distribution of pawnshops confirms this. In 1870 84 per cent of
pawnbrokers were located in cities and boroughs as against 50
per cent of the population, so that in the agricultural county of
Hereford there was one pawnbroker for every 62,000 people, in
industrial Warwickshire, it was one for every 2,600. Non-
industrial cities such as Oxford, Cambridge, and Brighton all
had a low density of pawnbrokers, but in industrial centres
there were roughly 4,000 people per pawnbroker, with a
slightly greater concentration in seaports.

This urban concentration of pawnbrokers gave rural
labourers little opportunity to raise loans on goods and chattels,
and made them overly dependent on shop credit or charity to
survive periods of financial inadequacy.[96] But for the urban
work-force it meant easy access to the mortgage facilities provided by the pawnbroker. Pawnshops were concentrated in city
centres, the areas of densely packed working-class housing. In
the 1930s it was claimed that one reason for the decline of
pawnbroking was the growth of working-class housing estates
on city outskirts. According to an editorial in the *Pawnbrokers'*
Gazette, its readers 'for years . . . have been content to sit still
and watch their customers leave the overcrowded districts in

    [94] *Pawnbrokers' Gazette*, no. 5265 (7 Jan. 1939), p. 3.
    [95] Women's Co-operative Guild, *Extension of Co-operation*, p. 20.
    [96] Rowntree, *How the Labourer Lives* (London, 1913), ch. 3.

which they are generally situated for more comfortable and congenial districts'.[97] But the absence of pawnbrokers on new housing estates did not stop the habit of pawning. In his survey of Becontree and Dagenham, Terence Young noted that 'On every Monday morning, the 9.30 bus from Five Elms to Barking was filled with women with bundles. There was a similar bus from "Church Elm". They were called "pawnshop buses". After 1931, this ceased because a pawnshop was opened in Dagenham village.'[98]

The usual concentration of pawnbrokers in city centres ensured a fair degree of competition. Although the rate of interest was regulated by statute, brokers could compete for pledges by manipulation of the capital advanced on any particular good. George Attenborough claimed that pawnbrokers were 'obliged to lend quite up to the hilt, and even above it',[99] in order to prevent custom going to competitors, and the result of this, according to one trade paper, was excessive competition. If pawnbrokers 'did not lend to the uttermost farthing upon goods offered in pledge their customers would go elsewhere; and only too frequently have they strayed beyond the bounds of wisdom in their desire to retain their trade'.[100] This was not just self-protective hyperbole. Of the six metropolitan pawnbrokers that closed in 1897, two did so because their owners were gazetted bankrupt.[101] This could be evidence of incompetence as much as competition, and bankruptcy was a rarity even during the years of decline between the two wars,[102] but there is little indication that pawnbrokers made extortionate profits. In 1949 it was estimated that pawnbrokers earned a gross profit on turnover of between 4 and 6 per cent,[103] and eighty years before it seems to have been much the same, with interest and ticket fees received equalling about 6.6 per cent of turnover.[104]

---

[97] *Pawnbrokers' Gazette*, no. 4960 (11 Mar. 1933), p. 100.

[98] Terence Young, *Becontree and Dagenham* (London, 1934), p. 76 n. I would like to thank Ross McKibbin for this reference.

[99] Ayrton Cttee., q. 695.

[100] *Pawnbrokers' Magazine and Record* i, no. 12 (23 Sept. 1891), p. 264.

[101] *Pawnbrokers' Gazette*, no. 3123 (1 Jan. 1898), p. 12.

[102] A. L. Minkes, 'The Decline of Pawnbroking', *Economica* xx (Feb. 1953), p. 22.

[103] Ibid., p. 14, footnote 1.

[104] Ayrton Cttee., appendix 9.

The business of pawnbroking was an expensive one to conduct. There was the risk of being unable to sell unredeemed goods for the amount loaned upon their security, either because the pawnbroker had been over-generous, over-competitive, or not alert enough to spot the 'duffer', the person who manufactured expensive-looking goods, usually jewellery, out of cheap materials with the intent of pawning them for considerably more than their true worth. Cases of 'duffing' or 'moskeneering' (a Yiddish slang word first recorded in 1883) were regularly reported in the trade papers, along with various chemical tests pawnbrokers developed to identify fake gold.[105] There was also a considerable cost in running a pawnshop, especially if a large 'industrial' (i.e. working-class) trade was carried on; not only were pawnshops normally in crowded areas with high rents, but the process of examining, recording, storing, and retrieving pledges was a labour-intensive one. Several assistants were required to tie up parcels, write out tickets in triplicate (one to pin to the parcel, one for the customer, one for the ledger), and store the pledges. In 1883 the *Quarterly Review* gave a description of what the observer would see if he ventured inside a pawnshop:

There he will understand the meaning of the familiar phrase 'up the spout', when he sees a kind of funnel or chimney communicating between the shop below and the warehouse above. Up this spout go all the soft goods pawned, to each of which a ticket is attached, the duplicate being in the hands of the pledger. They are drawn up by a boy stationed in the warehouse above, who stores them away upon shelves or racks according to the date when they were deposited. So, in redeeming a pledge, a bell rings, and in obedience to it the boy draws up the canvas bag from below, in which is the ticket of the article. The date of the ticket tells the boy on which shelf to find the package that he wants, and with incredibly little delay it is dropped down the spout and restored to its owner.[106]

The average cost to the pawnbroker of taking in each pledge was reckoned by George Attenborough to be 1.6*d.*, and in the

[105] On duffing, see Ayrton Cttee., qq. 700, 2613; *Pawnbrokers' Gazette*, no. 4963 (1 Apr. 1933), p. 130.
[106] *Quarterly Review* clv (Jan. 1883), p. 133. For other descriptions see A. S. Jasper, *A Hoxton Childhood* (London, 1969), pp. 22–3; Walter Greenwood, *Love on the Dole* (Harmondsworth, 1969), ch. 4.

Liverpool sample it stood at 2.1*d*.,[107] so pledges valued at 4*s*. or less which were redeemed within a month did not yield a profit, as interest and ticket fee came to only 1½*d*. On the other hand, it was commonly the case that unredeemed goods would not realize at auction or sale enough to cover the sum loaned and interest due, and for the twelve months they were sitting in the pawnshop they tied up both capital and storage space. Pawnbrokers therefore gambled upon the likelihood of a good being redeemed. As a Salford pawnbroker explained to the Select Committee on Pawnbrokers, 'We do not care about destitute customers . . . our trade is a regular one, and our profit is got where the money is lent and lent again and not from the person who wants to get the money and leave the goods.'[108] It seems that about 5 per cent of goods were forfeited, whilst 80 per cent were redeemed within three months,[109] though popular opinion had it that the chance of redemption was much less. The pawnbrokers' traditional sign of three golden balls was taken to mean two to one that pledges would never be redeemed.[110] During the periods of acute industrial distress caused by unemployment or strikes, forfeits increased, redeems declined, and pawnbrokers' profits fell as a consequence.[111] 'The popular fancy', reported one trade paper, 'is that the Pawnbroker thrives upon the distress and poverty of his fellow-creatures. Nothing can well be further from the truth than such a supposition.'[112] Distress and poverty led to large stocks, slow turnover, a high rate of forfeiture, and low prices for goods at the 'sale' counter. An attempt by the government to use pawnbroking returns as an index of financial distress among the working population failed because, as the report pointed out, 'Broadly speaking it appears that activity in pawnbroking is rather a sign of prosperity than of exceptional distress.'[113]

---

[107] Ayrton Cttee., q. 714; appendix 9.
[108] Ibid., q. 963.
[109] Ibid., qq. 191, 222.
[110] Paul, *Poverty—Hardship but Happiness*, p. 18.
[111] See comments on the effect of unemployment and strikes in *Pawnbrokers' Gazette*, no. 2184 (5 Jan. 1880), pp. 4–5; ibid., no. 2497 (2 Jan. 1886), pp. 4–5; ibid., no. 4951 (7 Jan. 1933), p. 5; *Pawnbrokers' Market*, no. 7 (8 Nov. 1912), p. 100.
[112] *Pawnbrokers' Gazette*, no. 1728 (17 Apr. 1871), p. 124.
[113] 'Distress and Unemployment', PRO LAB 2 1599/L1129/1905.

It was true, though, that poverty was the reason why people turned to the pawnshop—they had an acute need for immediate liquidity. What pawnbrokers wanted was a random distribution of this need, rather than a concentration of it among a particular population at a particular time. The unpredictable nature of sickness and death ensured some regular business for pawnbrokers. 'Bereavement', said the Secretary of the Glasgow Pawnbrokers' Association, 'is very often the cause of an individual coming first to us . . . either illness or death in the family is often sufficient to make a beginning.'[114] The temporary unemployment which afflicted most manual workers other than a fortunate few with scarce skills or in government or railway company service was also the cause of pawning, especially so in ports with their large pool of casual dock labour.[115] The economic hardships of unemployment paid little respect to middle-class moral judgements; the Superintendent of Detective Police of the Metropolis felt that 'a provident man, when he is out of work, probably as often goes to the pawnbroker as another'.[116] This need for ready money affected almost all families from time to time. Arthur Newton, recalling his childhood as a shoemaker's son in Hackney before the First World War, wrote, 'there were very few people indeed who could truthfully say that at no time in their lives they had not pawned something to get ready cash. I have even known my parents to do this. Not more than two, perhaps three times, but they did it, nevertheless.[117]

What was the ready cash used for? Doctors' fees or undertakers' charges sometimes, but other expenditure was more common. A Chief Constable claimed that 'as a rule, they expend it in the purchase of whisky or other intoxicating liquors',[118] and undoubtedly some of the loans were used to quench a fiery thirst, but Saturday, the day of greatest intemperance, was also the day of large-scale redemptions, of money flowing into the pawnshop rather than out of it. The loans

---

[114] Ayrton Cttee., q. 2110.
[115] Ibid., q. 3044.
[116] Ibid., q. 1648.
[117] Arthur Newton, *Years of Change* (London, 1974), p. 23.
[118] Ayrton Cttee., q. 1330.

received on Monday went to pay the rent collector, insurance and tally-men, to buy food, and to pay for occasional extravagances—Christmas junketings, a holiday, or, in Lancashire in particular, to buy new clothes for the children to wear in the Whit parade.[119] If credit was needed there was often much to be said for turning to the pawnbroker. It was thought that, in the short run at least, 'shopkeepers charge more for such credit than the pawnbroker does for the loan of his money'.[120]

There was widespread agreement, even among stern critics of pawnbroking, that at times of real distress, the pawnshop was useful and necessary. The heavy-handed moralizer who wrote 'a Cyclopaedia of Cottage Management and Practical Economy for the People', conceded that:

Notwithstanding all that is justly said against the pawnshop, there are special trials and extreme emergencies wherein the wage earning classes may be, of all others, most excused for resorting to it. In exceptional times of real adversity, the pawnshop may be, and often is, a beneficent institution.[121]

Mrs Bosanquet, despite her strictures referred to above, realized that 'To many thousands the pawnshop is their one financial recourse, their one escape from charity or the Poor Law. . . . To raise money on the home is not among the lower class the last expedient of despairing misfortune, but the ordinary resource of the average man.'[122] These critics had a good understanding of the economic problems of working-class households; theirs was not blind prejudice, but informed condemnation, and the condemnation was directed against both the pattern of pledging and the very notion of working-class credit.

The weekly pattern of pawning—redeeming goods on a Saturday when wages were received, pledging them on a

[119] Aside from many references in evidence heard by the Ayrton Cttee. see *Pawnbrokers' Gazette*, no. 1694 (22 Aug, 1870), p. 282; ibid., no. 4951 (7 Jan. 1933), p. 5; *Pawnbrokers' Market*, no. 43 (18 July 1913), p. 25; Northcote Cmmn., Second Report, q. 1426; *The Liverpool Citizen* (2 Jan. 1889), p. 11.

[120] Ayrton Cttee., qq. 1023, 4468. Also Standish Meacham, *A Life Apart* (London, 1977), p. 74.

[121] *Thrift Book: A Cyclopaedia of Cottage Management and Practical Economy for the People* (London, n.d., *c*.1883), p. 6.

[122] Bosanquet, *Rich and Poor*, p. 99.

Monday when the collection agents called—this was seen as the real curse of the system. It was not a way of meeting sudden emergencies but a way of funding normal expenditure, a habitual system resting on the inability of the working class to plan ahead, both a cause and an indicator of the demoralization and dependency of the masses. What made this worse still, in the eyes of these critics, was that resort to the pawnbroker was in many cases quite conscious and deliberate. In 1883 C. S. Loch wrote:

Pawnbrokers are the bankers of the unthrifty. They give them advances on goods and household gear, and thus help them at a pinch. In a sense pawnbroking is a kind of inverse method of saving—taking credit for stock. And the poor will buy things quite prepared to make capital out of them, in a time of need, and even estimating their prospective value for this purpose.[123]

But this sort of capital accumulation, although clearly seen for what it was, drew continued criticism on what can only be called moral grounds. Pawning household goods, even those deliberately purchased for that purpose, was thought of not as realizing capital but as 'forestalling future earnings'.[124] For the comfortably-off—comfortable enough to be able to indulge in the hobby or profession of social observation—goods and chattels were inalienable, something to be used whilst required and to be disposed of when redundant, but not something to be converted into liquid assets when funds were required. A quite distinct system of cash accumulation was used to provide for such contingencies. No matter how close these observers came to the realities of working-class life, they could never understand it from the perspective of the observed, because they had quite different views of social and economic propriety. As Ross McKibbin has pointed out, they saw the profligacy and lack of foresight of the masses as a function of 'working classness' rather than low income and wealth.[125]

For the people forever trying to live on the economic knife-edge between sufficiency and want, deliberate and habitual

[123] C. S. Loch, *How to help cases of distress* (London, 1883), p. 101.

[124] Bosanquet, 'Small Debts', p. 217.

[125] R. I. McKibbin, 'Social Class and Social Observation in Edwardian England', *Transactions of the Royal Historical Society*, 5th ser., xxviii (1978), p. 184.

pawning was neither as useless nor as ill-considered as it appeared to those who made sorties into the 'infernal wen'. In households without storage space, the pawning of best clothes was the only way to make sure they would be properly hung until next needed. In 1872 a London magistrate thought this was a common, though not very provident, response to the problem of living in damp, overcrowded, and ill-furnished accommodation,[126] and the recollections of one East Ender born in 1886 suggest that little had changed by the turn of the century: 'Wardrobes were practically unknown when I was a child. You put the same things on the next day. It was a question of sticking them on the chair when you went to bed of a night. If you had any best clothes you kept them in the pawnshop.[127] Miss Llewelyn Davies heard exactly the same claim several times in her survey of poor urban areas.[128] It may not have been provident behaviour, but it was within the financial compass of the poor when the alternative of the purchase of a wardrobe and possibly the move to larger premises often was not.

Another pattern of pawning was determined by the seasons. Loch's observation that people assessed purchases with one eye on their pledgeability was an acute one; they did indeed treat the acquisition of durable goods as thrift in reverse. It was a coherent form of forward planning, and not just the result of a need to gratify desires for immediate consumption. Two government inquiries, one in the 1870s and one just before the First World War reported that, in London at least, workers bought goods in periods of full employment with the deliberate intention of pawning when jobs were scarce and money short, or when some other economic crisis hit the family.

Summer is usually a better time for work, but this summer [1907] there has been no recovery, and the work is scarce. The people live on by pawning. It is their way of saving. Everybody pawns ... In summer they buy a clock or table cloth or hearth rug. They get the sense of joy and of possession for a time. It is their way of preparing for illness. When the pressure comes they part with their belongings.[129]

[126] Select Committee on the Pawnbrokers' Bill, PP 1872 xii (288), q. 460.
[127] Samuel, *Arthur Harding*, p. 99.
[128] Llewelyn Davies, *Co-operation*, p. 13.
[129] Hamilton Cmmn., app., vol. xvii, PP 1909 xliii (Cd. 4690), p. 8. See also SC Pawnbrokers' Bill, qq. 54, 379.

Even Thomas Mackay, bastion of the COS and one of the administrators of the Mansion House Fund in 1886, recognized this pattern: 'These dock labourers—there are very few artisans—get fair wages in the summer, and buy furniture and Sunday suits of clothes, and in winter they put them into pawn, and get them out in spring. They do this every year.'[130] A survey of the life-styles of casual labourers in Liverpool in 1907–8 revealed, much to the surprise of the investigators, that:

for the great majority the curve of income and expenditure is to some extent smoothed by the help of the pawnbroker, or moneylender, or both. Resort to these is, of course, in its effects a sort of retrogressive saving. In bad weeks clothes and furniture are pledged and debts incurred. In good weeks the surplus is spent in getting straight again, and if anything is left it is turned into negotiable securities of more clothing and more furniture. So far as the pawnshop goes, the disadvantages of this plan over 'saving forwards' do not seem so very serious, in spite of the popular impression to the contrary. The security being good, the rate of interest charged is only moderate ... The articles most generally pawned are the Sunday clothes of the whole family.[131]

The practice of casual labourers pawning their goods during winter months of slack employment had been common in the 1830s,[132] and little seems to have changed over the course of a century. In the mid-1930s a Pilgrim Trust investigation of unemployed families in Liverpool found that two out of three admitted to having goods in pawn.[133] The COS view, however, concentrated not on the convenience of this pattern, nor its likely benefits, but on its costs. In the uncompromising words of Mrs Bosanquet, 'but for the vicious habit of drawing upon the future they might with less hardship to themselves get through

---

[130] Charity Organisation Society, *Report on the best means of dealing with exceptional distress* (London, 1886), q. 1192. For some interesting comments on both Mackay and the COS in general, see J. W. Mason, 'Thomas Mackay: the Anti-Socialist Philosophy of the Charity Organisation Society' in K. D. Brown (ed.), *Essays in Anti-Labour History* (London, 1974), pp. 290–316.

[131] Liverpool Joint Research Committee, *How the Casual Labourer Lives* (Liverpool, 1909), p. xv. See also Dearle, *Problems of Unemployment*, pp. 139–40; H. A. Mess, *Casual Labour at the Docks* (London, 1916), p. 45.

[132] *Provident Societies Recommended* (London, 1833), pp. 7–8.

[133] Pilgrim Trust, *Men Without Work* (Cambridge, 1938), pp. 183–4.

the winter and have the use of their furniture into the bargain'.[134]

For poor households this system of thrift in reverse could make good sense. It had the advantage over almost all institutional thrift of extreme liquidity. Pawnshops were open six days a week from 8 a.m., with early opening on Monday mornings and late closing on Saturday nights. The only delay between needing and getting cash was the time it took to walk to the nearest pawnbroker, and in any sizeable town this was insignificant. The extent of this need is illustrated by the rapid development of the POSB 'withdrawl on demand' facility noted in chapter 4. Before the introduction of this service in 1905 no major thrift institution gave the same degree of liquidity as the pawnshop, so it would be reasonable to say that for working-class households portable durable goods were the near-money equivalent of demand deposits today. The financial status of these goods began to change as savings banks became more immediately accessible and as the mortgage market for household goods began to contract after 1914, but at least up to this date estimates of working-class thrift based just upon the accounts of financial institutions are likely to underestimate the extent and sophistication of attempts at economic management.

It would be wrong to think of liquidity as the only, or even main, reason for a widespread working-class preference for real rather than financial assets. For families with relatively few possessions, any extra good was of great value, both for the services it provided and the potential it had for display, aside from its financial worth in time of need. As long as the utility gained from possession of a good outweighed the cost of occasionally pawning and redeeming plus the interest forgone on an alternative financial asset, then it made sense to accumulate goods rather than save cash. If a family had insufficient bedding, the advantage derived from money spent on more blankets would almost certainly outweigh the 2½ per cent interest that might be earned on the same money if left in a savings bank for a whole year. But this is not so obviously the case if the expenditure was not on blankets but on something merely decorative like a

[134] Bosanquet, 'Small Debts', p. 217.

string of china ducks. In an article on 'Thrift in the Home' Mrs
Barnett complained that: 'In most rooms there is too much furniture and there are too many ornaments . . . I have counted as
many as seventeen ornaments on one mantelpiece—three, or
perhaps five are ample. She who aims to be thrifty will fight
against yielding to the artificially developed instinct to
possess.'[135]

That possession of ornaments and thrift could be one and the
same thing Mrs Barnett did not see, but there may be some
point to her observations; it hardly seems realistic to explain
away all seventeen ornaments by reference to their liquidity or
their usefulness. Part of this 'instinct to possess' sprang from the
same root as that mentioned in the section of this chapter dealing with HP—a desire for status in a society in which position
was judged in a large part by what one owned. For these social
reasons it often made more sense to buy something bright and
showy that could be admired by neighbours than to put cash
into the bank. A savings book could hardly be flaunted in front
of friends, whereas an overmantel, for instance, was a tangible
sign of living above the poverty line. Arthur Harding recalls
that:

Everybody bought overmantles. It was a new fashion about 1900.
The poor always wanted an overmantle. Couldn't have a house without an overmantle. We had one in Queen's Buildings. The bigger the
better. . . . They was very ornate, black and gold. Ours was polished
walnut. Overmantles wasn't expensive at all. The cheapest ones were
ten bob new in a shop. When you looked at them you couldn't realise
how cheap they was.[136]

The role of goods in improving or maintaining status can be
seen to be even more important in determining patterns of
weekly pawning. The reasons for real asset preference
advanced to explain occasional or regular seasonal pawning do
not account well for the high cost or repetitive nature of regular
weekly pawning; if the need for liquidity was so great at such
predictably frequent intervals, then the most sensible response
would have been to hold cash rather than pay the conversion
charges which, as noted above, could exceed 250 per cent p.a.

[135] Mrs S. A. Barnett, 'Thrift in the Home' in *Thrift Manual*, p. 20.
[136] Samuel, *Arthur Harding*, pp. 97–8.

To understand why the apparently foolhardy habit of weekly pawning was so common, we need to look closely at the pattern of pawning and the type of goods pledged.

The daughter of a Victorian pawnbroker recalled that 'Saturday nights and Monday mornings were, of course, the busiest times. On Mondays the women brought in their family's Sunday best.'[137] This use of Sunday clothes for weekly pawning seems to have been common from at least the 1860s to the 1930s,[138] and most of the reports of it mention regularity. According to a pawnbroker's assistant who started work in 1922, 'The busiest time was Monday, of course. The pledge used to come on Monday and then be redeemed on Friday. Bank Holidays and the day before Christmas, they were very busy times . . . Of course, we knew our customers and we knew the goods they were pledging regularly.'[139]

But regularity did not necessarily mean continual pawning all year round. As one pawnbroker explained to the Select Committee, 'the people have been behind, and it is some time before they can, as it were, get up so that they are able to pay', but they would never come in every week for a whole year. 'There never is such a thing.'[140] So, for any particular family the initial loan made at a time of want might be cancelled each Friday or Saturday and renewed each Monday until such time as the amount loaned could be repaid. But the weekly cancellation and renewal of the loan was a costly affair, and it might be thought that the sensible policy would be to leave the goods in pawn until such time as they could be lastingly redeemed. Was the use of a different set of clothes for one day a week really worth so much?

'No' was the response of the COS, but the pawners seem to have taken a different view. Although poor households had

---

[137] *The Times* (10 Oct. 1961), p. 14.

[138] See, for instance, T. Turner, *The Three Gilt Balls* (London, n.d., c.1864), p. 21; *Thrift Book*, p. 6; B. Seebohm Rowntree, *Poverty, A Study of Town Life* (London, 1901), p. 59; Roberts, *Classic Slum*, p. 26; Pilgrim Trust, *Men Without Work*, p. 124.

[139] Transcript of an interview with Mr Sidney Shipps carried out by Kenneth Hudson in 1981 for his book on pawnbroking. This and other transcripts and questionnaires are in the possession of Mr Hudson, but may be deposited with the Pawnbrokers' Association at a later date. See Kenneth Hudson, *Pawnbroking*.

[140] Ayrton Cttee., qq. 4464–8.

many other uses to which their limited funds could be put, they were willing to pay very high rates of interest to secure the use of Sunday clothes on the Sabbath, rates that seemed to bear little relation to the intrinsic value of the Sunday best. In 1899 Thorstein Veblen wrote:

No-one finds difficulty in assenting to the commonplace that the greater part of the expenditure incurred by all classes for apparel is incurred for the sake of a respectable appearance rather than for the protection of the person. And probably at no other point is the sense of shabbiness so keenly felt as it is if we fall short of the standard set by social usage in this matter of dress.[141]

As hats are to Royal Ascot, so Sunday best was to working-class communities at the weekend. The Sunday suit was a sign of financial sufficiency, the most public sign possible as it was paraded around the streets, while its non-appearance was a public confession of want. As Robert Roberts noted, 'News of domestic distress soon got around. Inability to redeem basic goods was a sure sign of a family's approaching destitution.'[142] The son of a plumber's mate recalls that 'Mother had another important job on Saturdays, as she had to redeem Dad's suit from the pawnshop, so that he could wear it over the weekend. He had to keep up appearances when he visited the pub for the weekend session with his mates.'[143] In a society in which status and wealth were intimately linked, the ritualized forms of wealth display were essential to maintain 'position'. An extravagant funeral was an occasional indicator of wealth, and for this reason burial insurance came to be almost universally regarded as a necessity, but regularly turning out in the Sunday best was an indicator of habitual respectability. Gareth Stedman Jones has pointed out that in working-class communities in Britain in the last three decades of the nineteenth century, 'Respectability did not mean church attendance, tee-totalism or the possession of a post office savings account. It

[141] Thorstein Veblen, *The Theory of the Leisure Class* (New York, 1899), pp. 167–8.
[142] Roberts, *Classic Slum*, p. 25.
[143] John Blake, *Memories of Old Poplar* (London, 1977), p. 11.

meant the possession of a presentable Sunday suit, and the ability to be seen wearing it.[144]

If the Sunday suit was of such social importance, why was it pawned in the first place? Because from Monday to Saturday it was an idle asset, a nuisance if anything, since it had to be stored somewhere. If cash were needed quickly in a household with few possessions, it made more sense to pawn clothes that would not be missed rather than articles of practical utility like pots and pans, or ones of constant social utility like ornaments, lace curtains, or any other item that was normally on display. Sunday clothes were unique among household assets in that they had no alternative use for six days of the week; if something had to be pawned, they were the obvious choice. The rate of interest over many weeks might seem exorbitant, but there was no certainty that it would be paid for weeks on end—next week might bring a new or better job, an end to the illness, a win on the horses. Only by considering both the economic uncertainty of working-class life and the social role of certain private possessions can the deeply entrenched and widely practised patterns of behaviour which seemed so profligate to people like Mrs Bosanquet be properly understood.

If the pattern of pawning was in part determined by a desire to conceal financial insufficiency whilst conforming to certain ritualized forms of display, then it would seem likely that the act of pawning would itself be shrouded in secrecy despite its commonplace nature. The evidence is ambiguous; entrances to the pledge counter were up alley-ways or in side-streets, the counter itself was divided by partitions into 'boxes' so that one customer could not see what another was pawning, yet some women would queue outside on a Monday morning, which clearly broadcast their intentions.[145] Pawnbrokers themselves seem to have accepted that their trade carried with it a certain amount of stigma. They pointed out that most people gave false names and addresses for entry on the pawn ticket, because 'To

[144] Gareth Stedman Jones, 'Working-Class Culture and Working-Class Politics in London, 1870–1900', *Journal of Social History* (1974), p. 475. See also Pat O'Mara, *Autobiography of a Liverpool Irish Slummy* (London, 1934), p. 63.

[145] Tebbutt, *Making Ends Meet*, pp. 58–9.

a respectable person the exposure that would result from the loss of a Pawn-ticket in the public streets, containing the true denomination and residence of the owner, would be an over-powering degradation ... Such a calamity is now avoided by the general adoption of fictitious names.'[146]

There was also often a strong desire to conceal any visit to the pawnshop because, as a pawnbroker's assistant said, 'the person who visits the pawnbroker has a great degree of shame, and does not want to be seen'.[147] There was a peculiar antithesis between the widespread use made of the pawnbroker's services and the social stigma attached to this use.

One way of not being seen was to pay someone else to incur the shame. Before the First World War, 'there was a woman in nearly every street of the East End of London who got a living taking neighbour's things to the pawn shop',[148] and sometimes children would be recruited to run errands to 'Uncle'.[149] The occasional or better-off customer might pawn in person but, by using the 'front shop' or sale counter, could give the appearance of being a purchaser rather than a pledger.[150] Many ruses were followed to disguise or conceal pawning from neighbours. In London, some people would travel to areas where they were unknown in order to pawn,[151] and in Lambeth, according to one man's recollection:

much ingenuity was used in arriving at the pawnshop without having one's neighbours made aware that that was the destination. There were even occasions if my mother felt that the neighbours suspected that she was visiting the pawnshop, when a penny ride would be taken in a direction away from the pawnshop, and from the alighting point a devious journey made back through side streets to the real destination.[152]

---

[146] *Pawnbrokers' Gazette*, no. 1723 (13 Mar. 1871), p. 84. Also Ayrton Cttee., qq. 77–84, 2684–724, 4857; Michael Winstanley, *The Shopkeeper's World, 1830–1914* (Manchester, 1983), p. 195.

[147] Ayrton Cttee., q. 3527.

[148] Samuel, *Arthur Harding*, p. 90.

[149] Thomas Callaghan, *A Lang Way to the Pa'nshop* (Newcastle upon Tyne, 1978), pp. 16–18.

[150] Questionnaire filled in by Mr G. H. Mobbs, son of East End pawnbroker. In the possession of Kenneth Hudson.

[151] SC Pawnbrokers' Bill, q. 42.

[152] *The Times* (28 Jan. 1957), p. 10.

Visiting the pawnbroker brought a sense of 'shame and degradation' which could not be shaken off.[153] In Edwardian Salford 'some families would go hungry rather than pledge belongings'.[154] But the shame of pawning was less than the shame of turning to the Poor Law. Pledging household goods was 'a rather degrading business, but not as degrading as going to the Board of Guardians or the Workhouse'.[155]

How far this sense of shame and loss of community standing was felt by regular as well as occasional pawners is not clear; it was, understandably, something that people tended not to acknowledge. As a socialist newspaper wrote in 1891, 'It is rude, and in flat contradiction of all the rules of polite society, even to breathe the word pawnshop. Everybody "pops", but very few have the hardihood—we will even say shamelessness—to own up to the transaction.'[156] It is likely, however, that in certain circumstances the shame associated with pawning was diminished because it ceased to become a significant social indicator. These circumstances were when, through strike, lock-out, or depression, all members of a particular community were forced to raise cash by mortgaging personal possessions—that is, when pawning became a community-wide response to a general problem. It is reported that during the dock strike of 1889 there was 'an unprecedented rush to the pawnbrokers',[157] in West London during the severe winter of 1885 'every available article of furniture or clothing was sold or pawned',[158] and in the engineering dispute of 1897–8 the respectable skilled artisans as a group resorted to all the expedients of borrowing and default they would normally eschew. The effect of the strike in Newcastle was that:

At the West End of Newcastle the landlords of houses, the occupants of which were as sure as the bank with their rents, have had to let the rent days pass over, hoping against hope that the tenant would soon be back to work again and recover his lost ground. A pawnbroker at

[153] Letter from Mr E. Codling, in possession of Kenneth Hudson.
[154] Roberts, *Classic Slum*, p. 26.
[155] Barnes, *Coronation Cups and Jam Jars*, p. 23.
[156] *The Reader and Workers' Advocate*, no. 68 (26 Sept. 1891), p. 18.
[157] G. von Schulze-Gaevernitz, *Social Peace: A study of the Trade Union Movement in England*, translated by C. M. Wicksteed (London, 1893), p. 259.
[158] Arthur Sherwell, *Life in West London* (London, 1897), p. 9.

Benwel has had to take the tenancy of two empty houses in which to
store the goods and chattels pledged with him, and three pawnbrokers at the West End have for a long time closed their books
against further pledges, the offers in that way being altogether
beyond the limits of their business. These facts will give but a slight
notion of the hardships that have been suffered by families; and there
must yet be many a day of steady employment before formerly comfortable homes recover their old appearance.[159]

There were two forms of pawnbroking that always invoked
some social opprobrium, no matter when they were used or by
whom, because they were such sure indicators of acute need.
One was resort to unlicensed (and hence illegal) pawnshops,
called 'dolly' or 'leaving' shops in England, 'wee pawns' in
Scotland. In 1871, according to George Attenborough, they
were found 'in low neighbourhoods, and are carried on under
various guises, such as rag shops, chandlers shops, old metal
shops, and such like'.[160] They operated by nominally purchasing
second-hand goods, and then offering them back for resale to
the original vendors a week or so later at an increased price, the
effective interest varying between $1d$. and $4d$. in the shilling per
week. No tickets were given, no records were kept, the rate
charged was at least twice that paid by weekly pawners to
licensed brokers, but the leaving shop had two advantages over
the official pawnshop—it could open on Sundays and public
holidays, and it could take goods that pawnbrokers would
refuse either because they were perishable or because they were
of so little value that the cost of ticketing and storing them was
not worth the likely financial return.[161] Even grocery shops
would take in goods. One woman, recalling her time as a ten-
year old working in a chandler's shop in Bethnal Green in the
1860s, explained that:

Articles of clothing and household goods were brought and left, something like a pawnshop, only food was given instead of money in return
for the goods, which would be redeemed when the poor things were
able to pay the money. Babies' pinafores, frocks, saucepans, candle-
sticks and all kinds of articles have been brought to hold for food. The

---

[159] Quoted in the *Pawnbrokers' Gazette*, no. 3126 (22 Jan. 1898), p. 57.
[160] Ayrton Cttee., q. 762.
[161] Ayrton Cttee., qq. 316–18, 413–15, 968, 1028, 1625–32, 4709; *Meliora*, iv, no.
15, 1861, p. 242; *Pawnbrokers' Gazette* (3 July 1871), p. 212.

practice was illegal, so all articles had to be brought in when no one was about, and I was trained to smuggle the things in.[162]

It seems probable that the improved interest rate for pawn-brokers ushered in by the Act of 1872, combined with more vigilant policing, undermined the position of leaving shops, although their very nature makes the estimation of numbers or extent of trade impossible. The only evidence of their existence after this date comes from a few scattered references, mainly from court reports of illegal pawnbroking.[163]

The other type of pawning that always drew forth condem-nation was that which involved goods bought on credit. The Select Committee heard that when people buying blankets and family bibles through clubs had difficulty keeping up pay-ments, they pledged these goods and often failed to redeem them,[164] and the same was noted among unemployed families in Liverpool in the 1930s where 'in some instances the whole econ-omy of the home is so much dominated by the pawnshop that as soon as the clothes are bought through a clothing club, they go into the pawnshop and are never redeemed'.[165] As the sur-veyors pointed out, this made purchases through clubs an even more uneconomical way of 'saving'. It was a sign of abject need—even more so when the goods pawned were being bought on HP, since the pawner did not have legal ownership of them, and so was committing a criminal offence.

The pattern and extent of pawning seems to have been fairly stable up to 1914, but thereafter the number of pawnbrokers and the pledge business done by the survivors declined, despite the economic problems of extensive unemployment and short-time working. The offer of immediate liquidity by banks and building societies has already been put forward as one reason for the decline of the mortgage market for durable goods after 1914, but pawnbrokers themselves identified two other causes. One was the rapid growth of HP which hurt the pawnbroker in a number of ways. The small size of down payment meant the 'people no longer need to pledge goods in order to purchase any

---

[162] Llewelyn Davies, *Life as we have known it*, p. 21.
[163] *Pawnbrokers' Magazine and Record* (23 Sept. 1891), p. 257; Cuthbert Keeson in Sims, *Living London*, ii. 40.
[164] Ayrton Cttee., qq. 4547–50, 4578–80.
[165] Pilgrim Trust, *Men Without Work*, p. 124.

new articles they require', the poor quality of much mass-produced furniture bought on credit made it almost worthless as security on a loan, and unredeemed items, especially furniture, were very difficult to sell against the heavily advertised goods of instalment traders.[166] The other cause was the growth of the welfare state. A Bristol pawnbroker commented that, after the First World War, 'social circumstances had altered, people were getting better pensions and earning more money, so there was no need for them to pawn'.[167] Surveys of trade in various cities published in the *Pawnbrokers' Gazette* claimed that 'the extension of pensions and public relief, of course, had a retarding effect on pledge business' and that 'today there were so many other ways of getting assistance—the dole and so on'.[168] Pawnbroking declined not because of a 'remoralization' of the working class, but because of institutional developments in financial and welfare systems.

BORROWING

With such an extensive pawnbroking market, the only reason for most working-class people to turn to a moneylender was lack of goods to pledge, since it was almost inevitable that interest charged by a pawnbroker on a secured loan would be less than that demanded for a loan dependent simply on a promise to pay. In Robert Roberts's Salford:

Only those in dire straits, and with a certainty of cash to come, patronized the local blood sucker; he charged 3*d.* in the 1*s.* per week. To be known to be in his clutches was to lose caste altogether. Women would pawn to the limit, leaving the home utterly comfortless, rather than fall to that level.[169]

Mrs Pember Reeves thought loans did not normally exceed five or six shillings, at a rate of a penny in the shilling,[170] a figure agreed on as common by the Anti-Moneylending Association in 1921,[171] although cases with a much higher nominal interest

---

[166] *Pawnbrokers' Gazette*, no. 4951 (5 Jan. 1933), pp. 4–5.
[167] Transcript of interview with Mr Jesse White, in possession of Kenneth Hudson.
[168] *Pawnbrokers' Gazette* (7 Jan. 1939), pp. 3–5.
[169] Roberts, *Classic Slum*, p. 27.
[170] Pember Reeves, *Round About a Pound a Week*, p. 73.
[171] H. H. Kelsey, *3000%, or the borrower's book on money-lending* (London, 1926), p. 34.

rate were often unearthed and publicized.[172] How many working men and women borrowed money on these terms is unclear. The Select Committees on Moneylending of 1897, 1898, and 1925 were concerned largely with technical issues of licensing and registration, on ways to limit high interest rates, and how to exempt bona fide banks or self-help organizations from proposed restrictions.[173] Much evidence was presented to the 1897 and 1898 committees of deception, extortion, and fraud practised by moneylenders, but it related to loans larger than those usually asked for by workers. Professional lenders often did not deal in very small loans of a few shillings; as one of them said of the working classes, 'they are too much trouble; they keep moving about from one place to another'.[174] Workers resorted not to the 'capitalists', 'private gentlemen', and 'loan companies' that advertised in the local and national press, but to some local lender. The pattern could be just like the weekly pawn cycle. According to a Liverpool judge, 'they borrow money . . . at the beginning of the week; they pay it with interest, which is hardly ever less than a penny in the shilling a week, on the Saturday, and then on the Monday they borrow it again. That is not at all an uncommon case.'[175]

One of the few sources of information on this low type of moneylending is a survey carried out in Limehouse and published in the *Sociological Review* in 1917. A sample of working-class women was drawn from applicants for relief from the Prince of Wales's fund, and from the list of 'dental cases' of the School Care Committee. All lodgers were excluded, so that the final sample consisted of those who 'might be described as fairly respectable'.[176] Of the first hundred women who were visited, 47 admitted to using or having used a moneylender, 10 others made the unlikely claim that they had borrowed but had paid no interest, 8 borrowed from a loan club, 32 claimed not to

[172] There are many examples in J. A. Dunnage, *The Modern Shylock* (London, n.d., c.1926), *passim*.
[173] See Select Committee on Moneylending, PP 1897 xi (364); SC on Moneylending, PP 1898 x (260).
[174] SC Moneylending 1897, q. 4201.
[175] SC Moneylending 1898, q. 299.
[176] V. de Vesselitsky and M. E. Bulkley, 'Money Lending among the London Poor', *Sociological Review* ix (Autumn 1917), p. 129.

borrow, though they did pawn, and 3 claimed neither to borrow nor pawn,[177] an indication that among this very needy
group, pawning was a preferred way of raising cash. All the
loans were raised locally; as Arthur Newton wrote of pre-1914
London, 'Each neighbourhood had its moneylender. Perhaps
Mrs. Buggins up the street had a bit more money than most,
perhaps a bit mercenary in her ways, and had a thick skin to resist the thoughts and slanders that could often be thrown at
her.'[178] The one thing they had in common was that they ignored the stipulations of the Moneylenders Acts; few bothered
with the complexities and cost (£15) of registration.[179]

What drove people to resort to these illegal loans at a penny
in the shilling, or a nominal annual interest rate of 433 per
cent? In the Limehouse survey the financial distress caused by
casual employment was the prevailing factor, and even in the
1930s, inadequate unemployment pay forced some out-of-work
breadwinners to raise loans.[180] But the loans were not, at least
initially, spent on the most basic requirement of food; they were
often used to maintain customary standards of behaviour:

in the majority of cases the object was harmless or even laudable, and
... the first loan often represented a clumsy attempt at independence;
the desire to escape from a pauper funeral, to keep the children off the
school meals list, to buy a pair of boots for the mother or a suit of
clothes for the eldest boy, who cannot go out to work in his habitual
rags, or to purchase little extras in time of sickness.[181]

This desire to maintain appearance was one reason why the
borrowers made every effort to repay the loans, despite their
being unlawful and so not recoverable by legal process. As a
writer on poverty put it in 1921, 'if there is undue delay in
repayment [the lender] may threaten to disgrace the borrower
in the eyes of the neighbours by creating a disturbance on the
doorstep; he may even resort to brutality'.[182] But there was also
the need for this very poor group of borrowers to keep on good

[177] Vesselitsky and Bulkley, 'Money Lending', p. 130.
[178] Newton, *Years of Change*, p. 23.
[179] Vesselitsky and Bulkley, 'Money Lending', pp. 132–3; Women's Group on
Public Welfare, *Our Towns*, p. 19.
[180] Women's Group on Public Welfare, *Our Towns*, p. 19.
[181] Vesselitsky and Bulkley, 'Money Lending', p. 133.
[182] Jamieson B. Hurry, *Poverty and its Vicious Circle* (London, 2nd edn. 1921), p. 55.

terms with the lenders because, as a social investigator explained in 1932, 'there will be other occasions of desperate need'.[183]

In households where one of the partners was a particularly bad manager, the financial pressures of dealing with a money-lender could be ruinous. Mrs W, the wife of a railway worker and mother of three children, explained:

I am in an awful muddle with a moneylender. I have been borrowing for years, I pay back when my money comes in and then borrow again. I had 10s. Sat: 5s. Mon: 12s. Tuesday to pay the rent, 5s. Wed. I pay about 4s. a week in trust [i.e. interest], if I could have a loan to get me straight it would mean I saved the interest and saved myself a heap of money, I would gladly pay back anything regularly in small amounts but I feel I don't know how to turn round with all this. I don't know how our debts started, it was expense with Elsie [daughter aged 2] and then my husband misses a week now and again with boils and we get no money.[184]

The cost of this 'muddle' was a nominal interest rate of 650 per cent per annum. On the other hand, the financially astute could combine borrowing with other forms of credit to obtain maximum purchasing power at minimum cost. In her reminiscences of life in Chelsea just after the First World War, Rose Gamble described the financial acumen of her mother who, with no home and no money, set about raising the six shillings advance rent necessary to move into new lodgings. First, she borrowed one shilling from the local street moneylender, at one penny a day interest. Then she went to a credit draper and signed for a pair of sheets at 15s. the pair, the borrowed shilling acting as down payment. The sheets she took to a pawnbroker where they were pledged for 7s. 6d. The six shillings rent could then be handed over, the loan and interest repaid to the moneylender, and still a precious 5d. was left. Mrs Gamble explained her financial dealings to her daughter:

A shilling a day borrowed at a penny a day interest for one week is seven pence, right?
Right Mum.

[183] Women's Group on Public Welfare, *Our Towns*, pp. 19–20.
[184] COS Case Papers, area 4, box 1, case 28995.

Six shillings borrowed for a week makes the interest come to three and sixpence, doesn't it?

Yes Mum.

Now, how much each week do we have to pay for the sheets?

A shillin' a week.

Well then, its not how much money we owe, but how much we have to find each week to pay back that matters. I could never find three and six a week to pay just for interest, not on top of everything else, and still have the six bob to find. But we can easily find a shilling, see?[185]

Borrowing was clearly at the bottom of the hierarchy of credit facilities open to working men and women because of its cost, but even so it was not the resort of simply the shameless and intemperate. Some loans were used to preserve the appearance of independence by avoiding the need for charity or state aid. This is another indication of the tenacious hold the idea of financial self-dependence had on many working-class families. Resort to credit, just like the attempts at saving, had both an economic and a social significance. They were both used to tide over periods of financial stringency, and at the same times to preserve a family's status by preventing a fall into public destitution, or to elevate it by permitting an accumulation of additional goods or services. They were opposite sides of the same coin that working-class households constantly juggled to maintain a financial balance.

[185] Gamble, *Chelsea Child*, pp. 38–9.

7

Wealth and Welfare

BETWEEN 1909 and 1920 the financial costs of three of the four spectres that haunted the poor—sickness, unemployment, old age, and death—were ameliorated by state action. Old-age pensions were introduced in 1909, health insurance benefits were paid to most manual workers from 1913, and unemployment pay was extended from the precarious trades covered in 1913 to include virtually all manual workers by 1920. Only the financial burden of death went unaided by the state, and was to remain so, in order to appease the commercial insurance companies, until 1948, when a £20 death grant was introduced as part of the Beveridge scheme.[1] The impact of these welfare measures on the economic, social, and moral standards of working-class life was a topic that drew forth much debate but little enquiry. It was claimed both that these welfare schemes would demoralize and pauperize the masses and that they would stimulate self-help and thrift, that they would destroy the family unit and that they would strengthen it, that they would precipitate socialism and that they would prop up capitalism, that they would make the nation weaker and that they would make the country wealthier. This chapter will examine some of these alternative claims, and set them against the background of the long-run trends in working-class saving outlined in the chapters above.

The belief that many forms of state welfare interfered with and diminished private thrift had a long heritage; it was a guiding principle in the drafting of the 'less eligibility' clause of the new Poor Law of 1834, and in the 'crusade' against the granting of out-relief to paupers during the last thirty years of the nineteenth century.[2] It is important to realize that long before

[1] Beveridge Report, p. 135.

[2] For a detailed account of the crusade against out-relief, see the second part of David William Thomson, 'Provision for the elderly in England, 1830–1908' (Cambridge University Ph.D. thesis, October 1980); and Mary MacKinnon, 'Poverty and Policy: The English poor law, 1860–1910' (Oxford University D.Phil. thesis, June 1984), chs. 1, 3, and 5.

the passing of the old-age pension legislation in 1908, many people believed that any apparently ameliorative action by the government would harm the country at large and the poor in particular, and this view was not confined to middle-class onlookers and political economists. In the early 1870s the Royal Commission on Friendly Societies heard a number of complaints that Poor Law relief, particularly out-relief, reduced private saving. People felt that 'the poor law is after all the best benefit club, because everything is taken out, and nothing paid in'.[3] The Chairman of the Madeley (Shropshire) Board of Guardians reported that some poor people 'think that they have a right to Poor Law relief, because they have paid "Loans all their lives". "Loans" is the local term for poor rates.'[4] These expectations were much resented by friendly societies, which believed their membership was being constrained by Poor Law largesse. The societies argued that in order to encourage private thrift, and all the virtues of manful independence associated with it, Poor Law guardians should give preferential treatment to any friendly society member who, through illness or other misfortune, was forced to make an application for Poor Law relief. Official policy was held to be a direct discouragement to joining any sort of sickness society;[5] in 1870 the Secretary to the Poor Law Board spelled out the legal position in the annual report:

With regard to the money allowance granted by the friendly society, the guardians cannot but take into account this allowance in estimating the resources of the applicant and his family, and if they acted in consistency with universally admitted principles of Poor Law administration, the guardians would not grant further aid than would be sufficient together with this allowance, to relieve the destitution of the applicant and his family to the same extent as they would relieve the destitution of any other applicant and his family, not being a subscriber to a friendly society.[6]

This ruling meant that 'By law, no assistance can be given except in the case of the absolutely destitute. The consequence

[3] Northcote Cmmn., Third Report, q. 26917.

[4] Ibid., q. 28132.

[5] Ibid., q. 28027.

[6] Twenty-second Report of the Poor Law Board, 1869–70, PP 1870 xxxv (C. 123), appendix, p. 109.

of this is to discourage the wage earners from making any provision whatever for old age.'[7]

As was so often the case with the Poor Law, regulations decreed in London had little bearing on administration in the provinces. Henry Longley, a Poor Law inspector, found that the majority of the boards of guardians of which he had knowledge took friendly society doles at half their actual value; that is, if a man received 10s. a week from his club, the guardians took this to represent 5s. of income, and made up the out-relief accordingly. Twenty years later the Royal Commission on the Aged Poor found this practice to be the norm, despite its illegality, and in 1894 it was belatedly authorized by the Outdoor Relief (Friendly Societies) Act.[8]

There was some unease about this favouritism directed towards friendly society members, because by implication it rated friendly society thrift above all other forms of prudence and foresight. The Friendly Society Commissioners considered at length the question of whether the man who accumulated funds in a savings bank was displaying more or less prudence than the man who joined a friendly society. There was an obvious asymmetry in treatment by guardians of the savings bank depositor, who generally received no relief until all his savings were exhausted, and the friendly society member, who was assisted even though the actuarial value of his contingent property right could be very large. This problem of how to distinguish prudent paupers from the profligate was even more acute when real assets were considered; how to compare the thrift that motivates the purchase of furniture with that which motivates the purchase of a deferred annuity? Octavia Hill explained to the Royal Commission on the Aged Poor why it was that workers did not buy annuities:

They feel that if they invest their money in other forms it brings in a better and happier return. They prefer educating their children well, and getting them into better positions; or buying a small business, or having a little house, or getting a quantity of furniture, or something which they have, and have to leave, and to give, and to use.[9]

---

[7] W. Moore Ede, 'Pensions for the Aged', *Economic Review* ii (Apr. 1892), pp. 179–80.
[8] Northcote Cmmn., Third Report, q. 27268; Aberdare Cmmn., Report, p. xlvii.
[9] Aberdare Cmmn., q. 10464.

In this view she found an unlikely ally in the trade unionist and Lib./Lab. MP Henry Broadhurst; in his dissenting report he wrote, 'For the large classes of workers who earn less than [30*s.* a week], thrift means, not the saving of any part of their weekly wage, but its judicious spending.[10] It was not Poor Law policy to break up homes; the destitution recognized was 'constructive', not 'absolute' destitution, and certain basic possessions—clothes and furniture at least—were regarded as a necessary minimum. But in households where real asset accumulation was the favoured form of thrift, possessions that exceeded this minimum could be disposed of by the relieving officer. Judicious spending was not a concept recognized by most Poor Law officials.

In so far as guardians made some allowance for friendly society members they encouraged a certain sort of private thrift, but there were widespread complaints that such allowances could not overcome the demoralizing effect of poor relief, especially lax out-relief. A typical comment was that of the Rector of St George's-in-the-East to the House of Lords Select Committee on Poor Law Relief in 1888:

The out-door relief has a great tendency to make the poor more improvident than they are already; it indisposes them to take advantage of savings banks and provident clubs ... I think it is very detrimental to the moral character of the recipients; it not only takes away their independence, but also has a very bad effect upon their relations; it prevents them from accepting their natural responsibilities. The children, for instance, learn to think that they have no responsibilities towards their parents, and that they need not take care of them in their old age. And then, again another important evil is that it certainly acts, that is in my opinion, as a stimulus to population; persons are disposed to marry even with more improvidence than they do now, when they think at any rate they will have out-door relief for their children if they are in distress.[11]

Poor Law relief increased rates, reduced personal independence and thrift, and undermined the moral sanctity of the family. It was to combat all these dangers that the 'crusade' against out-relief was launched in the 1870s, and the stigmati-

---

[10] Ibid., Report, p. xxix.
[11] House of Lords Select Committee on Poor Law Relief, PP 1888 xv (363), q. 1610.

zation of the pauper so eagerly pursued by relieving authorities—the social cost of poor relief, at least, could be made a very heavy one. It is important to realize that before the introduction of pensions and national insurance, Britain had, in the Poor Law, a primitive welfare system, and this system was recognized as having some impact on both the form and the scale of private thrift.

The discussion about the private effects of state welfare became much broader when the government began seriously to consider a range of proposals for some sort of national old-age pension. A scheme for an insurance-based old-age pension put forward by Canon Blackley in 1878 is usually taken as the starting-point of the campaign that led to the passing of the Liberal government's non-contributory pension legislation thirty years later,[12] though it seems clear that similar ideas were being voiced a year earlier by, amongst others, W. E. Forster.[13] Joseph Chamberlain joined the debate with his own proposals for state-assisted contributory pensions, Charles Booth advocated non-contributory pensions for all persons above 65 years, and all three schemes were examined in detail by the Royal Commission on the Aged Poor in 1895.

The anodyne Majority Report, which concluded that none of the pension schemes analysed could or should command whole-hearted support, and which was heavily influenced by self-interested friendly society views that contributory state pensions would undermine independent working-class insurance,[14] did not truly reflect the profound differences among both commissioners and witnesses about the likely impact of state welfare on working-class thrift. The battle lines were sharply drawn between the self-helpers like G. C. T. Bartley,

[12] W. L. Blackley, 'National Insurance: A cheap, practical and popular means of abolishing poor rates', *Nineteenth Century* iv (1878). For an account of the development of contributory and non-contributory pension scheme proposals see Pat Thane, 'Non-Contributory Versus Insurance Pensions, 1878–1908' in Pat Thane (ed.), *The Origins of British Social Policy* (London, 1978).

[13] Both Forster and John Walter, the proprietor of *The Times*, made speeches in the autumn of 1877 advocating insurance for old age. Accounts of these can be found in *The Economist* xxxv (6 Oct. 1877), pp. 1178–9. I would like to thank Peter Ghosh for this reference.

[14] James H. Treble, 'The Attitudes of Friendly Societies towards the movement in Great Britain for State Pensions, 1878–1908', *International Review of Social History* xv (1970).

Thomas Mackay, and the Secretary of the Charity Organisation Society, C. S. Loch, who believed that independent provision for old age was within the compass of all prudent (and abstinent) working men, and those like Booth, Henry Broadhurst, and Charles Ritchie, who argued that the economic uncertainties of working-class existence prevented the regular and long-run accumulation necessary to provide an old-age annuity. There was dispute over the extent of old-age poverty, with Booth claiming that over half of all persons aged 65 and above were living in or on the verge of pauperism, and Loch countering these claims with much more optimistic estimates.[15] More important were the differences over whether pensions would increase or decrease working-class independence; this question drew forth many assertions but little investigation, and the commissioners concluded that further 'careful consideration' was needed before any irrevocable decision might be taken. What instead happened was that the exchange of invective continued, and continued at a higher pitch from July 1899 when the National Committee of Organised Labour on Old Age Pensions was established to support Booth's pension plan.

Booth had no doubt that both thrift and popular welfare would be increased by a non-contributory pension scheme. In 1892 he wrote:

Will the assurance of 5s. a week after 65, on the whole, make those who can lay by at all unwilling to do so? This sum may be enough to keep an old man or woman out of the workhouse. Except when illness rendered them helpless, or love of drink made them reckless, I believe it would have this effect. But so much secured, every shilling would tell on comfort. The spiritual truth that 'To him that hath shall be given' is clinched by the wordly observation that 'He who has wants more', and I am inclined to think that the greater certainty of the enjoyment of saving (now by no means certain) would make thrift more attractive ... I am therefore inclined to think that such a provision as we are considering, underlying the whole social structure, would have no adverse effect on the business of thrift agencies, but might rather be expected, by raising the whole standard of life, to increase demand for their services.[16]

[15] Aberdare Cmmn., Report, pp. civ–cxvii, and q. 10909.
[16] Charles Booth, *Pauperism and the Endowment of Old Age* (London, 1892), p. 66.

Henry Broadhurst was in complete agreement: 'If a State pension of 5*s.* a week were secured to everyone, it would give a new impetus to the provision through Friendly Societies, Trades Unions and the Post Office', and even J. Frome Wilkinson, the historian of the friendly society movement, concurred—the reason for a lack of private provision for old age was 'the hopelessness of being able to save enough to live on'.[17]

These views did not go unchallenged. In a published debate between Frederick Rogers, the secretary of the National Committee of Organised Labour, and Frederick Millar, secretary of the Liberty and Property Defence League, Millar presented an alternative prediction:

Old age pensions would encourage wasteful expenditure, as the wage-earning classes, having no motive to save, would be more prodigal in their expenditure than they are at the present time. The remark is frequently heard that our working classes are really no better off for being better paid, owing to the fact that improvement in their habits has not kept pace with improvement in their circumstances. High wages in many instances lead to self-indulgence; and every one who is familiar with the habits of the English wage-earning classes knows that improvidence is far more common than prudence. . . . The Poor Law is in a large measure responsible for this. It discourages thrift, raises the unthrifty to the pecuniary level of the thrifty, and creates a fictitious notion of right to aid.[18]

This staunchly individualistic view saw the problem of financial provision in old age as a strictly moral issue, and therefore one to be overcome by moral education. Millar likened the lack of foresight of the labouring masses to that of a careless child,[19] and emphasized the role of the Poor Law in training workers to adopt a more forward-thinking approach to their budget management. The possibility that working-class families did not have the economic resources to achieve long-run security was seldom considered by the individualists, who seemed to think of a worker's financial dependency on the state as both a moral and an economic crime which demonstrated a loss of respectability and manful independence on the part of the individual,

[17] Aberdare Cmmn., Report, p. c; q. 5843.
[18] Frederick Rogers and Frederick Millar, *Old Age Pensions* (London, 1903), pp. 160–1.
[19] Ibid., p. 162.

weakened the moral fibre of the nation, and placed an unfair burden on self-sufficient property-owners. Rowntree's identification of a poverty cycle that prevented many working-class couples from accumulating large financial reserves during the years of full-time employment did not have an obvious impact on the individualist's reading of the problem of old-age poverty. The Committee on Old Age Pensions established by the COS in 1903 to attack Booth's proposals maintained that 'State pensions would prejudice thrift,'[20] and on the second reading of the Old Age Pensions Bill in the House of Lords in 1908 Lord Wemyss continued the attack with even greater vehemence, telling the supporters of the bill that 'you will establish a system of demoralisation amongst the working classes, that you will do away with thrift, that families will cease to regard it as an obligation to maintain those of their members whose working days are passed, and that self-reliance will be diminished.'[21] This was no mere backwoods belief. In 1923 Stanley Baldwin spoke of 'the discouragement of thrift at present associated with the working of the Old Age Pensions Act. The encouragement of thrift and independence must be the underlying principle of all our social reforms.'[22] During the Second World War the same sort of moral opposition was voiced against the Beveridge Report: '"Social Security" as defined in the Beveridge Report is a panacea for the ills of a populace declining in virility and enterprise, to whom a "State guarantee" of a regular income is more attractive than the reward of effort and self-reliance.'[23]

In responding to his critics, Booth attempted to separate moral issues about pauperism and dependency from economic issues about the motives behind working-class saving. In reply to claims that old-age pensions would merely create a new class of pauperized 'loafers',[24] he argued that the stigma of pauperism lay not in the receipt of funds, but in the humiliating system of enquiry and administration of relief. 'Benefits which all may

---

[20] Committee on Old Age Pensions, *Old Age Pensions* (London, 1903), pp. 9–10.
[21] Hansard, 4th ser., vol. cxcii, col. 1347 (20 July 1908).
[22] Quoted in Joseph L. Cohen, *Social Insurance Unified* (London, 1924), p. 11.
[23] C. Clive Saxton, *Beveridge Report Criticised* (London, 1943), p. 3.
[24] Rogers and Millar, *Old Age Pensions*, p. 166.

enjoy', he said, 'carry with them no slur. Educational endowments as enjoyed by the rich, free elementary education as bestowed upon the poorer classes, the facilities offered by free libraries, etc.—are cases in point. Pensions open to all and paid for out of taxation would have nothing either morally or economically in common with pauperism.'[25] In answer to the assertions that giving the poor a pension would allow them to become more profligate and more intemperate, he suggested that aged poverty arose from a general financial inadequacy in earlier life which made long-run saving for old age an economically irrational act for most workers; there were other more pressing and more rewarding calls upon the family purse:

Even amongst the quite poor, with whom, if at all, it might be supposed that fear of future destitution would be effective, savings are seldom deliberately made for any object more doubtful or remote than sickness or funeral expenses. If money is laid by the aim is rather the security of position that is afforded by a small balance at the bank. The fact that this will surely be exhausted in old age, if the owner survive, is no stimulus to further accumulations, but even the contrary. Nor is striving after security of position the principal motive for saving in this or any other class. Amongst the poor who save it is more usually some immediate advantage that is sought, the offspring not of fear, but of hope, for which people are ready to pinch and scrape. In such aims, and not on the dread of being some day destitute, lies the chief cause of thrifty accumulation.[26]

The belief that economic insecurity undermined attempts at self-help gained support from professional economists. In a treatise on *Interest and Saving* published in 1906, E. C. K. Gonner, Professor of Economics at Liverpool, explained why 'all or nothing' savings decisions could be sensible:

The alternative before the man who deliberates whether he will save, is the enjoyment of certain additional pleasures or comforts in the present and the immediate future, or the sacrifice of these in favour of security from certain risks and dangers. Unless he can save enough, he will be tempted not to save at all but to enjoy. In other words, security, if that be his aim, must be complete, or fairly complete. The same

---

[25] Charles Booth, 'Pensions for All' in National Committee of Organised Labour, *Ten Year's Work for Old Age Pensions, 1899–1909* (London, 1909), p. 43.
[26] Ibid., pp. 33–4.

may be said of those economies practised in view of retirement, for here too, unless there be some chance of saving enough to make retirement safe and a legitimate aspiration, its influence as an incentive to present sacrifice will vanish.[27]

Some thrift institutions agreed with this economic interpretation. Just after the introduction of National Insurance, the Perth Savings Bank was anticipating a general increase in working-class saving to supplement the small state allowances. Workers, it was suggested, 'now have the assurance that any little savings which they accumulate will not be robbed from them by the grim spectres of sickness and unemployment which have hitherto menaced their lives'.[28]

Savings propaganda directed at workers during the First World War was effective in maintaining or increasing levels of working-class accumulation, and it was felt that the habits of thrift learnt by many during the war would be of permanent importance.[29] During the 1920s, with the pension and National Insurance schemes firmly established and being gradually extended, discussion of the adverse effects of state welfare on private thrift moved into the shadows; Booth's ideas appeared to have won the day. But changes in the administration of the unemployment insurance scheme in the early 1930s revived fears that the government might prejudice attempts at self-help through its own efforts to relieve poverty. In 1931, by the Unemployment Insurance (National Economy) (No. 2) Order, unemployed workers whose insurance contribution had lapsed became entitled to 'transitional payments' subject to a means test administered by local Public Assistance Committees.[30] There was a working rule that savings below £100 should be disregarded in the assessment of the means of any applicant for assistance, but the relative generosity or severity of committees in their interpretation of this rule varied greatly from place to place, with the result that, according to the Trustee Savings Banks Association, thrift was diminished. A survey by the Association early in 1932 found:

---

[27] E. C. K. Gonner, *Interest and Saving* (London, 1906), p. 8.
[28] Perth Savings Bank, *A Brief Sketch of the History, Aims and Practice of the Savings Bank of the County and City of Perth, 1815–1915* (Perth, 1915), p. 38.
[29] *War Savings*, Feb. 1917, p. 60. PRO NSC 3/1.
[30] Percy Cohen, *British System of Social Insurance*, pp. 145–6, 177–82.

a widespread feeling that the man or woman who saves is not suffi-
ciently encouraged today, that the spendthrift is given as much or
more assistance from public funds as the prudent, that those who have
accomplished small savings are well advised to spend them on
immediate comforts or luxuries before they are compelled to use them
for other purposes and that money not so spent is best kept at home
where there is no fear of enquiry by the Government, Local Authority
or other Public Body.[31]

According to this report, there had in practice been a return to
the Poor Law principle enunciated in 1870.

Despite the wide diversity of views expressed in the seventy
years before the Second World War about the impact of state
welfare provisions on private, and particularly working-class,
thrift, no serious attempt was made to test the different assumptions, to see whether working-class saving had been unwittingly
reduced in amount or altered in form. Part of the reason for this
was that the wealth of the 'small investor class' appeared to be
rising quite rapidly throughout the period, at least as measured
by the funds accumulated in institutions designed for this
group. However, as was made clear in chapter 4 above, a large
share of the funds in these institutions did not belong to workers
or their dependants. Many writers assumed that all the funds
lodged in friendly, building, and co-operative societies, industrial assurance companies, savings banks, savings certificates,
and Post Office government stock belonged to the working
class,[32] but this obviously overestimated the workers' share, and
possibly misrepresented the pattern of change over time. With
the estimates made in chapter 4, it is possible to construct a
more reliable picture of the financial accumulation of the working population from 1900 to 1939 than has hitherto been the
case. It must be remembered, of course, that estimates of financial assets take no account of household possessions, which
served as realizable assets for many working-class households
before the First World War and for a smaller number later, nor

[31] 'The "Means Test". Its Effect upon Savings Bank Deposits and Withdrawals'.
PRO NSC 9/762.
[32] Chiozza Money, *Riches and Poverty*, pp. 48–9; Rowntree, *Poverty and Progress*, pp.
198–202; First Annual Report of the National War Savings Committee, PP 1917–18
xviii (Cd. 8516), p. 14; Estimate by Prof. John Hilton of 'Small Savings' in 1934 and
1938, PRO NSC 9/264/9.

---

do they take account of the indebtedness of workers, which may well have increased with the inter-war growth of hire-purchase.

Nevertheless, it is possible to obtain a good idea of the financial dealings of the working population; estimates are presented in Table 7.1. The first column shows the total wealth accumulated in 'small saver' institutions from 1901 to 1936, with all figures given in current prices. This is an obvious overestimate of working-class wealth; column 2 gives a revised figure for working-class assets which takes into account the fact that some of the funds in 'small saver' institutions represented middle-class capital. On the basis of evidence presented in chapter 4, 30 per cent of savings bank funds have been allocated to workers, 5 per cent of TSB Special Investment Department and Post Office government stock funds, and 30 per cent of the assets in National Savings Certificates. For building societies, 10 per cent of shares and deposits are deemed to be working-class, though only 5 per cent of increases in total society assets after 1930 are allocated to workers. The inrush of capital from 1930, attracted by the generous interest rates the societies offered, did not come primarily from working-class savers, so it seems wrong to impute 10 per cent of the post-1930 growth to this section of the population. Atkinson and Harrison assumed that the proportion of the increase of funds in building societies after 1930 due to working-class investors was only half that before 1930, and a similar assumption has been followed here.[33]

For the obviously working-class thrift institutions—industrial life assurance companies, friendly and co-operative societies—other assumptions have been made. Ninety per cent of the funds in friendly societies and industrial life assurance companies have been allotted to the working-class population because, as shown in chapter 3 above, these institutions were dominated by their working-class membership. Some of the less fraternal societies, like the National Deposit Friendly Society, did attract some members from outside the manual working group. so the exclusion of 10 per cent of these assets from the working-class total seems plausible. With co-operative societies it has been assumed that three-quarters of the capital was

[33] Atkinson and Harrison, *Distribution of Personal Wealth*, p. 303.

Table 7.1. Estimates of working-class wealth

	Total assets in 'small saver' institutions £m.	Total working-class assets £m.	Adult per caput working-class assets		Percentage of working-class assets in different savings institutions						
			Current prices £	Constant 1913 prices £	Savings Banks %	Industrial Life Assurance %	Friendly Societies %	Building Societies %	Co-operative Societies %	POSB & TSB Stock %	National Savings Certificates %
1901	356.7	140.5	8.8	10.0	41.1	17.4	22.8	4.1	13.5	0.6	—
1906	421.3	172.7	10.1	11.1	36.3	22.7	22.6	3.9	13.7	0.8	—
1911	478.0	205.9	11.2	11.8	33.4	26.0	22.3	2.9	14.3	0.9	—
1916	627.7	252.2	13.1	9.2	29.8	27.9	20.5	2.4	16.9	2.4	0.1
1921	1,249.2	449.0	22.3	10.0	22.5	24.2	14.3	2.0	15.1	2.9	19.0
1926	1,568.9	599.4	28.1	16.6	18.3	30.4	13.7	3.0	13.8	2.1	18.8
1931	1,969.5	739.4	32.8	22.6	14.9	34.1	13.7	5.0	15.2	2.0	15.1
1936	2,561.3	963.6	41.8	29.0	17.2	36.6	13.2	5.0	14.4	1.5	12.2
	(1)	(2)	(3)	(4)	(5)	(6)	(7)	(8)	(9)	(10)	(11)

Sources

Above, Tables 2.1, 3.1, 4.1, and 4.6.

owned by workers or their dependants. Although there can be
no doubt that co-operative societies were largely working-class
institutions, they did attract both middle-class patronage and
middle-class capital. How much capital came from manual
workers, and how this share may have changed over time it is
impossible to say; the figure of 75 per cent is no more than an
informed guess, which places co-operatives between savings
banks and friendly societies in terms of working-class domina-
tion of the capital stock.

The working-class share of funds in 'small saver' institutions
has remained fairly stable over time at around 40 per cent of
the total, but there have been some quite dramatic changes in
assets per caput. Column 3 of Table 7.1 shows the average per
caput wealth measured in current prices of working-class adults
aged 20 and above in Britain between 1901 and 1936, and
column 4 gives the same figure in constant 1913 prices.[34] Both
sets of numbers show a gradual rise in average per caput
working-class wealth in Edwardian Britain, though from a very
low base. When set against average annual earnings before the
First World War for an unskilled worker of £63 and for a
skilled worker of £106,[35] they illustrate starkly the precarious
financial position of most working-class households in this
period. Two months of unemployment or sickness could render
an averagely prudent and wealthy working-class family completely destitute.

The early years of the war appear to have damaged working-
class finances; although the cash value of working-class savings
rose between 1911 and 1916, the inflation of the first two years
of the war reduced the buying power of these savings to something below their 1901 level, and despite enormous cash
accumulation over the next five years which raised the current
value of working-class savings from £13 to £23 per caput, the
buying power was still no greater than the 1901 level, because

[34] The working-class adult population has been taken to be three-quarters of the
total adult population; this conforms with Routh's income estimates of the size of the
working class and Langley's wealth estimates (above, p. 103). Feinstein's retail price
index has been used as the deflator. Feinstein, *National Income*, table 65.

[35] Routh, *Occupation and Pay*, p. 120.

retail prices had more than doubled between 1914 and 1921. Although war savings propaganda clearly worked to produce an historically high rate of working-class accumulation, it did not leave workers any better off than they had been in 1913. The post-war depression, however, gave a considerable boost to the real value of these savings; the falling price level throughout the 1920s meant that those who had savings were getting richer without doing anything. Whereas the cash value of working-class savings rose by 47 per cent between 1921 and 1931, the purchasing power rose by 126 per cent. For those workers who did not have to deplete their savings to support themselves during periods of unemployment, the 1920s and 1930s appeared to be quite prosperous times. This prosperity is indicated by the rise in the current value of working-class savings throughout the inter-war period; falling prices and stable wage-rates gave an increased opportunity for cash accumulation. There is, therefore, no support in these figures for the idea that the extension of state welfare facilities in the inter-war years inhibited the thrift of those workers who were in employment and therefore who had the financial capacity for thrift. It could be argued, of course, that working-class savings would have been even higher in the absence of state pensions and national insurance. This is a difficult proposition to test, but some econometric results reported elsewhere[36] suggest that the pension scheme actually increased working-class saving rather than reduced it, thereby supporting the contention of Booth and Broadhurst that financial security in old age would raise workers above a threshold of hopelessness and encourage them to make some additional private provision for their old age.

The analysis of working-class savings by institution given in columns 5 to 11 of Table 7.1 adds weight to this view. The most striking feature is the pronounced inter-war growth of the share of working-class funds directed towards industrial life assurance companies. As was noted in chapter 2 above, the type of industrial life assurance that experienced the fastest growth between the wars was endowment assurance, which was designed to

---

[36] Paul Johnson, 'Self-Help versus State Help: Old Age Pensions and Personal Savings in Great Britain, 1906–1937', *Explorations in Economic History* (Oct. 1984), pp. 329–50.

produce an annuity at a certain age (usually at retirement)
rather than simply a lump sum at death. If the arguments of
Loch and Bartley about the disincentive effects of state welfare
had been true, there should have been a noticeable fall in this
sort of insurance relative to other, more short-run, forms of
working-class accumulation. Instead there was a reduction in
the share of working-class funds deposited with savings banks,
which dealt with a great deal of short-run working-class saving,
and this indicates a clear limit to the amount of short-run
accumulation, or 'saving for spending' desired by working-class
households. If workers wanted to embark upon relatively long-
run and relatively liquid cash saving they probably turned
from the savings banks to the slightly less accessible but slightly
more profitable National Savings Certificates. As one working-
class respondent told a Mass-Observation investigator, cash
savings went 'Half in the post office and half in certificates. The
certificates pay a good interest, but its a lot of palaver to get the
money out again quickly, so we keep up the post office in case
we ever want the money out quickly.'[37]

Only in the case of friendly societies does the argument of
Loch appear to have some plausibility, with a sharp decline in
the share of working-class assets held in these institutions. But
as column 7 shows, the decline came not after the payment of
pensions in 1909 or of national insurance benefits in 1913, nor
after the introduction of the contributory pension payments in
1928, but instead during the five years from 1916 to 1921. The
reason for this decline in the share of working-class assets was
not that funds were moved from friendly societies to alternative
financial institutions (Table 3.1 above shows the current value
of friendly society funds to be increasing throughout the inter-
war period), but rather that friendly societies did not share in
the great rise in working-class saving in the last two years of
the war and during the post-war boom of 1919–20. Friendly
societies maintained their rather tired pre-war rate of capital
accumulation at a time when other institutions were surging
ahead; one reason for this relative lack of attractiveness was the

[37] M-O, 'A Savings Survey (Working Class)', p. 20.

existence of a rival state insurance scheme for sickness and unemployment benefit, and of a more efficient form of private old-age provision provided by the industrial insurance companies, but it should be remembered that the societies were stagnating in terms of membership from the turn of the century.

In aggregate, the statistics or working-class wealth between 1900 and 1939 suggest a continuation , or even a strengthening, of support for contractual saving, though with a shift from friendly societies to life assurance, the maintenance of relatively small cash sums in savings banks (which showed a marked stability over time in buying power but a decline in terms of the share of total working-class assets), a great initial enthusiasm for national savings certificates during the prosperous years 1916–20 (which was not maintained at the same level thereafter), and a very stable wealth-holding in co-operative societies, as might be expected for an institution that was very largely an automatic savings bank index-linked to working-class expenditure. But what the figures show above all else is the very low average level of wealth available to each working-class adult. Even writers as conscious of the financial tribulations of working-class existence as Rowntree failed to comprehend the flimsy nature of the workers' savings. Because he did not appreciate how large a part of the capital held in 'small saver' institutions belonged to middle-class investors, he estimated that the average working-class family in York in 1936 had savings valued at £275;[38] the evidence of Table 7.1 suggests a true figure of little over £80.

The overall picture of stability in working-class saving in the inter-war period painted by these aggregate statistics can be compared with some more local and more impressionistic evidence from the early years of the Second World War. At the behest of the National Institute of Economic and Social Research, Charles Madge, lately of the Mass-Observation team, conducted a series of investigations into patterns of saving during the war, and his conclusions can be compared with

---

[38] Rowntree, *Poverty and Progress*, p. 202.

similar evidence for the Edwardian period given in the preceding chapters. He found, first, that in Coventry, Islington,
Blackburn, Bristol, and Leeds, life assurance was a majority
habit practically unaffected by the war, and the same was true
of other club and society saving.[39] He wrote:

Regular weekly saving is typical of the lower income levels. As income
rises there is increasingly more of another sort of saving. This is the
occasional deposit in a Post Office or Trustee Savings Bank; more
rarely, but with local variations, in a building society Deposit
account, a Co-operative Bank, or in a Joint-Stock Bank.[40]

Some impression of this hierarchy of saving can be gained
from Table 7.2, which reports the 1940 surveys of Coventry,
Blackburn, and Bristol. The Coventry survey is of particular
interest as it gives information for an upper/middle-class group
(A/B), as well as for skilled (C) and unskilled (D) manual
workers, although the limitations of the figures should be
noted. First, they refer to the percentage of families making use
of the specified institutions, not the amount of money saved,
and this certainly diminishes the importance of middle and
upper-class funds. Secondly, there is likely to be some overlap
in terms of income between the different class categories.
Thirdly, some of the information given to the interviewers may
be incorrect, either because an important saving institution was
omitted from the inquiry (in Bristol and Blackburn this was
true of building societies), or because certain saving categories
were ambiguous (does 'sick club' include trade unions or affiliated friendly societies?), or because the same term could be
interpreted in different ways by different people (for class A/B,
life assurance would invariably be ordinary life assurance for
substantial sums, with premiums paid quarterly or annually,
for groups C and D it would normally mean industrial assurance).

Nevertheless, there are some general patterns in the figures.
In Table 7.2 the first three saving methods, which together
make up 'National Savings', all show a clear dominance by

---

[39] Charles Madge, 'War-time saving and spending—a district survey', *Economic
Journal* (June–Sept. 1940); Madge, 'The Propensity to Save in Blackburn and Bristol',
Economic Journal (Dec. 1940); Madge, *War-time pattern of saving*, p. 41.

[40] Madge, *War-time pattern of saving*, p. 42.

Table 7.2. *Usage of savings institutions in Coventry, Blackburn, and Bristol in 1940*

	Coventry %				Blackburn %	Bristol %	
	A/B	C	D	Total		All	Working-class
National Savings							
Savings Certificates	38	20	9	21	17	23	20
Savings Groups	31	26	17	25	15	24	25
Defence Bonds	7	1	0	1	1	2	1
Deposit Saving							
TSB	9	7	2	7	10	1	0.4
POSB	17	22	6	19	6	20	17
Co-op Bank	2	8	2	6			
Joint-Stock Banks	39	9	2	12	5	11	5
Other banks					2	5	5
Building Societies	11	3	0	4			
Contractual Saving							
Clothing Club	4	13	20	13	9	19	24 (62)[a]
Hospital Fund					49		36
Sick Club	9	50	28	42	26	32	76
Life Insurance	57	70	54	68	82	71	76
Endowment Policy	20	37	19	32	19	22	24
Superannuation	11	15	0	12	8	14	15
Trade Union					36	31	36
Private Saving	4	17	6	14	9	11	12
Other Saving	0	15	2	12	7	15	13

Note

[a] This figure comes from Herbert Tout's 1937 social survey of Bristol. It is reported in: Herbert Tout, 'A Statistical Note on Family Allowances', *Economic Journal* 1 (Mar. 1940), p. 58. Tout's preliminary report of this social survey, *The Standard of Living in Bristol* (Bristol, 1938) promised a further volume that would include an analysis of working-class expenditure on life insurance but no further publication emerged. Some unpublished material from the survey is preserved in Bristol University Library, including a number of typewritten tables summarizing the survey data, but tables 50–6, covering life insurance and friendly society payments, have not survived.

Sources

For Coventry: Charles Madge, 'War-time saving and spending—a district survey', *Economic Journal* 1 (June–Sept. 1940), p. 331.
For Blackburn and Bristol: Charles Madge, 'The Propensity to Save in Blackburn and Bristol', *Economic Journal* 1 (Dec. 1940), p. 416.

class A/B, and lowest use by class D. This may not accurately reflect the pre-war pattern of usage, since the survey found that National Savings had 'shot up' since the start of the war;[41] if it does, it would seem to correspond closely with the pattern of usage of National Savings facilities suggested in chapter 4—that is, greater working-class saving through groups than through the private purchase of saving certificates, and negligible working-class holding of bonds purchased through the post office register.

The next group of institutions, those for deposit saving, displays a mixed pattern. Joint-stock banks and building societies are seen to provide facilities used overwhelmingly by the upper and middle-class group; this is true of TSBs also, although in them classes C and D are relatively well represented. The POSB is seen to be marginally class-sensitive, in that use rises with income within the working class, but falls slightly in class A/B, whilst the co-op bank shows a clear dominance by skilled manual workers. The greater proportionate representation of middle and upper-class depositors in the TSB is compatible with the larger deposit in Trustee compared with Post Office savings banks mentioned in chapter 4. However, the relative strength of the local TSB *vis-à-vis* the POSB varied abruptly from place to place as the Blackburn and Bristol surveys show, and it may be that the proportionate use by different classes varied also.

Contractual saving in Coventry is seen to be less popular with middle-class than with working-class savers, although within the working class it is generally more popular amongst those with higher incomes. The only exception to this is the case of clothing clubs, use of which falls consistently as income rises. This does not seem to be a maverick result; it reflects the pattern found in Merseyside in 1934. The Merseyside survey revealed that the bulk of families living below or just above the poverty line bought clothes through clubs, although less than half of working-class families living significantly above the poverty line belonged to clothing clubs: 'the more prosperous

---

[41] Madge, 'War-time saving', *Economic Journal* (1940), p. 332.

families, instead of spending small sums from week to week, buy more expensive articles of clothing out of their savings at less frequent intervals.[42]

Saving through sick clubs in Coventry is seen to be strongly class-sensitive, with little use being made of this facility by class A/B; this was less true of whole-life and endowment assurance, though this would alter if industrial assurance alone were considered. The only type of contractual saving that shows a surprising pattern is superannuation, where it might be expected that salaried middle-class employees would be much more heavily represented than skilled manual workers. Little is known about superannuation schemes other than that they varied in type and coverage greatly from town to town, depending on the initiative of local employers, and that they were relatively new.[43] Bowley and Hogg found few retired workers in receipt of private pensions in their 1924 survey.[44] Private saving is also class-sensitive, though this may bear little relation to pre-war patterns since it was the skilled working class who benefited most from the rapid rise of incomes caused by war production, and Madge thought the private accumulation of this group was an abnormal response to abnormal income.[45]

The conclusion of these surveys, about the ineffectiveness of National Savings propaganda in attracting extensive working-class wartime saving, is of less importance here than the comments on the long-run pattern:

the whole working class attitude to saving . . . has not been fundamentally modified by the war, though it has been deflected. Few working people save in order to get rich or to have a large capital sum. Working class saving is a margin for spending next year, or within a few years, to a very large extent. Often short-term saving is tied to the cycle of the year and its seasons, spring-clean, summer suit, autumn holiday, Christmas party. Or it is a standard weekly payment towards the problems of illness and ultimate death, still kept up outside the formal saving pattern by many non-savers. As long as a cer-

[42] D. Caradog Jones, *Social Survey of Merseyside* (Liverpool, 1934), p. 213.
[43] Madge, *War-time Pattern of Saving*, p. 45.
[44] Bowley and Hogg, *Has Poverty Diminished?*, pp. 81–2, 108, 131, 165–6.
[45] Madge, 'War-time saving', *Economic Journal* (1940), p. 339.

tain amount is going into savings, most working people feel satisfied.
A big increase in money by no means necessarily means a big increase
in savings . . .

Working class saving is largely a subsidiary activity, a subsidiary
function of spending. It is essentially a form of self-protection against
the insecurity and instability of industrial democratic working life. It
is a thing you do with some future objective in view, and usually on a
defined and fairly limited scale. The whole atmosphere of working
class saving is that it is something put aside, and this tradition
becomes a difficulty when large amounts are required to be saved.
Saving is a matter of shillings, spending a matter of pounds.[46]

Whilst insurance saving was common to most working-class
families, National Saving was much more concentrated, particularly among high earners, although the amount saved by
any family was found to vary widely even among families of
similar composition and income.[47] Some families with high
excess income saved little but spent heavily on furniture, which
was commonly seen as an 'obvious competitor' with National
Savings.[48] Although financial capacity imposed constraints on
savings, habit was seen to play a large role in determining how
to save, and what to do with abnormal or transitory income. As
long as insurance payments were up to date and enough liquid
funds were held to ensure that limited sense of security required
by most working-class people, extra income was likely to be
spent on some fairly conspicuous form of consumption—drink,
holidays, entertainment, ornaments, and jewellery. But the
'rudimentary providence' that Miss Butler found in Oxford in
1912[49] persisted throughout the inter-war period, despite the
expansion of state welfare services. The correspondence
between the aggregate statistics and the detailed local surveys
points to a fairly standard attitude to thrift across the country.
Some form of saving, particularly contractual saving, continued to be a primary, and if the figures in column 6 of Table
7.1 are to be believed, a growing call on working-class income.
The build-up of cash reserves in savings banks was an important, though not major, part of working-class thrift, and the

[46] M-O, 'A Savings Survey (Working Class)', p. 37.
[47] Madge, *War-time pattern of saving*, p. 66.
[48] Ibid., pp. 73–4.
[49] Butler, *Oxford*, p. 242.

details of average per caput wealth show quite clearly why this cash saving was more often short-run than long-run in its object. The idea of saving to achieve independence in old age was beyond the financial horizons of most workers. To secure an income of 5*s.* per week (the rate at which pensions were paid from 1909) from a private investment earning 2½ per cent p.a. in the POSB would have required a capital of £520; in 1911 the average adult working-class wealth in all 'small saver' institutions was just over £11.

The analysis of working-class savings before and after the introduction of old-age pensions and national insurance gives little support to the individualists' view that state welfare would increase improvidence and reduce working-class thrift. The major constraint on savings faced by workers and their families was the economic one of low pay, and the saving schemes usually adopted were those suited, by virtue of their small and regular contributions, to working-class income. The impossibility for most workers of accumulating their way out of the working-class environment added a psychological barrier to the economic constraints on thrift, and although this barrier was lowered by the introduction of old-age pensions, as shown by the growth of endowment assurance, it was not removed altogether. High incomes during the Second World War were not readily channelled into new forms of thrift; habits developed over many years of low income were not quickly changed when the immediate economic constraints were relaxed. Yet the demise of the friendly societies does show that habit was not immutable, but rather linked to generations. After the First World War the societies attracted few new, young members, because both the economic security and social esteem hitherto associated with membership were now of less consequence. The idea that a habit formed by the economic environment and integrated into the working-class way of life may change less rapidly than the economic conditions themselves did not seem to occur to many observers of the working-class economy. They argued that the moral character of the workers had to be developed in order to rid them of their latent 'working classness' before they could be helped to improve their economic lot. Increase the means of the masses, wrote Samuel Smiles, and one would 'merely furnish them with increased means for gratifying animal indulgences, unless their moral character keeps pace with their physical advancement'.[50] For Smiles, as for many other individualist writers, the idea that the 'moral character' or the social behaviour and value systems of workers might be determined ultimately by their low and precarious income was beyond belief.

[50] Smiles, *Thrift*, p. 28.

8

Conclusion

Work and leisure, earning and saving, spending and spar-
ing—such are the necessary elements of economic life, and on
the maintenance of a due balance between them does its success
depend.[1]

THE importance of the 'due balance' that Charles Booth was
writing about in 1902 was apparent to practically all working-
class families in Britain from the mid-Victorian period to the
Second World War. The millions of insurance policies and savings bank accounts, the thousands of private savings clubs and
medical aid schemes, the countless pledges taken in by pawnbrokers and the tick books opened by shopkeepers—all these
are evidence of extensive and often intricate efforts to anticipate fluctuations in income and expenditure, or to cope with
them once they had happened. The statistics of poor relief,
public assistance, and court claims for debt show that, despite
this great effort, success in the balancing act was by no means
guaranteed. It depended on prudence, some self-sacrifice, and
personal commitment, but it rested also on the chance of
having good health, a small family, and secure employment.

It was this element of chance that conditioned the type and
extent of working-class thrift, and the way it was viewed by
many middle-class observers. Not all middle-class social investigators, it should be said, were advocates of the late nineteenth-century self-help ethic so fervently publicized by the
Charity Organisation Society. Charles Booth does not fit this
stereotype, nor does Maud Pember Reeves and the other members of the Fabian Women's Group. But self-help ideas pre-
dominated in middle-class newspapers and journals, and were
a powerful force in government, as witnessed by the number of
COS members who sat on the Royal Commission on the Poor
Law. In their comments, these individualists never took proper

[1] Booth, *Life and Labour*, final volume, p. 92.

2 I 8 *Conclusion*

account of the precarious economic circumstances of working-
class life, and so, despite all the detailed and well-meaning
investigation, they failed to understand the life of mean streets
from the perspective of mean streets. Almost every work that
comes from the pen of an individualist writer displays this; here
are samples from Smiles, Jebb, Loane, and Bosanquet:

Even the best paid English workmen, though earning more money
than the average of professional men, still for the most part belong to
the poorer classes because of their thoughtlessness. In prosperous
times they are not accustomed to make provision for adverse; and
hence, when a period of social pressure occurs, they are rarely
found more than a few weeks ahead of positive want. This habitual
improvidence—though of course there are many admirable exceptions—is the real cause of the social degradation of the artizan.[2]

... it is not so much the poverty as the ignorance of the poor that prevents them from saving. Where there is a penny or two left over at the
end of the week after the weekly expenses have been met, they do not
pause to think of a day when even pennies may be wanting, or if they
do think of it they know of no means of preserving the small surplus of
today against a future need.[3]

The great hindrances to saving are laziness and self-indulgence,
slavery to impulse, mental apathy, narrowness of outlook, feeble or
dangerous misconceptions as to the origins and functions of capital,
untrained imagination, undisciplined will, ignorance of practical
arithmetic and entire neglect of accounts, contempt of housewifely
arts, and lack of a proper spirit of independence and desire for self-
realization.[4]

The weekly wage has an illusory appearance of regularity, which has
much to do with the difficulties of the 'poor'. Their mental horizon
tends to be limited to a stretch of seven days, and many feel that they
have amply satisfied the claims of providence if they can see their way
clear to next Saturday.[5]

Workers were seen almost as a species apart, separated from
the civilized section of the community not by their economic
weakness, but by their entire way of life. Nurse Loane even

[2] Smiles, *Workmen's Earnings*, p. 14.
[3] Eglantyne Jebb, *Cambridge: A brief study in social questions* (Cambridge, 1906), p. 116.
[4] Margaret Loane, *The Common Growth* (London, 1911), p. 105.
[5] Bosanquet, 'Wages and Housekeeping' in Loch, *Methods of Social Advance*, p. 136.

thought it was 'open to question whether the poor as a whole may not have developed a more economical digestive system'.[6] Not surprisingly, Mrs Bosanquet, the most careful and thoughtful investigator of this group, came closest to an understanding; she at least realized that the economic foundation of the weekly wage was a crucial determinant of thrift, but her interpretation was wrong. It was not the 'illusory appearance of regularity' of income that curtailed thrift, but its inevitable chanciness. J. B. Hurry, in his study of the 'circles of poverty', explained:

The uncertainty of the future is one reason why even in prosperous days the working man so often spends his wages as soon as earned. He fears that any small economies within his reach will prove insufficient to save him from misery in the event of unemployment. Uncertainty is the enemy of thrift.[7]

This was true even after the introduction of national insurance. In 1938, Pilgrim Trust social investigators wrote: 'one of the main differences between the "working" classes and the "middle" classes is the difference in security. This is probably a more important distinction than income level.'[8]

The insecurity of working-class income prevented the adoption of long-term saving plans that might conform to middle-class models of saving over the life-cycle. There was little point in thinking about saving for retirement when there were more immediate calls on funds—payment of the quarterly rent or purchase of new boots. Nor was there much point in attempting to save for a goal beyond the financial means of a typical working-class wage—as, for instance, was the purchase of an old-age annuity. The COS case-workers expected almost superhuman efforts from poor families to make ends meet on a low income. As Mrs Pember Reeves complained, 'they argue as though the patent fact that 30s. misspent may reduce its value to 18s. could make 18s. a week enough to rear a family upon.'[9] That this middle-class hectoring of working-class improvidence

[6] Loane, *From their point of view*, p. 162.

[7] Hurry, *Poverty*, p. 82.

[8] Pilgrim Trust, *Men Without Work*, p. 144.

[9] Pember Reeves, *Round About a Pound a Week*, p. 76. Margaret Loane reckoned that a family of six could live decently on 20s. a week. See *From their point of view*, p. 161.

caused resentment there is no doubt. A senior officer of the North London Oddfellows wrote a stinging attack on the pompous prescriptions of the 'man who spends as much, perhaps, on his cigars as another man has for the maintenance of his whole family'. Thrift should be a means to an end, but for many of these middle-class improvers, it was seen as an end in itself, suitable for all people in all circumstances. For many working men it was economically inappropriate and socially deadening, as it dammed the stream of human kindness, killed off all sentiments of charity and fellowship.[10]

All people dependent on a weekly wage needed to pay some attention to financial planning, both to stretch their income over seven days, and to cope with fluctuations in incomings and outgoings from week to week, but it was not obvious that the most efficient means of doing this was by accumulating a private stock of savings. Because the incidence of some major financial crises was unpredictable, it made good sense to pool risks with others in mutual insurance organizations. There were, of course, administrative costs to this insurance which would not be borne by a private saver, but there was the benefit of increased security, and this security could be very valuable. Unless the individual had a discretionary income large enough to allow the accumulation of a stock of funds that could provide as much financial security as insurance policies, then insurance was likely to be preferred. The great difference between the middle-class observers and their working-class specimens was that the former could support this level of private accumulation, the latter could not.

This difference in income affected not only the institutional form of saving, but the specific method of saving as well. As noted in chapter 4, middle-class savers built up their stock of funds by placing the income they had not spent at the end of each month in a savings account. For them, savings were a residual, albeit a planned one. For many working-class families, there was no residual; the income level afforded little more than a subsistence standard of living, and there were usually pressing physical needs of food, clothing, or shelter that remained unfulfilled. Yet the unpredictability of income and

---

[10] *Oddfellows' Magazine* xxxv (Sept. 1903), p. 240.

expenditure made some financial provision for the future essential. The way most households chose to cope with this problem was by committing a set portion of income each week to financial planning—this was the insurance or club money. Small regular deductions were not missed in the way lump-sum payments would be, and they imposed a degree of external discipline on the saving scheme. Will-power was seldom strong enough to permit accumulation in a week when money for food and rent was short, but the power of a contract often was. Some housewives in London in the early 1920s feared that 'the saving of twenty or thirty shillings in the house would have led their husbands into temptation.'[11]

It was for exactly the same reasons of convenience and discipline that payment-by-instalment was used so extensively, especially by the poorest families, for the purchase of clothes, boots, coal, and durable goods; housewives could never accumulate on their own a lump sum large enough to permit purchase of these goods. The same is true today for low-income families; in his pioneering study of the household economy of poor families in New York, David Caplovitz found that:

Some family heads felt that it was *easier* to buy on credit than to save and pay cash. They made it plain that they were referring to the discipline required for advance saving. This they found difficult to achieve. Faced with many day-to-day demands upon their resources, they found it hard to build up substantial reserves. For them credit provided a system of enforced savings with the discipline imposed from without.[12]

The use of clothing clubs, for instance, is still very extensive among poor families in Britain living on supplementary benefits, because they lack the means of accumulating privately the capital sum large enough for cash purchases.[13] To reiterate the key point made in a Mass-Observation survey, 'people tend to save because they haven't enough money to budget . . . without saving, not because they can spare enough money to save.'[14]

[11] Brown, *London Co-operation*, p. 158.
[12] David Caplovitz, *The Poor Pay More* (New York, 1963), p. 97.
[13] David Piachaud, *Do the poor pay more?* (Poverty Research Series 3, Child Poverty Action Group, London, Feb. 1974), p. 17; Louie Burghes, *Living from Hand to Mouth* (Poverty Pamphlet 50, Family Service Unit, London, Dec. 1980), chs. 3 and 7.
[14] Above, p. 99.

The general working-class preference for insurance or club saving rather than private accumulation, and an extensive reliance on short-term credit, did not mean that workers were insensitive to all economic costs and benefits, but rather that they did not value them in the same way as middle-class savers. Whereas the middle class was concerned with interest rates, the working class was concerned with absolute amounts. Because the discretionary income of workers was low, the only practicable form of borrowing or saving was that conducted through small payments; the limit to credit or thrift was the contribution that could be afforded weekly. And because the income of workers was insecure, planning periods were short, so the annual interest rates, keenly calculated by groups such as the Anti-Moneylending Association, were immaterial. Weekly pawning was a ruinously expensive activity if contemplated and conducted over the long run, but there was always the expectation that next week would bring a higher income, the redemption of the pledge, and the return to financial self-sufficiency. If this did not always happen, then it was the over-optimism rather than the moral degeneracy of the workers that was to blame. It was an over-optimism that was not surprising, since the alternative was the anticipation of dependence on charity or public relief, and with it a drastic reduction of self-esteem. The 'failure' of working-class savers to realize, after a number of burial insurance lapses, that they were incapable of maintaining policy payments was in fact an indication of their financial optimism, or their refusal to accept the idea of economic dependence.

The seven-day time horizon of the poor that Mrs Bosanquet bemoaned was a myth—almost everyone indulged in some club saving and some credit purchasing that extended beyond the weekly cycle. But because the financial status of the household was uncertain from week to week, there was little point in embarking upon long-term plans for large-scale accumulation, since they would almost certainly fail. Similarly, there was scant incentive to save any excess income that might be left over at the end of the week, since there was a good chance that it would be required in the near future. If the money was put in the savings bank, for instance, its liquidity was reduced (at least before 1905) but it did not earn interest, since that was only paid on multiples of £1 invested for a twelve-month period. It could be better spent on the purchase of some good that at least provided a service until sold or pawned. Middle-class people were seldom able to comprehend this behaviour because they had little need for or experience of the mortgage and resale market for second-hand goods. Nor could they appreciate that in small-scale borrowing, saving, or spending on durable goods, workers were demonstrating not their fecklessness but their true desire for financial stability. It was almost inevitable that the middle-class individualists would misunderstand the effect of pensions and national insurance on working-class thrift, because they failed so often even to identify thrifty behaviour, resting content to describe that which they did not do themselves as improvident, short-sighted, thoughtless, inefficient, and degenerate. Their economic outlook on the world was a curious amalgam; they believed in the efficiency of a free market untrammelled by state interference, yet at the same time they viewed the majority of economic agents—the workers—as being incapable of responding to economic forces in an efficient and self-interested way. This was a moral problem, the solution to which was the moral re-education of the poor. They could not comprehend that a middle-class economic outlook might be inappropriate to working-class economic circumstances.

If the broad institutional forms and methods of working-class credit and thrift were determined by these economic circumstances, the specific choices between varieties of these institutions were not. Economic rationality determined that savings or borrowings be paid for in small weekly instalments, that planning should be over the short run, that long-term aims of 'accumulating' one's way out of the working class be generally dismissed as impractical. But economic rationality did not cause burial insurance to be thought of as a call on income ahead of sickness insurance, or a Sunday suit to be valued more than a tablecloth. To understand the value system within the boundaries set by economic factors, the social structure of working-class life must be looked at. At the heart of this social structure lay the idea of personal competition.

This was not competition to rise from the ranks, to acquire the traits of the bourgeoisie (though there was a desire to acquire some of the material trappings), but rather to establish a position or status within the ranks. Some historians have been so beguiled by the intensity of the middle-class proclamation of 'independence', 'respectability', 'thrift', that they feel these terms were part of a language and value system imposed on workers. But twenty-five years ago Richard Hoggart was pleading for caution:

There is, I think, a tendency among some writers on the working-classes to think of all who aim at thrift and cleanliness as imitators of the lower middle-classes, as in some way traitors to their own class, anxious to get out of it. Conversely, those who do not make this effort tend to be regarded as more honest and less servile than those who do. But cleanliness, thrift and self-respect arise more from a concern not to drop down, not to succumb to the environment, than from an anxiety to go up.[15]

Thrift made as much sense to the worker as to the clerk or the banker, because none of them would willingly contemplate a fall in their physical standards or social standing. But the fear of the banker was not that of sinking to the level of a wage-earner, nor the hope of the worker that of rising to the position of banker; hopes and fears were articulated with reference to points of comparison nearby.

The narrowness of the social spectrum of each individual was reflected and emphasized by the importance of community. This is difficult to detail from contemporary sources because, as François Bédarida has recently noted, the early social surveys were based on local government administrative units, not on neighbourhood morphology, and it was not really until after the Second World War that an anthropological approach to the social survey broke down this rigid analytical framework.[16] Some of the work of oral historians is useful for describing personal perceptions of the boundaries of community, and of competition within the community. Michael Winstanley's study of Victorian and Edwardian Kent led him to conclude:

People were slotted into the appropriate rung on the social ladder by a variety of factors: their job, income, cleanliness, material welfare, whether they had lace curtains up, whether they had a table cloth or

[15] Richard Hoggart, *The Uses of Literacy* (Harmondsworth, 1958), p. 78.
[16] François Bédarida, 'La vie de quartier en Angleterre: enquêtes empiriques et approches théoriques', *Le Mouvement Social* (Jan.–Mar. 1982), no. 118, pp. 12–18.

a newspaper on their dining table, whether they frequented the pub or not, and most important of all, where they lived ... The physical layout of the town, therefore, reflected the divisions within it. Each town consisted in reality of a cluster of separate little communities each operating its own set of rules and living apart from the rest of society.[17]

Writing of the community of Rothschild Buildings, Jerry White says, 'the boundaries of the area were clear cut and some people strayed outside them hardly at all. Knowledge even of the rest of the East End was sometimes very limited.'[18] One resident of Edwardian Wapping recalled that 'if you crossed the Dock Bridge, or lived beyond it, you were said to be "on the other side". Neither the grown-ups nor the children "on the other side" had anything to do with us. They were a community on their own and so were we, although we were all in one parish.'[19] This intense isolationism was reported by Mrs Pember Reeves of the working-class inhabitants of Lambeth:

A family who have lived for years in one street are recognized up and down the length of that street as people to be helped in time of trouble. These respectable but very poor people live over a morass of such intolerable poverty that they unite instinctively to save those known to them from falling into it. A family which moves two miles away is completely lost to view. They never write and there is no time and no money for visiting. Neighbours forget them.[20]

Isolationism fostered a sense of social exclusivity. Arthur Harding's wife prevented her children playing with the boys and girls from around the corner because, living in a terraced house, she considered her family to be above those living in the adjacent flats.[21] Ron Barnes records how one of his working-class grandmothers looked upon the other as 'one of the upper classes' because, though coming from the same area of the East End, she had a little more money (thanks largely to a widow's pension) and a slightly higher status. But this was in a community where even single streets were divided by their

[17] Michael Winstanley, *Life in Kent at the Turn of the Century* (Folkestone, 1978), pp. 165–6.
[18] White, *Rothschild Buildings*, p. 137.
[19] Foakes, *Between High Walls*, p. 22.
[20] Pember Reeves, *Round About a Pound a Week*, pp. 39–40.
[21] Samuel, *Arthur Harding*, pp. 224–5.

226

inhabitants into 'rough' and 'respectable' ends.[22] In his oral
history study of Edwardian Britain, Paul Thompson remarks
that:

No firm lines can be drawn to separate the different styles of life
within the urban working classes, for each merged into the next. Even
the generally recognized distinction between the rough and respectable was a flexible one, raised or lowered according to the standpoint
of the observer.[23]

Competition was based on being able to demonstrate more
respectability or social worth than the next man, but not necessarily more than the man in the next street, since he might be
living in a quite different social environment. Respectability
was a relative term, not a definitive position, and what might
be respectable to some would be shocking to others. Respectability was conditioned by where one lived, what one did, and
what one owned, and all three were themselves determined by
money; as Thorstein Veblen wrote in 1899, 'the basis on which
good repute in any highly organized industrial community ultimately rests is pecuniary strength'.[24] Pecuniary strength had to
be displayed effectively if the maximum amount of social
advantage were to be gained from it, and it was not surprising,
therefore, that some of the working-class savings institutions
that provided financial security were also manipulated to display this security. The Oddfellows and Foresters, the trade
unionists, the co-operators, accumulated a vast and colourful
paraphernalia of banners, sashes, and medals to distinguish
their processions through town. Being known as an Oddfellow
or 'in the Buffs' was a much more significant social cachet than
simply being thought of as financially self-sufficient. Since it
was so difficult to maintain financial self-sufficiency on a precarious working-class wage without resort to some mutual
insurance organization, membership of these organizations
came to be an accepted way both of obtaining and of signifying
pecuniary strength. The other main way of doing this was by
accumulating goods and indulging in specific acts of conspicuous consumption.

The importance of the Sunday suit in working-class life, both

[22] Barnes, *Coronation Cups and Jam Jars*, pp. 31–43.
[23] Paul Thompson, *The Edwardians* (London, 1977), p. 54.
[24] Veblen, *Leisure Class*, p. 84.

as an indicator of status and as a realizable asset, has been discussed in some detail; other highly visible goods, like net curtains, could function in the same way. In the East End of London, where a curtained window implied a certain degree of status and financial sufficiency, the curtains could be paid for weekly by those households which could not afford outright purchase but wished to acquire the prestige.[25] In Worktown, curtains were for seeing, not using; one woman remarked to a Mass-Observation interviewer that she was 'amazed at curtains being put up in rooms where they could not be seen from the street'.[26]

Within each street there was a curious mixture of neighbourliness and isolation. As the extract from Mrs Pember Reeves given above makes clear, there was a strong element of genuine charity among the very poor, a feeling (based in part, perhaps, on keen calculation) that those on hard times should be assisted. There was also a vibrant street life—local gossip and scandal to be exchanged, children to be watched over, infants to be nursed—yet neighbours could pose a threat, they could end up prying. Therefore, despite the charity, the gossip, the strong sense of community,

the inhabitants keep themselves to themselves, and watch the doings of the other people from behind window curtains, knowing perfectly that every incoming and outgoing of their own is also jealously recorded by critical eyes up and down the street.[27]

Margaret Loane, whose work as a district nurse allowed her a privileged view of the domestic life of working-class households, felt that:

Secrecy is strongly developed among the poor, and although often sustained by deceitfulness and even fraud, is closely connected with self-respect and independence. Wages and the expenditure of money are always shrouded in thick darkness, but all details connected with food are trebly secure from observant eyes, however kindly ... Schoolchildren are constantly forbidden to tell one another what they have had to eat—unless occassionally, when there may be something to boast of.[28]

[25] Samuel, *Arthur Harding*, pp. 87–8.
[26] M-O, box W17. Bundle headed 'Budgets: Expenditure', paper GW 10/11/38.
[27] Pember Reeves, *Round About a Pound a Week*, pp. 3–4.
[28] Loane, *From their point of view*, pp. 74–5.

Alexander Paterson explained the jealousy and mutuality of South Londoners before the First World War as follows:

It is, perhaps, the only form left to each family of asserting a certain inherent pride, for it is by contrast that men most easily come to respect themselves. By mutual contrast the families are each led to think themselves a superior unit set in a strangely inferior company. But this is only the theory on which they rely to prove their own importance, and it rarely colours their daily conduct or their natural kindness.[29]

The mutual contrast was heightened at times of traditional social display. The traditions varied from place to place—in Lancashire, for instance, there was the Whit parade, when children would process in their new summer clothes—and they changed over time as new patterns, such as the seaside holiday, emerged. One form of display that seemed to be more or less universal was the celebration of death. Mrs Bosanquet, with her typical mixture of insight and disapproval, wrote:

the greatest festival of all is the funeral. The women especially are incorrigible in this particular form of extravagance, and one sympathizes with them in so far as they regard it as the last mark of respect in their power. But mingled with this not unnatural feeling there is a great love of display, a desire to exceed the expectations of the neighbours, and a determination to make the most of the opportunity.[30]

Sunday suits were worn, doorsteps scrubbed, curtains hung, ornaments collected and put on view, friendly society feasts attended, not to appeal to the sentiments of passing middle-class observers, but to impress the peer group, the local community. As one worker explained, 'if you were keeping up with the Jones's, you had a piano and had your front door open so that people could hear'.[31] It was through these actions that people were informally assessed and placed on the ladder of social status, and that is why great efforts were made to maintain this behaviour even in straitened circumstances when it could not really be afforded. Position and status were nothing if they could not be manifested by some possession or activity;

---

[29] Alexander Paterson, *Across the Bridges* (London, 1911), p. 45.
[30] Bosanquet, *Rich and Poor*, p. 124.
[31] John Langley, *Always a Layman* (Brighton, 1976), p. 11.

this is why working-class life appeared so materialistic to out-side observers. In London in 1911, Paterson felt that:

there is a well-nigh universal tendency to cling to the visible and con-crete, and ignore all else. . . . A laurel-wreath or a letter of commen-dation is nothing to a silver cup and a gilt-lettered page. There must be 'something to show' for every effort . . . Goodness that is not trans-lated into tangible symbols and rewards is an alien plant.[32]

Thirty years later, Mass-Observation found the same senti-ments to exist in the pub life of Worktown, and in the clubs, societies, and games organized in each pub. Behaviour was 'governed by motives of exceeding and beating the other man, of being the best of the group. And it must be recognized in a concrete form, by regalias and medals, by prizes and cups and diplomas.'[33] Friendly society regalia was finely graded, so that every rank in the hierarchy, and progress from one to another, could be seen clearly by all members. Even so, some societies had difficulty in controlling their members' desires for ever more flamboyant aprons, medallions, and sashes.[34] As Stephen Yeo has pointed out in his study of Reading at the turn of the century, 'devices for maintaining discipline, exciting mutual emulation, or creating a hierarchy which looked attractive to climb, were deliberately employed ... Badges, tests, certifi-cates, ceremonies, uniforms multiplied from Sunday School upwards.'[35]

Patterns of display were not static, and changes in economic circumstances could alter the way in which people demon-strated their pecuniary strength. The most striking example of this is the stagnation of membership and decline in sociability of affiliated friendly societies in the inter-war years; once national insurance provided sickness benefit for all, there was little social advantage to be gained from parading the fact of membership of private insurance schemes—better to save cash in the post office for the down-payment on some consumer dur-ables to be bought on HP. As mutual insurance became a less significant indicator of financial and social status, so other

[32] Paterson, *Across the Bridges*, pp. 47–8.
[33] Mass-Observation, *The Pub and the People*, p. 312.
[34] See, for instance, *AOF Quarterly Report* (Oct. 1892), p. 5.
[35] Yeo, *Religion*, p. 167.

forms of expenditure took its place, but the element of display continued, and continues still.

Whether changes in the nature of local communities after the First World War affected the patterns of display indulged in it is impossible to say. The growing national influence of a metropolitan culture disseminated by the popular press, and latterly by broadcasting, together with an increase in the geographical mobility of the population, may well have weakened local hierarchies; greater economic security, to a large extent the result of state welfare policies, has allowed families to rely less on sharing risks with others and given the opportunity for more self-centred, domestic enjoyment of wealth. Yet even in areas like new housing estates, where there was little sense of community life and little evidence of mutuality, the competitive pressures of working-class life lived on through the 1930s with as much force as ever. In their study of the Bedminster estate on the outskirts of Bristol, Jevons and Madge reported a case where, 'when the wife took the instructions of the Housing Department seriously, and installed a bed in the front downstairs room, the remarks and curiosity of her neighbours quickly drove the bed upstairs again. The strong feeling against having beds in the parlour is based on social prestige.'[36] Ruth Durant's survey of social conditions in Watling found that 'many Watling residents, men as well as women, are, in fact, deterred from mixing with others because of the embarrassing consciousness that their outfits are shabby'.[37] Working-class housing estates which from afar appeared to be as socially homogeneous as they were architecturally, on closer inspection showed themselves to be riven with minor distinctions which were used competitively to establish social gradations. Jevons and Madge concluded that:

It is easy to think of all families with approximately the same incomes as constituting a single uniform class, but experience indicates numerous rifts and social distinctions. These are partly based on what appear to be very small wage differences. More important factors are differences in the standard of education, the type of work and, particularly, the degree of security enjoyed. It is not pleasant to be

[36] Rosamund Jevons and John Madge, *Housing Estates* (Bristol, 1946), pp. 51–2.
[37] Ruth Durant, *Watling* (London, 1939), p. 89.

reminded of persistent insecurity by having as neighbours casual or unemployed workers, whose worries and cares are unavoidably infectious.[38]

A necessary condition for these social distinctions is the existence of a coherent and stable community culture within which the display and competition can take place on known terms. This is as true for high society as it is for low, but the cultural norms will be different and the competition will follow different paths. In a society in which there are few economic constraints, the competition will be based on style and fashion; where financial constraints loom large, less subtle distinctions are used— competition is based on possession and wealth and economic security. The tension in working-class life between collective action and inter-personal competition has been underemphasized in most studies of late nineteenth and early twentieth-century social history, because of a bias in the research towards production rather than consumption, towards earning rather than spending. A close analysis of the domestic economy tends to undermine the views of monolithic class structures which commonly, and not surprisingly, emerge from studies of the workplace; the working class is decomposed into many strata with slightly different value systems, aspirations, interests, and incomes. The economic basis of working-class life—the sale of labour-power week by week or day by day—and the economic insecurity consequent upon this sort of wage-labour, certainly prompted collective action in terms of insurance, saving, and borrowing, but the existence of mutual institutions within a working-class community is not in itself an incontrovertible demonstation of the 'basic collective idea' which Raymond Williams sees as the essence of working-class culture.[39] Although E. P. Thompson nominates the friendly society as one influence making towards the growth in working-class consciousness,[40] and Eric Hobsbawm regards the unbroken increase in co-operative society membership from 1880 as an element and indicator of a 'growing class consciousness' which

[38] Jevons and Madge, *Housing Estates*, p. 69.
[39] Raymond Williams, *Culture and Society, 1780–1950* (Harmondsworth, 1961), p. 313.
[40] E. P. Thompson, *The Making of the English Working Class* (Harmondsworth, 1968), pp. 456–69.

united workers of all strata and sections,[41] a detailed examination of the economic and social role of these institutions points
to as much or more concern with self as with class or com-
monality. The belief that class-consciousness is manifested by
formal, paid-up mutuality is based upon a rigidly deterministic
view of the social psychology of workers which allows little or
no role for family, community, or neighbourhood in the formation of working-class attitudes. Hobsbawm asserts that 'local
differences did not run counter to the sense of a single class consciousness',[42] but does not explain how this class-consciousness
was to rise above the minutiae of keeping up appearances for
the sake of the neighbours, and of outdoing them if possible.
Mere reference to the size of membership of mutual organizations or the proclamations of leaders is not a good guide to the
interests and actions of the majority of members, as the study of
the co-operative movement in chapter 5 demonstrated.

To examine and understand the interests of working people,
to discover 'what really mattered' to them, requires an analysis
of the choices they made. This book has looked at one particular set of choices working people made about money matters—
choices that were important because they helped to determine
the material conditions of life, and they revealed something
about people's perceptions of their own future, their hopes and
fears. The range of choices was severely constrained by the low
and unpredictable income of most workers; this forced them to
share risks, pool funds, and pay by instalments in an attempt to
attain a reasonable degree of economic security and independence. The security and independence was desired both for
what it prevented—reliance on charity or public assistance—
and for what it permitted—the maintenance or improvement
of personal status within the local community. Although the
means adopted were sometimes mutual and collective, the goal
was personal and competitive; self-help sometimes, self-interest
always.

[41] Eric Hobsbawm, *et al.*, *The Forward March of Labour Halted?* (London, 1981), p. 8.
[42] Ibid., p. 10.

Bibliography

I. UNPUBLISHED SOURCES

(a) Archives

Britannic Assurance Company, Birmingham: Policy Registers.

Calderdale District Record Office: Friendly Society Records.

Co-operative Union Library, Manchester: G. J. Holyoake Papers.

Greater London Council Record Office: Charity Organisation Society Case Papers; Royal Standard Benefit Society Membership Registers.

Guildhall Library, London: St Andrew-by-the-Wardrobe with St Anne, Blackfriar Provident Clothing Fund Rules and Receipt Books; George Attenborough (Pawnbroker) Receipt Books.

Liverpool Municipal Library: Blackburn Philanthropic Friendly Collecting Society Membership Registers.

Mass-Observation Archive, University of Sussex: File Reports, Directive Replies, and Worktown Survey.

Pearl Assurance Company, London, Undated typescript by Arthur James Barry, 'Notes on the History of the Pearl Assurance Co. Ltd'.

Prudential Assurance Company Library, London: Annual Reports of the Company.

Public Record Office, Kew: Friendly Society Papers; National Savings Committee Papers.

In the private possession of Mr Kenneth Hudson, Bath: Transcripts of interviews with pawnbrokers.

(b) Theses, Reports, and Papers

Goldstrom, J. M., 'The cost of disposal of the dead in Metropolitan London, 1830–1870'. Appendix to Social Science Research Council Final Report on grant HR 2662, 1977.

Johnson, Paul A., 'Credit and Thrift: working class household budget management in Britain, 1870–1939'. Oxford University D.Phil. thesis, 1982.

MacKinnon, Mary E., 'Poverty and Policy: the English poor law, 1860–1910'. Oxford University D.Phil. thesis, June 1984.

Thompson, David William, 'Provision for the elderly in England, 1830–1908'. Cambridge University Ph.D. thesis, October 1980.

Whiteside, Noel, 'Wages and Welfare: trade union benefits and

industrial bargaining before the first world war'. Unpublished
paper, December 1983.

2. PUBLISHED SOURCES

(a) Periodicals

Aberdeen Savings Bank Reports.
Assurance Herald.
Ancient Order of Foresters Annual Directory.
Ancient Order of Foresters Quarterly Reports.
Building Societies Yearbook.
Co-operative Congress Annual Reports.
Co-operative News.
The Economist.
Foresters' Miscellany.
Hire-Purchase News.
Hire Traders' Guide and Record.
Hospitals Yearbook.
Independent Order of Oddfellows Quarterly Reports.

Insurance Agent and Insurance Review.
Insurance Mail.
Insurance Mail Yearbook.
Journal of Domestic Appliances and Sewing Machine Gazette.
Liverpool Citizen.
Meliora.
Oddfellow's Magazine.
Pawnbrokers' Gazette.
Pawnbrokers' Magazine and Record.
Pawnbrokers' Market.
Quarterly Review.
Reader and Workers' Advocate.
The Times.

(b) British Parliamentary Papers

(i) Series

Abstract of Statistics.
Abstract of Labour Statistics.
Judicial Statistics.
Annual Reports of the Chief Registrar of Friendly Societies.
Annual Reports of Customs and Excise.
Annual Reports of the Industrial Assurance Commissioner.
Annual Reports of the Inland Revenue.
Annual Reports of the National Savings Committee.
Annual Reports of the Postmaster-General.
Statement of Accounts of Life Insurance and Annuity Business.
House of Commons Debates, third, fourth, and fifth series.

(ii) Special Reports and Returns

Select Committee on Investments for the Savings of the Middle and
Working Classes, PP 1850 xix (508).
Select Committee on Pawnbrokers [Ayrton Cttee.], PP 1870 viii
(377).

Report of the Poor Law Board, 1869–70, PP 1870 xxxv (C. 123).

Royal Commission on Friendly and Benefit Building Societies [Northcote Cmmn.].

First Report, PP 1871 xxv (C. 452).

Second Report, PP 1872 xxvi (C. 514).

Third Report, PP 1873 xxii (C. 842).

Fourth Report, PP 1874 xxiii (C. 961).

Reports of Assistant Commissioners for Ireland and Wales, PP 1874 xxiii (C. 995).

Reports of Assistant Commissioners for Cheshire, Derbyshire, etc., PP 1874 xxiii (C. 996).

Reports of Assistant Commissioners for the Southern and Eastern Counties, PP 1874 xxiii (C. 997).

Select Committee on the Pawnbrokers' Bill, PP 1872 xii (288).

Statement showing estimated number of Deposits in the Post Office Savings Banks of the undermentioned Amounts for the year 1879, PP 1880 xl (342 Sess. 2).

Report of the Chief Registrar of Friendly Societies on the Royal Liver Friendly Society, PP 1886 lxi (C. 4706).

Select Committee on National Provident Insurance [Maxwell Cttee.], PP 1884–5 x (270); PP 1886 xi (208); PP 1887 xi (257).

House of Lords Select Committee on Poor Law Relief [Kimberley Cttee.], PP 1888 xv (363).

Interim Report of the Commissioner appointed to inquire into the affairs of the Trustee Savings Bank in Cardiff, PP 1888 xliv (C. 5287).

Select Committee on the Friendly Societies Act, 1875, PP 1889 x (304).

Select Committee on Yorkshire Provident Insurance Company, PP 1889 xvi (262).

Returns of Expenditure by Working Men, PP 1889 lxxxiv (C. 5861).

Royal Commission on Labour, Assistant Commissioners' Reports on the Agricultural Labourer, PP 1893–4 xxxv (C. 6894).

Royal Commission on the Aged Poor [Aberdare Cmmn.], PP 1895 xiv (C. 7684).

Select Committee on Moneylending, PP 1897 xi (364); PP 1898 x (260).

Departmental Committee appointed to consider the question of encouraging the Life Assurance system of the Post Office [Farrer Cttee.], PP 1908 xxv (311).

Royal Commission on the Poor Law [Hamilton Cmmn.].

Appendix, volume i, PP 1909 xxxix (Cd. 4625).

Appendix, volume iii, PP 1909 xl (Cd. 4755).

Appendix, volume v, PP 1909 xli (Cd. 4888).

Appendix volume vii, PP 1910 xlvii (Cd. 5035).

Appendix, volume xvii, PP 1909 xliii (Cd. 4690).

Report of the Committee on War Loans for the Small Saver [Montagu Cttee.], PP 1916 xv (Cd. 8179).

Departmental Committee on the Business of Industrial Assurance Companies and Collecting Societies [Parmoor Cttee.], PP 1920 xviii (Cmd. 614).

Report of the Committee of Enquiry into Savings Certificates, PP 1923 xii (Cmd. 1865).

Committee on Industrial Assurance and Assurance on the lives of children under ten years of age [Cohen Cttee.], PP 1932–3 xiii (Cmd. 4376).

Social Insurance and Allied Services [Beveridge Report], PP 1942–3 vi (Cmd. 6404).

Report of the Committee on Consumer Credit [Crowther Cttee.], PP 1970–71 (Cmnd. 4596).

(c) *Books and Articles*

Abel-Smith, Brian, *The Hospitals 1800–1948* (London, 1964).

Ackland, Joseph, 'The Failure of Co-operation', *Economic Review* vii (1897).

Acland, A. H. D., and Jones, Ben, *Working Men Co-operators* (London, 1884).

—— *Working Men Co-operators* (6th edn., revised by Julia P. Madams, Manchester, 1932).

Anderson, Gregory, *Victorian Clerks* (Manchester, 1976).

Ashton, T. S., 'Fluctuations in Savings Bank Deposits', *Transactions of the Manchester Statistical Society* (1929–30).

Atkinson, A. B., and Harrison, A. J., *Distribution of Personal Wealth in Britain* (Cambridge, 1978).

Aves, Ernest, *Co-operative Industry* (London, 1907).

Baernreither, J. M., *English Associations of Working Men* (London, 1899).

Bailey, Peter, '"Will the real Bill Banks please stand up?" Towards a role analysis of mid-Victorian working-class respectability', *Journal of Social History* xii (1979).

Barnes, Ron, *Coronation Cups and Jam Jars* (London, 1976).

Barnsby, G. J., *Social Conditions in the Black Country, 1800–1900* (Wolverhampton, 1980).

Bédarida, François, 'La vie de quartier en Angleterre: enquêtes empiriques et approches théoriques', *Le Mouvement Social*, no. 118 (1982).

Bell, Lady, *At the Works* (London, 1907).

Bellman, Sir Harold, 'Building Societies—some economic aspects', *Economic Journal* xliii (March 1933).

—— *The Building Society Movement* (London, 1927).

Benson, John, 'The Thrift of English Coalminers, 1860–1895', *Economic History Review*, 2nd series, xxxi (1978).

—— *British Coalminers in the Nineteenth Century* (Dublin, 1980).

—— *The Penny Capitalists* (Dublin, 1983).

Beveridge, Lord, and Wells, A. F. (eds.), *The Evidence for Voluntary Action* (London, 1949).

Blackley, W. L., 'National Insurance: a cheap, practical and popular means of abolishing poor rates', *The Nineteenth Century* iv (1878).

Blake, John, *Memories of Old Poplar* (London, 1977).

Boddy, Martin, *The Building Societies* (London, 1980).

Bonner, Arnold, *British Co-operation* (2nd edn., Manchester, 1970).

Booth, Charles, *Life and Labour of the People in London* (London, 1889–1903).

—— *Pauperism and the Endowment of Old Age* (London, 1892).

—— *The Aged Poor in England and Wales* (London, 1894).

Booth, 'General' William, *In Darkest England and the Way Out* (London, 1890).

Bosanquet, Helen, 'The Burden of Small Debts', *Economic Journal* vi (1896).

—— *Rich and Poor* (London, 2nd edn., 1898).

—— *The Strength of the People* (London, 1902).

—— Review of Mrs Pember Reeves, 'Round About a Pound a Week', *Economic Journal* xxiv (March 1914).

Bowley, A. L., and Hogg, Margaret, *Has Poverty Diminished?* (London, 1925).

Brabrook, E. W., *Provident Societies and Industrial Welfare* (London, 1898).

Braithwaite, Constance, *The Voluntary Citizen* (London, 1938).

Brett, R. Dallas, *Usury in Britain* (London, 1946).

Brown, K. D. (ed.), *Essays in Anti-Labour History* (London, 1974).

Brown, W. Henry, *A Century of London Co-operation* (London, 1928).

Bullen, Frank, *Confessions of a Tradesman* (London, 1908).

Burghes, Louie, *Living from Hand to Mouth* (Poverty Pamphlet 50, Family Service Unit, London, Dec. 1980).

Burnett, John, *A Social History of Housing 1815–1970* (London, 1980).

Butler, Violet, *Social Conditions in Oxford* (London, 1912).

Callaghan, Thomas, *A Lang Way to the Pa'nshop* (Newcastle upon Tyne, 1978).

Cannan, Edwin, 'The Stigma of Pauperism', *Economic Review* v (July 1895).

Caplovitz, David, *The Poor Pay More* (New York, 1963).

Carr-Saunders, A. M., Sargant Florence, P., *et al.*, *Consumers' Co-operation in Great Britain* (revised edn., London, 1942).

Casson, Herbert N., *Debts! How to Collect Them* (London, 1930).

Chamberlain, Mary, *Fenwomen* (London, 1975).

Chapman, S. D. (ed.), *The History of Working-Class Housing: A Symposium* (Newton Abbot, 1971).

Charity Organisation Society, *Report on the best means of dealing with exceptional distress* (London, 1886).

Chiozza Money, L. G., *Riches and Poverty* (3rd edn., London, 1906).

Cleary, E. J., *The Building Society Movement* (London, 1965).

Clegg, Cyril, *Friend in Deed* (London, 1958).

Clegg, H. A., Fox, Alan, and Thompson, A. F., *A History of British Trade Unions since 1889. Volume 1, 1889–1910* (Oxford, 1964).

Cohen, Joseph L., *Social Insurance Unified* (London, 1924).

Cohen, Percy, *The British System of Social Insurance* (London, 1932).

Committee on Old Age Pensions, *Old Age Pensions* (London, 1903).

Cox, Jas., *Royal Standard Benefit Society. The History of the Society, 1828–1928, with part 2, 1929–1966 by A. C. W. Mell* (London, 1967).

Crick, W. F., *The Economics of Instalment Trading and Hire-Purchase* (London, 1929).

Crossick, Geoffrey (ed.), *The Lower Middle Class in Britain* (London, 1977).

—— *An Artisan Elite in Victorian Society* (London, 1978).

Davies, Maud E., *Life in an English Village* (London, 1909).

Deans, James, *Credit Trading in Co-operative Societies* (Glasgow, 1903).

Dearle, Norman B., *Problems of Unemployment in the London Building Trades* (London, 1908).

Dennis, Norman, Henriques, Fernando, and Slaughter, Clifford, *Coal is our Life* (London, 1956).

Douglas, Mary, and Isherwood, Baron, *The World of Goods* (London, 1979).

Dunnage, J. A., *The Modern Shylock* (London, *c.*1926).

Durant, Ruth, *Watling* (London, 1939).

Economic Club, *Family Budgets: Being the income and expenses of twenty-eight British households 1891–1894* (London, 1896).

Ede, W. Moore, 'Pensions for the Aged', *Economic Review* ii (April 1892).

Ehrlich, Cyril, *The Piano, A History* (London, 1976).

Elkington, George, *The National Building Society 1849–1934* (Cambridge, 1935).

Elliot, W. H., *Reflections on Credit Trading* (Manchester, 1909).

Elliott, Sydney R., *Co-operative Store-keeping* (London, 1925).

Feinstein, C. H., *National Income, Expenditure and Output of the U.K., 1855–1965* (Cambridge, 1972).

'Fieldman, A.', *The Industrial Assurance Agents' Companion* (London, *c*.1935).

Foakes, Grace, *Between High Walls* (London, 1972).

Foley, Alice, *A Bolton Childhood* (Manchester, 1973).

Gamble, Rose, *Chelsea Child* (London, 1979).

Gamgee, Sampson, *The Origin of Hospital Saturday* (Birmingham, 1882).

Garnett, R. G., *A Century of Co-operative Insurance* (London, 1968).

Gilbert, Bentley B., 'The Decay of Nineteenth-Century Provident Institutions and the Coming of Old Age Pensions in Great Britain', *Economic History Review*, 2nd series, xvii (1965).

—— *The Evolution of National Insurance in Great Britain* (London, 1966).

Gisborne, Frederick H., *Life Assurance. How to Conduct an Agency* (Windsor, *c*.1897).

Gonner, E. C. K., *Interest and Saving* (London, 1906).

Gorer, Geoffrey, *Death, Grief and Mourning* (London, 1965).

Gosden, P. H. J. H., *The Friendly Societies in England 1815–1875* (Manchester, 1961).

—— *Self-Help* (London, 1973).

Grant, Clara, *Farthing Bundles* (London, *c*.1931).

Gray, J. C., *The System of Credit as Practised by Co-operative Societies* (Manchester, 1889).

Gray, R. Q., *The Labour Aristocracy in Victorian Edinburgh* (Oxford, 1976).

Greenwood, James, *Low Life Deeps* (London, 1876).

Greenwood, Walter, *Love on the Dole* (Harmondsworth, 1969).

Grossmith, George and Weedon, *The Diary of a Nobody* (Harmondsworth, 1977).

Guide Book of the Friendly Societies Registry Office (HMSO, 1912).

Hanson, C. G., 'Craft Unions, Welfare Benefits, and the case for Trade Union law reform, 1867–75', *Economic History Review*, 2nd series, xxviii (1975).

Hardaker, A., *Brief History of Pawnbroking* (London, 1892).

Harrison, Brian, *Peaceable Kingdom* (Oxford, 1982).

Heales, H. C., and Kirby, C. H., *Housing Finance in Great Britain* (London, 1938).

Heath, F. G., *Peasant Life in the West of England* (London, 1880).

—— *British Rural Life and Labour* (London, 1911).

Henderson, Thomas, *The Savings Bank of Glasgow: One Hundred Years of Thrift* (Glasgow, 1936).

Hewins, W. A. S., 'The Co-operative Movement', *Economic Review* i (1891).

—— *Apologia of an Imperialist* (London, 1929).

Higgins, H., *The District Manager* (London, 1924).

Hilton, John, *Rich Man, Poor Man* (London, 1944).

Hinton, J. P., *Britain's First Municipal Savings Bank* (London, 1927).

Hobsbawm, Eric, *et al.*, *The Forward March of Labour Halted?* (London, 1981).

Hoggart, Richard, *The Uses of Literacy* (Harmondsworth, 1958).

Honigsbaum, Frank, *The Division in British Medicine* (London, 1979).

Horne, H. Oliver, *A History of Savings Banks* (OUP, London, 1947).

Hospital Almoners' Association, *The Hospital Almoner* (London, 1935).

Hough, J. A., *Dividend on Co-operative Purchases* (Manchester, 1936).

Hudson, Bramwell, *History of Co-operation in Cainscross and District* (Manchester, *c.*1913).

Hudson, Kenneth, *Pawnbroking. An Aspect of British Social History* (London, 1982).

Hughes, Thomas, and Neale, E. V., *Manual for Co-operators* (Manchester, 1881).

Hunt, E. H., *British Labour History 1815–1914* (London, 1981).

Hurry, Jamieson B., *Poverty and its Vicious Circle* (London, 2nd edn. 1921).

Industrial Life Offices, *Industrial Assurance Explained—A Reply to Criticisms* (London, 1944).

—— *Twenty Questions about Industrial Life Assurance* (London, 1949).

Insurance Guide and Handbook (London, 5th edn., 1912).

Jasper, A. S., *A Hoxton Childhood* (London, 1969).

Jebb, Eglantyne, *Cambridge: A brief study in social questions* (Cambridge, 1906).

Jevons, Rosamund, and Madge, John, *Housing Estates* (Bristol, 1946).

Johnson, Paul, 'Self-Help versus State Help: Old Age Pensions and Personal Savings in Great Britain, 1906–1937', *Explorations in Economic History* (Oct. 1984).

Joint Anti-Credit Committee, *Suggestions for the control and limitation of credit trading in Co-operative societies* (Manchester, 1912).

Jones, Ben, 'Co-operation and Profit-Sharing', *Economic Journal* ii (1892).

Jones, D. Caradog, *Social Survey of Merseyside* (Liverpool, 1934).

Katona, George, *Psychological Economics* (New York, 1975).

Kelsey, H. H., *3000%, or the borrower's book on money-lending* (London, 1926).

Lady Margaret Hall Settlement, *Social Services in North Lambeth and Kennington* (OUP, London, 1939).

Lancet, The Battle of the Clubs (London, 1896).

Langley, John, *Always a Layman* (Brighton, 1976).

Langley, Kathleen M., 'The Distribution of Capital in Private Hands in 1936–38 and 1946–47', *Bulletin of the Oxford Institute of Statistics* xii, no. 12 (Dec. 1950).

Leppington, C. H. d'E., 'The Charity Organisation System Today', *Economic Review* viii (January 1897).

Liverpool Joint Research Committee, *How the Casual Labourer Lives* (Liverpool, 1909).

Llewelyn Davies, Margaret, *Co-operation in Poor Neighbourhoods* (Women's Co-operative Guild, Manchester, 1899).

—— (ed.), *Life as we have known it* (London, 1977 reprint).

Loane, Margaret, *From their point of view* (London, 1908).

—— *Neighbours and Friends* (London, 1910).

—— *The Common Growth* (London, 1911).

Loch, C. S., *How to help cases of distress* (London, 1883).

—— (ed.), *Methods of Social Advance* (London, 1904).

Madge, Charles, 'War-time saving and spending—a district survey', *Economic Journal* i (June–Sept. 1940).

—— 'The Propensity to Save in Blackburn and Bristol', *Economic Journal* i (Dec. 1940).

—— *War-time pattern of saving and spending* (NIESR Occasional Paper iv, Cambridge, 1943).

Mallet, Sir Bernard, and George, C. Oswald, *British Budgets, 1913–14 to 1920–21* (London, 1929).

Mass-Observation, *The Pub and the People* (London, 1943).

Maxwell, Williams (ed.), *First Fifty Years of St. Cuthbert's Co-operative Association Ltd., 1859–1909* (Edinburgh, 1909).

McKendrick, Neil (ed.), *Historical Perspectives: Studies in English thought and society in honour of J. H. Plumb* (London, 1974).

McKibbin, R. I., 'Social Class and Social Observation in Edwardian England', *Transactions of the Royal Historical Society*, 5th Series, xxviii (1978).

Meacham, Standish, *A Life Apart* (London, 1977).

Memoranda for Life Assurance Agents (London, 8th edn. *c.*1892).

Mess, H. A., *Casual Labour at the Docks* (London, 1916).

Minkes, A. L., 'The Decline of Pawnbroking', *Economica* xx (Feb. 1953).

Mitchell, B. R., and Deane, Phyllis, *Abstract of British Historical Statistics* (Cambridge, 1962).

Moffrey, R. W., *A Century of Oddfellowship* (Manchester, 1910).

Morrah, Dermot, *A History of Industrial Life Assurance* (London, 1955).

Moss, Les, *Live and Learn* (Brighton, 1979).

Nash, V., *The Relation of Co-operative to Competitive Trading* (Manchester, *c.*1887).

National Committee of Organised Labour, *Ten Years' Work for Old Age Pensions, 1899–1909* (London, 1909).

Neal, Lawrence E., *Retailing and the Public* (London, 1932).

Neale, E. V., *The Economic Aspect of Co-operation* (Manchester, *c.*1884).

New Statesman iv, no. 101 (13 March 1915), 'Special supplement on Industrial Insurance by the Fabian Research Department', ed. S. Webb.

Newton, Arthur, *Years of Change* (London, 1974).

Ogden, J. H., *Failsworth Industrial Society Ltd. Jubilee History 1859–1909* (Manchester, 1909).

O'Mara, Pat, *Autobiography of a Liverpool Irish Slummy* (London, 1934).

Ormerod, J. Redman, *The Essentials to Success in Life Assurance* (London, 2nd edn. 1906).

Parry, Noel and Jose, *The Rise of the Medical Profession* (London, 1976).

Parry, Noel, Rustin, Michael, and Satyamurti, Carole (eds.), *Social Work, Welfare and the State* (London, 1979).

Paterson, Alexander, *Across the Bridges* (London, 1911).

Paton, D. N., Dunlop, J. C., and Inglis, E. M., *A Study of the Diet of the Labouring Classes in Edinburgh* (Edinburgh, 1901).

Paul, Albert, *Poverty—Hardship but Happiness* (Brighton, 1974).

Pember Reeves, Maud, *Round About a Pound a Week* (London, 1913).

Perth Savings Bank, *A Brief Sketch of the History, Aims and Practice of the Savings Bank of the County and City of Perth, 1815–1915* (Perth, 1915).

Phelps Brown, E. H., *A Century of Pay* (London, 1968).

Piachaud, David, *Do the poor pay more?* (Poverty Research Series 3, Child Poverty Action Group, London, Feb. 1974).

Pilgrim Trust, *Men Without Work* (Cambridge, 1938).

Pinker, Robert, *English Hospital Statistics 1861–1938* (London, 1966).

Potter, B., *The Co-operative Movement in Great Britain* (London, 1891).

Pownall, George H., *Savings Banks and their Relation to National Finance* (London, 1903).

Provident Societies Recommended (London, 1833).

Prudential, *A Century of Service* (London, 1948).

Puckle, Bertram S., *Funeral Customs; their origin and development* (London, 1926).

Radice, E. A., *Savings in Great Britain 1922–1935* (OUP, London, 1939).

Readshaw, T., *History of the Bishop Auckland Industrial Co-operative Flour and Provision Society Ltd. 1860–1910* (Manchester, 1910).

Redfern, Percy, *The New History of the C.W.S.* (London, 1938).

Roberts, Robert, *The Classic Slum* (Harmondsworth, 1973).

—— *A Ragged Schooling* (London, 1978).

Robinson, Joe, *The Life and Times of Francie Nichol of South Shields* (London, paperback edn. 1977).

Robinson, M. F., *The Spirit of Association* (London, 1913).

Robson, William A. (ed.), *Social Security* (London, 1943).

Rogers, Frederick, and Millar, Frederick, *Old Age Pensions* (London, 1903).

Routh, Guy, *Occupation and Pay in Great Britain, 1906–1979* (London, 1980).

Rowntree, B. Seebohm, *Poverty, A Study of Town Life* (London, 1901).

—— *How the Labourer Lives* (London, 1913).

—— *Poverty and Progress* (London, 1941).

Royal Liver, *A Brief Survey of the History, Objectives and Achievements of the Royal Liver Friendly Society* (Liverpool, 1950).

Samuel, Raphael, *East End Underworld 2: Chapters in the Life of Arthur Harding* (London, 1981).

Saxton, C. Clive, *Beveridge Report Criticised* (London, 1943).

Schulze-Gaevernitz, G. von, *Social Peace: A Study of the Trade Union Movement in England*, translated by C. M. Wicksteed (London, 1893).

Seligman, Edwin, R. A., *The Economics of Instalment Selling* (New York, 1927).

Shanas, Ethel, and Sussman, Marvin B. (eds.), *Family, Bureaucracy and the Elderly* (Durham, NC, 1977).

Sheppard, David K., *The Growth and Role of U.K. Financial Institutions 1880–1962* (London, 1971).

Sherwell, Arthur, *Life in West London* (London, 1897).

Sims, G. R. (ed.), *Living London* (London, 1902).

Sinclair, J. G., *Evils of Industrial Assurance* (London, 1932).

Smiles, Samuel, *Workmen's Earnings, Strikes and Savings* (London, 1861).

—— *Thrift* (revised edn., London, 1875).

—— *Self-Help* (revised edn., London, 1878).

Smith, F. B., *The People's Health 1830–1910* (London, 1979).

Smith, F. S., *Credit Trading in Retail Co-operative Societies* (Manchester, 1928).

Smith, Henry, *Retail Distribution* (OUP, London, 1937).

Snell, Lord, *Men, Movements and Myself* (London, 1936).

Spender, Humphrey, and Harrison, Tom, *Britain in the 1930s— Worktown by Camera* (Royal College of Art, London, 1975).

Spooner, M. C., *Emergency Funds and their Application* (London, c.1910).

Stedman Jones, Gareth, *Outcast London* (Oxford, 1971).

—— 'Working-Class Culture and Working-Class Politics in London, 1870–1900; Notes on the Re-making of the Working Class', *Journal of Social History* vii (1974).

Stone and Cox Industrial and Monthly Tables (London, 1928).

Stone, Richard, and Rowe, D. A., *The Measurement of Consumers' Expenditure and Behaviour in the United Kingdom 1920–1938, Vol. 2* (Cambridge, 1966).

Stratton, Revd J. Y., 'Farm Labourers, their Friendly Societies, and the Poor Law', *Journal of the Royal Agricultural Society*, 2nd Series, vi (1870).

Suthers, R. B., 'The Mystery of National Savings and Spendings', *The People's Year Book, 1931* (Fourteenth Annual of the English and Scottish Co-operative Wholesale Societies, Manchester, 1931).

Tebbutt, Melanie, *Making Ends Meet* (Leicester, 1983).

Thane, Pat (ed.), *The Origins of British Social Policy* (London, 1978).

——— 'Craft Unions, Welfare Benefits, and the Case for Trade Union Law Reform, 1867–75: A Comment', *Economic History Review*, 2nd series, xxix (1976).

Thompson, E. P., *The Making of the English Working Class* (Harmondsworth, 1968).

Thompson, Paul, *The Edwardians* (London, 1977).

——— and Haskell, Gina, *The Edwardians in Photographs* (London, 1979).

Thrift Book: A Cyclopaedia of Cottage Management and Practical Economy for the People (London, c.1883).

Thrift Manual (London, 1906).

Titmuss, R. M., *Essays on 'The Welfare State'* (London, 1958).

Tout, Herbert, 'A Statistical Note on Family Allowances', *Economic Journal* I (March 1940).

Treble, James H., 'The Attitudes of Friendly Societies towards the movement in Great Britain for State Pensions, 1878–1908', *International Review of Social History* xv (1970).

——— *Urban Poverty in Britain, 1830–1914* (London, 1979).

Tressell, Robert, *The Ragged Trousered Philanthropists* (St Albans, 1965).

Turner, T., *The Three Gilt Balls* (London, c.1864).

Useless Thrift, or how the poor are robbed (London, c.1893).

Vallance, Aylmer, *Hire-Purchase* (London, 1939).

Veblen, Thorstein, *The Theory of the Leisure Class* (New York, 1899).

Vesselitsky, V. de, and Bulkley, M. E., 'Money Lending among the London Poor', *Sociological Review* ix (Autumn 1917).

Walker, R. B., and Woodgate, D. R., *Principles and Practice of Industrial Assurance* (London, 2nd edn. 1943).

Warren, Edward C., *Credit Dealing* (London, 1939).

Watkins, E. S., *Credit Buying* (London, 1939).

Webb, Sidney, *The best means of bringing co-operation within the reach of the poorest of the population* (Manchester, 1891).

Webb, Sidney, and Webb, Beatrice, *The Consumers' Co-operative Movement* (London, 1921).

Whaley, Joachim (ed.), *Mirrors of Mortality* (London, 1981).

White, Jerry, *Rothschild Buildings* (London, 1980).

Whitelock, W. H., 'Industrial Credit and Imprisonment for Debt', *Economic Journal* xxiv (March 1914).

Wilkinson, J. Frome, *The Friendly Society Movement* (London, 1886).

—— *Mutual Thrift* (London, 1891).

Williams, Raymond, *Culture and Society, 1780–1950* (Harmondsworth, 1961).

Wilson, Sir Arnold, and Levy, H. J., *Industrial Assurance: An Historical and Critical Study* (Oxford, 1937).

—— *Burial Reform* (Oxford, 1938).

Winstanley, Michael, 'The Rural Publican and his Business in East Kent before 1914', *Oral History* iv, no. 2 (Autumn 1976).

—— *Life in Kent at the Turn of the Century* (Folkestone, 1978).

—— *The Shopkeeper's World, 1830–1914* (Manchester, 1983).

Wolveridge, Jim, *'Ain't it Grand'* (London, 1976).

Women's Co-operative Guild, *The Extension of Co-operation to the Poor* (Manchester, 1902).

Women's Group on Public Welfare, *Our Towns, A Close-up* (OUP, London, 1943).

Woolf, H. W., 'Co-operation and the Poor', *Economic Review* xiii (1903).

Wright, L. C., 'Consumer Credit and the Tally Man', *Three Banks Review* 44 (1959).

Yeo, Stephen, *Religion and Voluntary Organisations in Crisis* (London, 1976).

Yonge, C. F., 'Friendly Societies', *Economic Review* xvi (July 1906).

Young, Michael, and Willmott, Peter, *Family and Kinship in East London* (Harmondsworth, 1962).

Young, Terence, *Becontree and Dagenham* (London, 1934).

Index

Abbey Road Building Society 117, 122, 124
Aberdeen Savings Bank 96, 106, 110
Acland, A. D. 131
Ancient Order of Foresters Friendly Society 50–4, 62, 65–7
Anti-Moneylending Association 188, 222
Ashton, T. S. 104–5, 112
Atkinson, A. B. and A. J. Harrison 103–4, 204
Attenborough, G. 167, 171–2, 186

Baernreither, J. M. 62
Baldwin, S. 200
Barnes, R. 225
Barnett, S. A. 180
Bartley, G. C. T. 197
Bath Friendly Society 64
Baxter, D. 75
Bédarida, F. 224
Bell, Lady 64, 149
Benson, J. 14
Beveridge, W. 41, 99, 193, 200
Blackburn Philanthropic Friendly Collecting Society 24, 62
Blackley, Cannon W. L. 83, 197
Bolton 24, 43, 64, 99, 123
Booth, C. 3, 22, 25, 81, 148, 197–8, 200, 202, 217
Booth, W. 156
Bosanquet, H. 22, 144, 158, 167–8, 175, 178, 218–9, 222, 228
Bowley, A. L. and M. Hogg 99, 213
Brabrook, Sir Edward 15, 20, 37, 60, 68, 82
Bristol 23, 211
Britannic Assurance Company 22
Broadhurst, H. 83, 196, 198–9
building societies
    class of members 117–8, 211–2
    membership and assets 118–22, 204–5
    rate of interest 123–4
    size of accounts 122–3
Bullen, F. 148
Butler, V. 59, 214

Carr-Saunders, A. M. 139

Chamberlain, J. 81, 197
Chapman, C. 59
Charity Organisation Society
    case papers 2, 26
    economic views of 178, 200, 217, 219
check trading 152–3
Chiozza Money, L. 11
Committee of Enquiry into Savings Certificates and Local Loans (1923) 110
Committee on Industrial Assurance and Assurance on the lives of children under ten years of age [Cohen Cttee.] (1932) 14, 32, 42
Committee on War Loans for the Small Saver [Montagu Cttee.] (1916) 107, 109
Cooper, W. 131
co-operative societies
    class of members 139–40
    control of 137–8, 141–3
    credit trading in 131–9
    dividend 127–30
    membership and assets 119–21, 126–7, 143, 204–6, 209
    prices 130
    social standing of 142
Co-operative Union 134–6, 142
Coventry 88, 210–13
credit
    cost of 147–8, 152–3, 175
    criticism of 150, 158–9
    cycle of 148, 175–7
    default on 163–5
    function of 150, 152–3, 161
    stigma of 160–1
credit clubs 149–50, 152, 211–3, 221
Crossick, G. 57, 60, 62, 67

Dark, S. 22, 150
Davies, M. 60
Degge, J. 32
Departmental Committee on the Business of Industrial Assurance Companies and Collecting Societies [Parmoor Cttee.] (1920) 20, 23, 32, 36
Durant, R. 230